AN INTRODUCTION TO EASTERN WAYS OF THINKING

By the same Author

- *Current Trends and Problems of Progressive Education*
- *Value Education : Theory and Practice*
- *A Search for Human Values*
- *Education and Values in Mahabharata*
- *New Education Policy – A New Era in Education*
- *Creativity and Values*
- *Anglo-Hindi-Sanskrit Practical Grammar*
- *Phonology of Banda Dialect*
- *Equality of Religions*
- *Contribution of Western Indologists*
- *Educational Ideals and Institutions in Mahabharata*
- *Cross-Cultural Communication : Global Perspective*
- *Humanistic Tradition of India*
- *Women Education : Through the Ages*
- *Human Values in Education*
- *Human Values for 21st Century*

About the Author

N.L. Gupta (*b.* 1940) is the first scholar to obtain a Ph.D. from two different faculties of Nagpur University. He has a series of Postgraduate degrees and many firsts at his credit. He is the first candidate to submit a thesis for D.Litt. in R.S. University, Raipur. Recently he has been awarded by Maharashtra Hindi Granth Academy for the best work on Literary criticism styled as "Nav-Manavatavadi Chintan" (Neo-humanistic Thought).

Dr. Gupta is a prolific writer. Besides many research papers, he has 46 books in both Hindi and English to his credit. Dr. Gupta's writings have a very broad spectrum of themes which include Literature, History, Culture, Education, Sociology, Philosophy,Theology and so on. He is considered to be the authority on 'Value Education' on which he has contributed as many as six books with different angles. Latest in the series was *Education and Values in the Mahabharata, Mulya Parak Shiksha* of about 400 pages published from Ajmer, has been profusely quoted by the scholars.

He retired as Assistant Commissioner, Kendriya Vidyalaya Sangathan, Bhopal, Madhya Pradesh and settled at Nagpur.

AN INTRODUCTION TO EASTERN WAYS OF THINKING

N.L. GUPTA D. Litt.

CONCEPT PUBLISHING COMPANY, NEW DELHI - 110059

ISBN 81-8069-003-2 (HB)

ISBN 81-8069-004-0 (PB)

First Published 2003

Published and Printed by

Ashok Kumar Mittal
Concept Publishing Company
A/15-16, Commercial Block, Mohan Garden,
NEW DELHI -110059 (India)

Phones : 5351460, 5351794
Fax : 091-11-5357103
Email : publishing@conceptpub.com

PREFACE

Great personalities may emerge and vanish, thinkers may come and go; but the thoughts remain for ever. The individuals, society or nations are as their thoughts have moulded them. It is the thought and not the personality, which has the paramount place in the sphere of culture. In America Vivekanand was asked – "Why he had not told the people about his great Master?" His reply to this was very candid — "I have already spoken about his thoughts. If the people accept them, people will automatically know about his personality also." About the force and vitality of thought he says:

- The character of any man is but the aggregate of his tendencies, the sum total of his mind. As pleasure and pain pass before his soul, they leave upon it different pictures and result of these combined impressions is what is called character. (I. 25)
- We are what our thoughts have made us. (VII. 12)
- Each thought is a little hammer blow on the lump of iron which our bodies are, manufacturing out of its what we want to be. (VII. 18)
- Words are secondary. Thoughts live; they travel far. And so take care of what you think. (I. 25)
- Thus the East is today what it used to think in past or what it thinks today. Various cultural trends in of the East are as its thoughts have mouled them. Similarly the character of the Eastern people is as has been their mind or the set of values they cherished in order to shape their lives and mouled their life-styles.

It needs mention here that cultural phenomena in the East also differ from country to country. In spite of certain common features, entire Eastern Asia does not display common cultural phenomena, as has already been established by great thinkers and philosophers. Hegel asserted that God or the Absolute in the East has the feature of "das Allegemeine" (the Universal): "The fundamental principles of the various religions of the East are that the single substance alone is the True, and an individual has no value in itself, nor is capable of attaining any value so long as it is by itself, apart from that which exists in and for itself, the Absolute, that an individual is only capable of assuming true value by uniting itself with substance, when this indivisual, however, is no longer a 'subject' but is dissolved into the unconscious." Further, regarding the difference between Eastern and Western thoughts he says: "On the contrary, with the Greek religion or Christianity the 'Subject' is aware of its freedom, and we ought to think in the manner." In the philosophy of the East, however, "The negation of the finite is real. But that negation is one in the sense that an individual only attains its freedom in unity with what is substantial."

A famous Japanese scholar once said, "If I were to write the history of Japanese thought it would be the history of Indian thought. This is equally true of our gods and pagodas from the Himalayans to Horyuja." For convenience we can apply this very analogy to China, Korea, Java, Sumatra, Thailand and host of other countries of South-Eastern Asia as there have been good many socio-religious trends in common. Under the geographic-conceptual schema the above subcontinents may be put under major headings of 'Asia' and 'Orient East'. Asia has no common characteristic, besides special coherence, that it is a continental landmass distinct from surrounding oceans.

According to Will Durant, "There are four Asias. There is the militaristic Asia of the Near East – Mohammedan Asia, the land of religion that came to bring not peace but the sword. Yet in the Near East what complexity of race and character! – Ottoman Turks, Semitic Arabs and Jews (as even these brothers so different), Persian and Afghans, Caucasians and Armenians. Then there is *mystic Asia,* the great peninsula of India, of which I trust that Siddha will speak to us. There is Siberia – Mongol and Russian, Korean and Japanese — again a complex mass defying ready formulas.

And there is China, the oldest and the youngest nation in the world." (*The Pleasures of Philosophy*, p.351).

This work is not a philosophical treatise in the technical sense of the term. It is an humble effort to highlight some threads of Eastern Thought in a very lucid, precise and simple manner; but keeping the fidelity and credibility of various trends, currents and cross-currents of the Eastern Thought. Besides two appendices the present book is comprised of fifteen chapters as under:

1. Ageless Communication between East and West
2. Thought Constructs of the East: Some Dimensions
3. Eastern Concept of Man
4. Karmite Laws
5. Status of Women-Folk
6. Religion: An Integral part of life
7. Knowledge: Material versus Spiritual
8. Work-Culture and Confucianism
9. Zen Cult: Fusion of Complexity and Simplicity
10. Message of Vedas
11. The Message of Bhagavadgeeta
12. Ways of Ajivikas
13. Mysticism: Eastern Context
14. Dr. Sun Yat-Sen and Chinese Nationalism
15. Religio-spiritual thought of Mahatma Gandhi

The philosophies of the Eastern Cultures have been studied from different angels. While pointing out the religious threads therein one has to elaborate their cults, doctrines and principles etc. But these philosophies do not have only religion or religious doctrines: but they do throw light on the ways of life, according to which one may form)ulate his lifestyle. Moreover, they incorporate very important value-components, both professional values as well as operational values, eternal values and contemporary values. In this book philosophical chapters have been dealt with the angle that may reflect the ways of life-ways of thinking, ways of feeling, ways of action, ways of devotion and so on.

Here we need to recall that schools of Indian Thought, like the school of Chinese thought appeared on the scene almost simultaneously. Japan, Korea etc. are indebted to China as far as religious doctrines and principles are concerned. Therefore, there are more points in common than the points of difference. They developed through mutual critisims by attempting to be self-consistent and comprehensive. Such developments took place during the course of centuries. For transcultural communication the credit goes to the Chinese pilgrims like Fa-Hien, Hieun-tsang. It-tsing etc. who came to Indian subcontinent all the way from China facing all sorts of hazards in order to quench their thrust of spiritual knowledge and host of monks and scholars went to China, Japan, Korea etc. Consequently the currents and cross-currents of thought found place in the accounts of various pilgrims and scholars.

Alike East-East cultural communication there had been East-West communication also particularly in the modern age. In the nineteenth and twentieth centuries people in Europe built various bridges to the tradition of the East being attracted by its spiritual wisdom with an apparent hope to create new springs of a synthesis of spiritual material life, synthesis of spirit and matter, synthesis of science and religion, synthesis of old and new and so on, which is the need of the hour not only for East or West but for the both. Except this there seems to be no other wayout for social peace and harmony, for the grace and unity of the mankind and peace on the planet earth at large.

I am thankful to the publisher who has takenup this project with a marked vision and verve. Here I would like to express my deep sense of gratitude to all those scholars whose works had been of direct or indirect help to me while working on the project.

N.L. GUPTA

117 Balpande Layout
Santaji Society
Narendra Nagar
Nagpur – 440015 (M.S.)

CONTENTS

ABBREVIATIONS USED

ABORI	Annals of Bhandarkar Oriental Research Institute, Pune
HASL	History of Ancient Sanskrit Literature
CHI	Cultural Heritage of India
HIL	History of Indian Literature
WOTEP	Ways of Thinking of Eastern People
CHOI	A Comparative History of Ideas
CRC-TTE	Contemporary Republic of China – The Taiwan Experience
CWMG	Collected Works of Mahatma Gandhi
MM	Mind of Mahatma Gandhi
HSL	History of Sanskrit Literature
NIAS	Netaji Institute for Asian Studies, Calcutta
IHQ	Indian Historical Quarterly
SBE	Sacred Books of the East
JRAS	Journal of the Royal Asiatic Society, London
Vol/Vols	Volume/Volumes
CWSV	The Complete Works of Swami Vivekanand, 8 Vols., Calcutta
VI	Vedic Index by Macdonell and Keith
SABCL	Shri Aurobindo Bibliography and Complete Literature
LD	The Life Divine
SIT	Sources of Indian Tradition, Vols I-II, Penguin

"Learning Without Thought is Labour Lost;
Thought Without Learning is Perilous."

— Confucious

"All that we are is the result of what
We have thought. It is founded on our
thoughts; it is made-up of our thoughts."

— Lord Buddha

"Chi-sun Hsing-fu only acted thinking
thrice. Twice is quite enough."

— Confucious

"A man can enlarge the principles which he follows;
Those Principles do not enlarge the man."

— Confucious

"When words are one-sided I know how *the mind of the speaker* is clouded over. When the words are extravagant, I know how *the mind* is fallen and sunk. When words are all-depraved, I know how *the mind* has departed *from principle.* When words are evasive, I know how *the mind* is at its wit's end."

— Mencius

1

AGELESS COMMUNICATION BETWEEN EAST AND WEST

"Some speculate that Plato of his predecessors had contact with India. It is in any case instructive to compare Plato's understanding of things with ideas in Hindu and Buddhist thought, comparative philosophy begins generally more enlightening between unconnected philosophies.

Leibniz's encounter with the philosophies of Neo-Confucianism and also the *I Ching* is the first case of a major Western thinker's seriously engaging in Asian philosophy. Interest in oriental thought developed gradually, until Hegel, commanding a more expansive view of History than any before him, declared his philosophy (not without justification) to be culmination of Western Metaphysics. *Eastern thought he considered to have remained in a state of relative immaturity – even though some of its products were worthy of being incorporated into his own system.* Schopenhaur, as more Asian text began to be available in better translation, saw greater depth in those philosophies, and maintained that *Western thought had much to learn from the wisdom of the East.* Nietzsche considered his "revaluation of all previous values" finally to have overcome the western metaphysical tradition. His understanding of Indian philosophy appears to have gone deeper than Schopenhaur's, and while his attitude towards Buddhism is ambivalent, he acknowledges parallels between aspects of Buddhist philosophy and his own subversive lines of thoughts."

— Graham Parkes[1]

Dichotomy of East-West

At the outset it needs mention here that dichotomy of East-West, by now at least, stand highly challenged and it has been strongly denied too.[2] Still individual differences exist in cultures as are obvious in persons. The medical term "Idiosyncrasy" meaning "mental constitution, view or feeling, or more of behaviour peculiar to a person"[3] apparently reveals that psycho-physical mechanism differs from person to person. That is why we observe differences among the individuals of the same family, what to say of the culture. Therefore, due to cultural differences, it is but natural to exist the differences in thinking, views, feelings etc. because the seeds of thought are sprouted on the basis of value-tenets, which invariably differ from culture to culture.

Bertrand Russell points out that man is perennially engaged in three basic conflicts: (1) against nature, (2) against other man, and (3) against himself.[4]

Inheriting this classification, Huston Smith says:

"Roughly these may be identified as man's natural, social and psychological problems. The great surviving cultural traditions are also three – the Chinese, the Indian and the Western. It helps us to understand and relate the unique perspectives of these three traditions if we think of each as accenting one of man's basic problems. Generally speaking, the West has accented the natural problem, China the social, and India the psychological."[5]

It was Rudyard Kipling, the British journalist who stayed for many decades in India, and said:

"East is East, and West is West
The twin shall never meet".

As the time rolled by the sane people started realizing superficiality of the statement, particularly when the people not only saw but also experienced the enjoyable marriage of the East and West. This synthesis or union of the two ways of life has given a entirely new dimension to the history of human glory. Some people like Mr. Nirad C. Chaudhary may be realizing or might have realized the superficiality of Westernization on the basis of the first hand experiences of their own, as Mr. Chaudhary says:

"Like all my countrymen who have read that dictum of Kipling's I rejected it violently. It was a believer in the accepted doctrine of the synthesis of the best in the East and the West, which, of course, meant substantial Westernization. Doubts, however, entered my mind as soon as I began to meet Occidentals in India, which I had not done except very casually until I had passed the age of fifty. By that time I had also seen the relapse of almost all my contemporaries into Hindu traditionalism of one kind or another.[6]

In spite of such individual positive experience and responses the historical fact about the clash between the East and West cannot be overlooked as it has been engaging the attention of scores of Oxidental as well as oriental scholars. This clash was but natural as it had its material as well as spiritual aspects. Both materially and spiritually Europe has thrown herself repeatedly upon Asia, Asia too upon Europe, to conquer, assimilate and dominate. There has been a constant alternation, a flowing backward and forward of these two seas of power. According to Shri Aurobindo: "All Asia has always had the spiritual tendency in more or less intensity, with more or less clearness, but for this essential matter India is the quintessence of the Asiatic way of being. Europe too in mediaeval times had a culture in which by the dominance of the Christian idea – but Christianity was of Asiatic origin the spiritual motive took the lead; then there was an essential similarity as well as certain difference. Still the differentiation of culture temperament has on the whole been constant. Since some centuries Europe has become material, predatory, aggressive, and has lost the harmony of the inner and outer man which is the true meaning of civilization and efficient condition of a true progress. Material comfort, material progress, material efficiency have become the gods of her worship."[7]

Mysterious East

The East could not remain unaffected with this materialistic order of the West. But this impact was more or less outward. Of course, it influenced the mind and body of the Eastern thinking, but its spirit (soul) remained intact. Hence, the very structure of Eastern Thought remained compact to a large extent. Joseph Conrad (Youth, 1902) has described the East through four words – mysterious East, perfumed like a flower, silent like death, dark like a grave.

In his small book titled as "Hindu view of life" Dr. S. Radhakrishnan has rightly remarked in this context. He says: "To the West religion in Indian tends to appear as a rich and rather baffling tangle of myth, with endless gods and goddesses worshipped in countless different forms. But this complexity, which spring as much from an exuberant lore of story-telling as any thing, is only the surface of Indian faith. Underlying it is a system of unifying beliefs that have guided the ordinary Indian family for thousands of years and provided inspiration for many other oriental peoples."

Once Paul Brunton was discussing with Raman Maharshi on the West. He reports: "It it easy for you to attain and keep spiritual serenity in this jungle retreat where there is nothing to disturb or distract you."

"When the goal is reached, when you know the knower, there is no difference between living in a house in London and living in the solitude of a jungle." comes the calm rejoinder.

And once I criticize the Indians for their neglect of material development. To my surprise the Maharshi frankly admits the accusation.

"It is true. We are a backward race. But we are a people with few wants. Our society needs improving, but we are contented with much fever things than your people. So to be backward is not to mean that we are less happy."[8]

After having his extensive tour to India for as long as 14 years in search of Yogis and their hermetic knowledge he had to change the allegiance to the Eastern creed. According to him he spent much of his spare time in the study of recondite books and in little-known by paths of psychological experiments. He delved into subjects which always have been wrapped in Cimmerian mystery. He writes :

"I did arrive at a new acceptance of the Divine. This may seem quite an insignificant and personal thing to do, but as a child of this modern generation, which relies on hard facts and cold reason, and which lacks enthusiasm for things religious, I regard it as quite an achievement. This faith was restored in the only way a sceptic could have it restored, not by argument, but by the witness of an overwhelming experience. And it was a jungle sage, an unassuming hermit who had formerly lived for six years[9] in a mountain cave, who promoted this vital change in my thinking."[10]

The very mystic character of the East had been vibrant throughout the ages in various spheres of life, may it be worship or meditation, perception or self-actualization. In past this has left a deep impact on other contemporary cultures particularly of the West. Will Durant has rightly observed, "The subtle infusion of an Asiatic soul into the wearied body of the master Greek was followed rapidly by the pouring of Oriental cults and faith into Greece along those very lines of communication which the young conqueror (Alexander) had opened up: *the broken dykes let in the ocean of Eastern thought upon the lowlands of the still adolescent European mind.* The mystic and superstitious faiths which had taken root among the proper people of Hellas were reinforced and spread about; and the oriental spirit of apathy and resignation found a ready soil in decadent and despondent Greece."[11]

Antiquity and Annals

The first real sources, from which Central European scholars drew information of India during the Middle Ages were, however, works writers of classical antiquity, various compilations from the period of the decline of the Roman Empire and writings from the Byzantine period. Frequently such works were wholly devoted to India or else contained passages on the country's history, natural conditions or on journeys along the basin of the river Indus and farther to the East. Among their authors' names we find those of Herodotus, Scylax of Caryanda, Ctesias, Megasthenes, Strabo, Pliny, Ptolemy, Arrian, Cosmos Indicopleusthes and many others. They have seldom come down to us complete and in original versions but as fragments, later selections, quotations and paraphrases, preserving many eyewitness reports and items of reliable information, apart from a great many fabrications and fantastic tales. Some of these manuscripts found their way on to the territory of Czechoslovakia (e.g. works by Pomponius Mela, Paulus Venetus and others).

A few passages on India are to be found in the Bible, which began to be translated in Bohemia and Moravia as early as the 9th century. These are, above all references to voyages by King Solomon's merchant ships from the Gulf of Aqabah to the shores of India and to Indian products imported by the Hebrews an assortment ranging from war elephants to perfumes and scents. Although the known Old Czech translation of all the parts of the Bible was not completed until the reign of Charles IV (1346-1378), King of Bohemia and Emperor of the Holy Roman Empire, Czech readers naturally had access to the original texts, in Latin or in other languages, before a translation into their own language was available.

The religious literature of medieval Bohemia contains interesting allusions to some legends current to this day among Christian believers in India. The first occurs in the manuscript of the *Old Czech Passional,* dating perhaps from the end of the 13th century: a prose tale of St. Bartholomew and his missionary work in India. The second relates to the Apostle Thomas who, as legend has it, also came to India to preach the words of God. In a manuscript poem from the end of the 14th century, *Pravenie o boziem umucenie a jebo svate krvi prolitie* (The Relation of Passion of God and the Shedding of His Holy Blood), the author begs the "King of the whole world" to strengthen him that he should do better than St. Thomas in the hour of his trial, who resisted the Lord's commandments by refusing to set out on a journey to India.

Old Czech renderings of the theme of the exploits of Alexander the Great enjoyed tremendous popularity with the reading public. For the most part they were based on a historical treatise by Q. Rufus Cutrtius and on a fantastic Greek romance, *the pseudo Callisthenes,* in version considerably modified by adapters at the beginning of the present millennium. Two *Czech Alexandreids,* both by anonymous writers, were circulated in many manuscript copies containing long passages on India. The first, a versified translation, dates from about the end of the 13th century and surpasses its models by its conception, topicality of adaptation, original variants and overall literary merit. It is regarded as one of the most notable works, not only in Czech but in contemporary European literature, which continued to be read extensively until the Hussite Wars (early 15th century). Readers, or rather listeners, learnt about India in the second half of the poem, narrating the story of the invasion, by Alexander's army, of the territory governed by Indian rulers, of Alexander's struggles with King Porus (the historical ruler of the Punjab kingdom of the Pauravas), the storming of the fortified town of the Sudrakas (the historical tribe of Malavas, with whom the Ksudrakas were allied) and so forth. And most interesting for Czech audiences, four Czech knights, of course purely fictitious, by the names of Jan., Mladota, Radota and Radvan took the journey to India in the ranks of Alexander's army.

East Meeting West Through Indology

Charles Wilkins in 1785 translated the Bhagavadgeeta for the first time; Kalidasa's Shakuntala was translated by William Jones in 1789, followed by Manu's Laws a few years later. Finally, at the turn of the century, Colebrook and Horace Haymond Wilson were the scholars whose important essays and translations enabled all Europeans, including the Germans, to have their first comprehensive view of Sanskrit and its literature.

Johann Cottfried Herder was the first to follow up these efforts in Germany. Though he didn't know much about the country or the language, Herder has given an idealistic description of India which was for a long time predominant in the fantasy of German poets.

Within the system of his Philosopohy of the History of Mankind, Herder gave an imaginative picture of India where according to him the origin of mankind is to be found: 'There the human mind got the first shapes of wisdom and virtue with a simplicity, strength and sublimity which has – frankly spoken – nothing, nothing at all equivalent in our philosophical, cold European world.' The Childhood of Mankind meant for Herder the Golden Age, which he believed existed in India of his time. He said:

"The Hindus are the most peaceful race of mankind. They do not like to offend any living being, they honour what brings life and eat the most innocent food, milk, rice, fruit of the trees, the healthy herbs which their ground offers them. Their tongue has never been enervated by the taste of fermented drinks or hot dishes.... Their stature is straight, slim and beautiful... Their way of walking and their stature is in the same kind as their original shape of kind... moderation and calmness, a gentle mood and a calm deepness of their soul characterise their work and pleasure, their ethics and mythology, their arts and even their tolerance under the heaviest yoke. Happy lambs, why could you not pasture on your meadow without any disturbance and distress?

Herder and Goethe

Herder's idealising glorification of India then was taken up by the romantic movement and it is one of his great merits that the poetical picture of India given by him paved the way for the development of German-Sanskrit philology.

Herder introduced the first Indian literary documents to Germany. First of all Shakuntala by Kalidasa. In 1791 the first German translation of the drama was published by George Forster, who sent one copy to his friend Herder. Here are some sentences of his reply: 'I cannot easily find a product of the human mind more pleasant than this one.... a real blossom of the orient, and the first, most beautiful of its kind... Something like that, of course, appears once every two thousand years.... '

Herder published three letters on Shakuntala. He studied Kalidasa's play in the light of drama rules evolved by Aristotle: 'The Greek postulates a development of the events which is in each part natural; the Indian, however, aims right from the beginning to the end at a sacred, divine, miraculous correlation.' Of course, Herder hurried to bring his discovery to Goethe's notice. His friend's enthusiasm about Kalidasa was not less exuberant. The instantaneous reaction of the poet after reading Forster's translations were penned in the following lines:

Shall I embrace in a name the blossoms of spring, the fruits of the autumn,
All that enchants and that charms, all that nurtures and fills,
Shall I embrace in a name All Heaven and the whole of the Earth,
Let me call, Shakuntala thee, and all is comprised in one name

Nearly forty years later Antoine de Chezy, a friend of Friendrich Schlegel, published an edition de luxe of Shakuntala, and having sent it to Goethe, he received the poet's reply of October 9, 1830, as follows :

"The first time I became aware of this inexhaustible work, it produced such an enthusiasm in me, attracted me so much that I did not cease from studying it and I even felt myself urged to try the impossible, namely, to adapt it for the German theatre. Through all these tough fruitless efforts I have become acquainted with this most valuable work to such an extent... that for the last thirty years I had not to read either the English or the German version... Only now I understand the enthusiastic impression which this work made upon me in former times. Here the poet apears in his supreme duty, as the representative of the most natural phase, of the finest way of life, of the purest ethical ideals, of the most dignified majesty and the most serious religion. But at the same time he remains the sovereign and master of his creation so that he may dare vulgar and ridiculous contrasts which, however, must be considered as necessary links of the whole organism."

Influence on Goethe

Two years before his death Goethe thus confessed that *Shakuntala* accompanied him throughout his lifetime.

And there is an interesting link between Kalidasa's masterpiece and Goethe's *Faust.* The plan for one of the three preludes, preceding the drama *Faust,* the so-called 'prelude on the stage' where the theatre manager, the dramatic poet, and the actor discuss the problem of a good play, came to Goethe from the similar prelude in the Indian *Shakuntala*.

Later on Goethe became acquainted with the *Meghaduta,* too, which was translated in 1813 by Horace Haymond Wilson. The poet mentions the small epic very often, sometimes calling it *Kamarupa*. But let us investigate now where Indian impressions are bearing fruit in Goethe's poetical creations.

A few years later, the triology 'Pariah' was published. Goethe found the story for these three poems in the same travel book. In the first part of Goethe's triology the despised Pariah prays to God:

For even to the dancing girls
You have given a goddess.
We others too want to hear of such a miracle
So that we can praise you.

The conclusion of the triology is the thanks of the Pariah to Brahma: (Great Brahma, now I understand that you are the creator of the worlds, I call you my sovereign for you approve of all.)

Between the prayer and thanks for the fulfilment, the central part of this triology gives the 'legend', the story of the inter-changed heads, which story was also told by Thomas Mann. Goethe narrates the story as follows:

"A Brahman kills his wife for unfaithfulness in thoughts. But then his son gets the order to re-connect the head and body of his mother. Because of his excitement, however, he makes a peculiar exchange, the head of the Brahmin wife is connected with body of a Pariah woman. Thus she learns all that had been unknowan to her as Brahmin wife. This means terrible suffering for her. But by enduring everything she becomes a goddess, whose duty is mediatorship, the goddess the Pariah was longing for.

It is always Kalidasa to whom Goethe turns time and again, full of admiration:

Kalidasa and others have attained their end;
They have with the neatness of the poet
Saved us from bad priests and grotesque images.
I would have lived in India myself
If there had not been any sculptors.

What can one imagine to be more pleasant,
Than Shakuntala and Nala, whom one must kiss,
And Megha-Duta, the cloud messenger
Who would not like to send him to those with mental affinity.

Let us return to Herder and the Romantic movement. Herder had combined the hypothesis of the Golden Age of mankind and the idea that originally man had been the very image of God. Thus the longing of Herder was for the oldest documents of mankind to rediscover the purest revelation of god.

Mythology and Romanticism

Novalis, the romantic poet par excellence, wanted to go back to Indian mythology. In his essay 'Christendom or Europe' he writes:

"The poetry full of charm and colour like a decorated Indian faces the cold dead peaks of this book-learning rationalism. In order to make India in the middle of the globe so full of warmness and beauty, a cold sea, dead cliffs, mist instead of a sky full of stars, and a long night, all this must make both ends of the globe desolate."

The famous romantic philosopher Schelling too grants India an important position in his *Philosophy of Mythology.* Max Muller writing about Schelling said that he was a great admirer of ancient Indian literature and he was especially delighted with the Upanishads….Schelling like Schopenhauer thought the Upanishads to be the genuine wisdom of the Indians and of mankind.

The contrast between the poetical, idealised India and the facts determined the poet Friedrich Schlegel's Indian studies. In his speech on Mythology, he explains the importance of mythology and its close connection with romantic poetry. "Mythology and its poetry, both are one and inseparable."

Friedrich Schlegel studied Sanskrit in Paris, the very first German to do so. He was able to read in this language and to translate from it. During that time, he wrote in one of his letters: "But now everything else has been pushed away by Sanskrit. Here is the very source of all languages, of all thoughts, and of all poetry of the human mind; everything originates in India, without any exception."

The inspiring power of Schlegel's book stimulated Friedrich's brother, August Wilhelm Schlegel, who, in 1818, became the first professor in Sanskrit at a German University; inspired Franz Bopp, and last but not least, stimulated the linguistic genius of the poet Friedrich Rueckert to give the most congenial translations of Sanskrit literature.

Poet Rueckert and Tamil

Friedrich Rueckert was one of the few outstanding scholars in the field of philology who was able to master some dozens of languages. Like Heinrich Schliemann, who discovered Troy, Rueckert used to learn even the most difficult of languages within six to eight weeks.

One day in the summer of 1839, for instance, a missionary who was to be sent to South India requested Rueckert to teach him Tamil. Rueckert answered that he could not understand a single word of Tamil at the moment, but that he should come in October, then he would be able to teach him.

In the meantime, the poet took the Grammatica Dumulica waritten by the missionary Ziegenbalg and published in Halle in 1716 and a Tamil translation of the Holy Bible, and composed a Tamil grammar and a Tamil dictionary and taught this difficult language marvellously.

During those times, it was very difficult and expensive to get texts and dictionaries of Oriental languages, and Rueckert was a poor poet and professor. So he copied the Sanskrit dictionary of Horace Haymond Wilson. There was no other one – a big book containing 1100 pages. This hand-written copy, corrected and enlarged by his own remarks, still exists.

The German scholar solved his problem in a similar way as the Indian pandit from Benaras who spoke fluent Sanskrit, but not a single word of English. One day he was persuaded to learn the despised language. Since he did not like to look for every word in the dictionary, he learned the whole dictionary, page after page, by heart. And later in his lifetime, he was proud to discover that there were only two words which he didn't know.

The poet Friedrich Rueckert being at the same time professor of Oriental Languges at the University of Erlangen, 1827-1841 translated quite a lot of Sanskrit poetry. Nala and Damayanti, Savitri and others were introduced to German literature through masterly translations by Rueckert. And even Jayadeva's Gitagovinda lost nothing of its beauty in Rueckert's German version.

Hermann Hesse

During the 20th Century many German poets were touched by impressions and influences from the East. One of them Rudolf Von Ems, the knight and German poet of the Middle ages, did not even know that his Barlaam and Josaphat story was of Indian origin. The German poets of the 18th and 19th centruies could meet India and try to understand by means of original literature, Sanskrit poems or at least their translations. Now in the 20th Century, we find poets who travelled to the romantic dreamland and learned by their own experience.

The most renowned of these Eastern wayfarers is Hermann Hesse. After his journey to the East in 1911, he published his Indian Diary in 1913, but could not record his experiences in the form of poetry. He confesses:

"Then I learned - not for the first time, of course, but harder than ever – that it is nonsense to warite down what you did not experience yourself and during the long interval when I had already abandoned the poetical work Siddhartha, I had to make up for practice of ascetic life and meditation before I could regain the scared and congenial world of the Indian spirit: my true home-land."

The first Czechoslovak Indologist to visit India was Otakar Pertold (1884-1965). He used his first stay from 1909 to 1910 for assembling a wealth of documentary material for further scientific work in the fields of ethnography, study of religion and philology. His travel sketches, which appeared in the daily press, found a responsive public and were published in book form in 1911 under the title *Cesty po Hindustanu* (Hindustan Travels).

At about the same time India was discovered by a pair of young Czech painters, Jaroslav Hnevkovsky (1884-1955) and Otakar Nejedly (1883-1957). Both also spent some time in Ceylon; the latter left India two years after but Hnevkovsky did not return home until 1913, when a comprehensive exhibition of his paintings from India was held at the Art Club Umelecka Beseda in Prague. Their adventurous wanderings, inspired by a romantic interest in the East and by the lure of the exotic flora, are to this day fondly recalled by many Czechoslovak artists of the older genearation. Practically without financial means and certainly free from prejudice, the two artists mixed with simple Indian villagers and fishermen, spending many months — and sometimes miraculously escaping grave dangers – in the towns, villages and jungles of South Asia. This was a period of unforgettable impressions and creative inspiration for them both. Both left their hearts in India. Hnevkovsky returned to the country once more after the war. They described their experience in books, which have lost little of their freshness to this day, as witnessed by a recent re-edition of Nejedly's Memories. With rare sincerity and frankness they spoke of their impressions, loves, hardships and art experimentation. Like the trips of some of their predecessors, Hnevkovsky's and Nejedly's tour greatly stimulated Czechoslovak interest in India before the first world war and after.

India's Impact on Western Thought

Eminent Indologists like Max Muller, Garbe and Winternitz agree that 'centuries before Christ there were in Persia, Asia Minor and Alexandria seats of learning which were visited, among others, by Greeks, and Brahmanas from India who played an important role in the intellectual fellowship promoted by these centres where Indian ideas were most popular.

Garbe says that the doctrines of the Indian Sankhya philosophy exerted great influence on Greek thinkers like Heraclitus, Empedocles, Anaxagorus, Democritus and Epicurus. He says that the theory of Heraclitus that "*all bodies are transformations of fire*" and of Empedocles of "*the eternity and indestructibility of matter*" are restatements of Sankhya ideas which were also the origin of the latter's belief in the transmigration of soul.

The Eleatic philosophers of Greece, says Hüszar, were profoundly influenced by the Upanishads. Their view that God and the universe are eternal and unchangeable was distinctly Upanishadic. Says Erdman: "*The absorption of all separate existence in a single substance*, as taught by the Eleatics seems rather an echo of Indian pantheism than a principle of Hellenic sprit."

Max Muller and other European authorities take the view that Pythagoras had contact with Indian scholars in Persia, from whom he learnt the forty-seventh theorem of the Euclidean geometry, which is found in the *Sulva Sutras* of Baudhayana, his ideas of the science of music, the importance of numbers, his doctrine of reincarnation, as also the holy tetractyls the meaning of which is found in the formula of diagrams for Vedic sacrifices to which again is traced the origin of the decimal system of notation. Colebrooke holds that they, Pythagorians, were indebted to their Indian instructors. Schrader declares that India is the birthplace of Pythagorian ideas.

Link With India

Both Plato and Aristotle had contact with India through Persia when the Achaemenian empire touched the borders of India and Greece. In the fifth century B.C. says Max Muller, there were in Grece 'Brahmanas' from India. That they were in Athens in the time of Socrates is corroborated by Eusebius, a Greek Church historian of the third century A.D. He mentions the meeting of an Indian with Socrates who was asked by the former what was the scope of his philosophy. "An enquiry into human phenomena," replied Socrates. At this the Indian burst out laughing "How can man enquire into human phenomena when he is ignorant of divine ones ?"

Urwick is convinced that India is the birthplace of many of the ideas of Plato. "Plato is full of Sankhyan thought worked out by him but taken from Pythagoras," says Hopkins. Max Muller says that "the similarity between Plato's language and that of the Upanishads is sometimes startling." Garbe holds that many of Plato's ideas were transferred from India to Greece. Gnotsticism and neoPlatonism are believed to have grown out of a synthesis of Christian and Indian ideas. The gnostic idea of the plurality of heavens and spiritual worlds are regarded as distinctly Unanishadic.

There can be no doubt, says Erdmann, that Plotinus, the founder of neo-Platonist school which profoundly influenced European thought, had deep knowledge of Indian mysticism and himself led the life of a Yogi often rising into states of Samadhi mentioned in the Yoga philosophy. His Universal Mind and 'World-soul' are clearly Vedantic. What he called "Nature" is identified with *Prakriti* of the Sankhya whose influence is traced by Garbe in the explanation Plotinus gave of creation.

Indian influence in pre-Christian Asia Minor is attested by Zenob, a fourth-century writer of Armenia, who relates how in the second century B.C. two Indian princes settled in Taron, West of lak Van, and erected temples for the worship of Giasne, identified with Krishna. To this is traced the influence of the Bhagavata or Krishna cult on Christianity in those regions where a little later it had as many as five thousand followers.

Buddhism's Role

Buddhism also had something to do with the growth of Christianity. In pre-Christian times there were Buddhists in Alexandria which had a number of them even in the second and third centuries A.C. Celment studied Buddhism with them. His tutor Pantaenus visited India as a Christian missionary. He is definite that the Greeks stole their philosophy from the barbarians (Indians).

The Therapeutics of Alexandria were no other than followers of the Buddha as their very name suggests. The Pali word *there*, derived from the Sanskrit word *sthira* meaning 'settled in peace' is a name of the Buddha, and the Pali word *putta*, derived from the Sanskrit word *putra*, means son follower. The essences of pre-Christian Palestine were also Buddhists. Historian Mahaffy says: "These Buddhist missionaries were the forerunners of the Christ."

Schelling, Schopenhaur, Mansel and Milman attribute the Buddhistic elements in Christianity to the Buddhist missionaries who came from India during the reign of Asoka. The parable style of the Bible is held to be an echo of the story-telling method of the Buddhist Jatakas, and says Vincent Smith, "Some Orthodox forms of Christian teaching owe some debt to the lessons of Gautama."

Winternitz believes that "in the combination of the Jewish and the Greek ideas on which the teachings of the Christian Gospels are based, there was also some admixture of Buddhist thoughts and legends. Some undoubted borrowings from the Buddhist religious literature are also found in the Apocryphal Gospels."[12]

The Gospel story of the Bible bears striking resemblance to the account of the Buddha's life given in such Buddhist works as the Lalita Vistara, which describes the Buddha's miraculous conception and birth, the star over the birthplace, the prophecy of the aged and temptation by Mara and the twelve disciples.[13]

Discussing the coincidence of the Jataka story of the pious disciple walking on the water with the similar story in the Gospels, Max Muller remarks that it can only be accounted for by some historical contact and transference, and the Jatakas are centuries older than the Gospels. The story of the prodigal son is found almost in the same form in the Buddhist work, the Suddhamma Pundarika.

Another fact which confirms the possibility of Indian influence on Christianity was revealed years ago in a book called 'The Unknown Life of Jesus Christ', translated from a manuscript discovered in a monastery of Tibet by the Russian explorer, Lutovitch. The book fills up the gap of the Christ's absence from Jerusalem for twelve years by describing his itinerary in Northern India during that period when he visited India's known cities and centres of learning and her great saints and scholars.

Indian knowledge was familiar to the Eastern Churches of the Levant. A notable instance is furnished by the presence of Indian ideas in the writings of Origen (third century A.D.), who was one of the greatest of the Greek fathers of the Eastern Church and a writer of many authoritative books on Christian theology. Origen believed in reincarnation and showed extreme eagerness to imbibe Indian wisdom, "those insights and illuminations from the Christians that were before Christ." He was thrice punished, the last time to death, for holding 'un-Christian' views, one of which must have been on reincarnation.

Lofty Idealism

An eminent Christian thinker says that, had not in the fourth century the Council of Chalcedon condemned reincarnation, then believed in the many Christian Fathers, the 'religion of love' would have been saved the disgrace of the cruel finality of everlasting punishment for the mistakes of this one life.

Many authorities have felt that in India there is a sourceland rich and constant enough in its yield of the Water of Life to have fed all mankind's ecclesiastical channels. They think that India influenced, directly or indirectly, that stream of lofty idealism and devotion which arose in the Rhine-land in the spring of the middle ages. Indian ideas were transmitted through a succession of teachers and disciples like the Arabian Monk Bar Saudali, also known as Dionysius the Areopagite, whose doctrines were more Vedantic than 'Synoptic'. This was as it were, a transplantation of Indian wisdom from the banks of the Ganga to those of the Rhine.

In his book 'The Flowering of Mysticism', Rufus Jones has traced quite clearly this movement of Indian ideas through Persia, Alexandria, Cordoba, Padua and thence by Paris on to the Rhine, 'influencing and forming the thought and practice of the first great schools of Western mysticism'. 'Scholarship', says Gerald Heard, 'has now proved as a fact of literature that the specific concepts which gave to Western religion its deepest insights and its most effective techniques were all imported from the Indian areas.'

It is well known that the stories of India form a substantial element in those of Europe, the Panchatantra, the Hitopadesha and the Buddhist Jatakas having played a most important part in this migration of stories from India. The famous Welsh story of Llewellyin and Gebert, many fables in La Fontaine's French work, a number of fairy tales in Grimm and Hans Anderson, many stories in the Gesta Romanorum, the Decameron, and Chaucer's Canterbury Tales, not to speak of the fables of Aesop, are derived from India.

Regarding the influence of Indian art Pandit Jawaharlal Nehru maintained that "Indian civilization took root especially in the countries of South-east Asia and evidence for this can be found all over the place today. There were great centres of Sanskrit learning in Champa, Angkor, Shrivijaya, Majapahit, and other places. The names of the rulers of the various states and empires that arose are purely Indian and Sanskrit. This does not mean that they were pure

Indian, but it does not mean that they were Indianized. State ceremonies were Indian and conducted in Sanskrit. All the officers of the state bear old Sanskrit titles and some of these titles and designationg have been continued up till now, not only in Thailand but in the Moslem states of Malaya. The old literature of these places in Indonesia are full of Indian myth and legend. The famous dance of Java and Bali derive from India. The little island of Bali has indeed largely maintained its old Indian culture down to modern times and even Hinduism has persisted there. The art of writing went to the Philippines from India."[14]

Search and Research

Recently, Professor J.V. Polisensky, of Charles University and P. Ratkos, a Slovak historian made a notable discovery in Bratislava, the Slovak metropolis; they identified a scroll of manuscripts containing fragments of an anonymous Description of a Voyage to India in the year 1502, supplements on the results of the voyage, data on the economic importance of some of the places visited, navigational data and a survey of Portuguese voyages to India between 1497 and 1517, as well as a description of a journey to India made in 1517 by a certain Lazarus Nuremberger. From a historical view point, the most interesting item is the account by a unknown participant in Vasco da Gama's second expedition to India which adds quite a lot to our knowledge of that voyage.

Interest in overseas countries and above all, in "both Indias" – East and West – was reflected in the great demand for cosmographic works. Contemporary maps were far from perfect but there is a marked difference in the quality of 16th century maps of South Asia and one of the first Czech maps of India, found in a circular picture of the world in the world Chronicle by Vavrinec of Brezova, a 15th century drawing (based on an older, so called Hereford map). The greatest popularity was enjoyed by Munster's monumental Cosmographia, which appeared in Prague in 1554, a short time after its publication in Germany. It was veritable mine of information on world geography, ethnography and history, both ancient and recent, presenting a compendium of contemporary knowledge of

India. A special edition of a Cosmography by J. Honter was published in Prague in 1595 by martin Bachacek of Naumerice (1538-1612).

Another popular work was Customs, Law, Regulations and Habits of All Nations, written by a Bavarian author, Johann Boehme (Boemius) Aubanus, at the beginning of the 16th century, translated into Czech by Jan Miroticky of Kromeriz and published at Olomous (Moravia) in 1579. The reader is immediately struck by the fact that pride of place is accorded to "Asia and the more noble nations of that part of the world" a total of nearly nine pages being devoted to India. Let us describe the work briefly.

India is presented as a country at the "Very extremity of Asia", with fertile soil and an abundance of all plants and products, mainly cinnamon, pepper, sweet calamus, ebony, also pearls and gems. The Indians are reported to be frugal eaters and fond of ornaments. As they trust one another in business transactions, they have no need of laws, seals and testimonies. The only law recognised by the "Brahmanic Nation" is never to violate the "natural law". Women meet men not out of lust but out of a desire for children. Seven estates are mentioned (among which it is possible to discern four Indian varnas). Our interest is aroused by a passage on the estate of the ploughmen, whom no one wrongs since all need their work, and by a reference to paper money. The King is said to be attended upon by bought women. Lest treacherous attempts should be plotted against him, the monarch changes his bed every four hour during the night. This rather confused yet on the whole sympathetic account of India contains, for the first time in Czech writing, allusions to certain specific features of Hindu society, such as self-torture practised by the sadhus and the burning of widows (Sati). Auban's work also reiterates some of the earlier fabrications and contains direct reference to Megasthenes' fables. Readers are, however, warned not to take these too seriously. In this respect the book markedly differs from the uncritical attitudes of many earlier and later writings on India.

Knowledge of India was greatly advanced by the publishing activities of Daniel Adam of Veleslavin (1546-99), a Prague humanist scholar. He was responsible for the publication of some original and translated works with passages on various Indian topics.

Valeslavin's *Politia Historica* (Historical Politics, Prague, 1584) states, *inter alia*, "the Old Indians... knew nothing of usury and were, therefore, so happy as to successfully resist, well-nigh alone, Roman Power". Indian geographical, zoological and botanical terms are assembled in *Nomenclator Quadrillinguis Bohemicolatino-graecogermanicus* (Tetralingual Nomenclature in Czech, Latin, Greek and German), while information about the Indian flora was provided by a beautifully illustrated Czech edition of Mattioli's Herber a Bylinar (Herbarium). The book states the places of origin of many imported plants. Readers are instructed that ginger is not the root of the pepper plant, as many apparently believed, but a different species also grown in India whence it is brought to Bohemia.

During the 16th century, the import of Indian spices to Europe again increased considerably. The merchants of Nuremberg now had goods shipped to the ports of Lisbon and Antwerp. It was only later that they were ousted from their position by their Italian rivals, who settled in Prague. Bohemia was conspicuous for her great consumption of spices. Thus, about 1500, cronicler Butzbach that "a Bohemia pig eats more saffron during a year than a German man during his whole lifetime". Interest in spices and other eastern products was also evidenced by a book by well-known Czech nobleman, Krystof Harant of Polzice and Bezdruzice (1564-1621), narrating his journey to the East and published in 1608. Although the author never seriously contemplated a journey to India, he devoted great attention to the country in his travelogue. Harant's *Putovani, aneb cesta z kralovstvi ceskebo do mesta Benatek: odtud po mori do zeme svate, zeme judske a dale do Egypta* (Journey from the Kingdom of Bohemia to Venice and Thence by Sea to Palestine, to Judaea and further to Egypt) is unparalleled in old Czech literature for enumerations of goods imported from India to Europe. A special list of about 30 Indian products known in Bohemia is given. The population of India is described as consisting of noble nations who, with the exception of Alexander the Great, "... were never subdued by a foreign king or monarch ... so that it is not known whether, since the beginning of the world, there has ever existed another nation which has so laudably defended and kept up its freedom and order as these Indians have." The writer contradicts the view that guns were invented in 14th century Europe, reminding his readers that the Indians had used them in war a thousand years before. When the Portuguese came to India they found hundreds of guns there, some of them so big that a hundred oxen had to be yoked together to pull one such fieldpiece. Thanks to its value as a source of information, Harant's book long ranked among the most successful travelogues by Czech authors.

In 1610 a voluminous work by H. Buenting, *Itinerarium sacrae scripturae* (Itinerations of the Holy Scriptures), appeared in Czech in Prague. The book contains an original map of the world, with Asia depicted in the shape of a Pegasus, and an account of voyages by King Solomon's ships to India. With this work we are about to wind up our survey of this category of reports. There remains a somewhat later book by Jiri Plachy-Ferus (1585-1655), a Prague Jesuit, librarian and prefect, which appeared under the title The Catholic Map or the Conversion of the Nations of the Whole World... to a knowledge of the Holy Catholic Faith, but its value as source of informations on India is very dubious. Plachy discusses the various realms of India from the narrow points of view of the spread of the Catholic faith, his approach, being, moreover, purely imaginative. His main "source" is a fictitious book in the Chaldean language, allegedly found on the Malabar shore. According to the book, St. Thomas founded eight archbishopries in India, of which only six are known (including one in China). The work is typical of the Catholic counter reformation movement in Bohemia. Even as regards knowledge of India, it is evidenced that the defeat of the Bohemian Estates at the battle of the white mountain in 1620 put an end to the promising development of Czech humanist literature, which found its greatest writer in Jan Amos Komensky-Comenius (1592-1670), the Teacher of Nations, author of a monumental work written in exile. His pedagogic and didactic writings give factual information on some realities of India and Indian life, rivers, worship of idols, script and so forth.

Regarding the impact of Indian thought on the East Dr. Radhakrishnan has rightly observed:

"Half the world moves on independent foundations supplied. China and Japan, Tibet and Siam, Burma and Ceylon look to India as their spiritual home. The civilization itself has not a short-lived one. Its historic records date back for over four thousand years, and even then it had reached a stage of civilization which has continued its unbroken, though at times slow and almost static course, until the present day. It has stood the stress and strain of more than four or five millenniums of spiritual thought and experience."[15]

Christopher Isherwood regarding contribution of Vivekanand has aptly remarked: "Who else had stood, as he stood impartially between East and West, prizing the virtues and condemning the defects of both of the cultures! We else could represent in his own person young India of the Nineties in Synthesis with Ancient India of the Vedas? Who else could stand forth as India's champion against poverty and oppression and yet sincerely praise American idealism and British singleness of purpose. Such was Vivekanand's 'greatness'. "[16]

Heideggar has more than any other European philosopher initiated dialogue between West and the Far East, and yet he takes upon his path the motives of the great traditions only in such a way that he incorporates them whole in his current point of departure – into the necessity into which his thinking is forced".[17] Today a relatively unified world civilization is being built which is meant to secure the survival of humanity, though it is not such security which could be man's first and last talk; in this situation it is imperative to have dialogue between the various traditions. Heidegger has provided a significant stimulus for such dialogue; and yet the task to which he applied himself has not been accomplished, but is being handed down to us open-ended.

REFERENCES

1. Graham Parkes (Ed.), *Heidegger and Asian Thought,* Intro, p.1.

2. For details please see – article 'Are comparison between the East and West fruitful for comparative philosophy?" of Laurence J. Roshan in *Philosophy East and West*, XI (4 January 1962) 239f.

3. *Concise Oxford Dictionary*, Ninth Edition.
4. Burtrand Russell, *New Hopes for the Changing World*, p. 18.
5. Quoted by Hajime Nakamura, *Ways of Thinking of Eastern People*, Introduction, p. 12.
6. Nirad Chaudhary, *Passage to India*, p. 33.
7. Shri Aurobindo, *The Foundations of Indian Culture*, (Seventh Impression, 1992), pp. 3-4.
8. Paul Brunton, *A Search in Secret India*, p. 202.
9. Here the indication is towards Raman Maharshi.
10. *A Search in Secret India*, p. 13.
11. Story, p. 97.
12. Winternitz, *History of Indian Literature*, Vol. II, part I, pp. 334-335.
13. *Ibid.*, p. 343. For details please see the chapter – "Buddhist Literature and Universal Literature," pp. 334-346.
14. Pt. J.L. Nehru, *The Discovery of India*, (1931), pp. 207-208.
15. Dr. S. Radhakrishnan, *The Hindu View of Life*, p. 11.
16. Christopher Isherwood's introduction p. XIX to *What Religion is*? in the words of Swami Vivekanand compiled by John Yale.
17. Graham Parkes (Ed.), *Heidegger and Eastern Thought*, p. 76.

2

THOUGHT CONSTRUCTS OF THE EAST
Some Dimensions

Divine mind in its waking state
Arises in far off distant places,
And does the same in sleeping states,
Weaving in dreams, so wondrous images,
    Unique light amidst lustrous objects
    Which swings far off in distant places,
    That my mind may develop so perfect,
    To reflect noble images,
Motivated by mind, the thoughtful pious,
Remain steadfast, above all vice
And offer themselves as a sacrifice
In struggles of life as oblations so nice.
    A luminous entity amongst all senses,
    An unheard of divine master of senses,
    That my mind may always reflect,
    Noble thoughts and deeds so perfect.[1]

— *Yajurveda*

"Learning without thought brings ensnarement. Thought without learning totters." Sayings of Confucious, II. 15.

धान्यानामुत्तमं दाढयं धनानामुत्तमं श्रुतम् ।
लाभानां श्रेयः आरोग्यम् सुखानां तुष्टिरुत्तमा ।।

—*Mahabharata,* Van 313.74

(The best of all laudable things is skill. The best of all possessions is knowledge. The best of all gains is health, and contentment is the best of all kinds of happiness.)

तपस्-स्वाध्याय-ईश्वरप्रणिधानानि क्रियायोगः ।

—Yoga Sutra 2.1

(Austerity, study and the dedication of the fruits of one's work to God – these are called Kriyayoga.)

> "The Four Noble Truths - viz. pain, the origin of pain, the cessation of pain, and the noble eightfold path that leads to the quieting of the pain"
>
> —Dhammapad 191

> "Merely reading the scriptures does not free the mind from anxiety. If for a moment thou restrainest thy mind, God will appear before thee."
>
> —Macauliffe, Sikh Religion, Vol. I, p. 177

> "*Jiva is Shiva* (all living beings are God). Who then dare talk of showing mercy to them? Not mercy, but service, service for man must be regarded as service to God."
>
> —Rāmakrishna

Beaconsfield says : "Meditation is culture". If it is true then thought is the root and meditation is fruit. First some thread of thought that comes to the mind and as per one's need and urge meditates upon that. At times the process is reversed also. Meditation comes up as a root for the thought. While continuously meditating on certain object or idea one gets a flash of novel idea or thought. In the educational system of the East, may it be Hinduism, Buddhism or Confucianism, two major points have been stressed upon ability to think and desire to learn.

Swami Vivekanand worked, *inter alia* other reforms, for an exchange of values. During his maiden American tour for participating in the parliament of religions (1893) he founded and recognised great virtues in the West – energy, initiative and courage – which he found lacking in Indians. Therefore, he said "India has to learn from Europe the conquest of external nature, and Europe has to learn from India the conquest of internal nature. Then there will be neither Hindus nor European's – there will be the ideal humanity which has conquered both the nature, the external and the internal. We have developed one phase of humanity, and they another. It is the union of the two that is wanted."[2] He was the great advocate of trans-cultural communication and believed in the synthesis of the East and the West.

Modern civilization relies solely on science, its achievements also have turned out to be partial and limited. The combination today of the spiritual energies of these two complementary disciplines in the life of man will produce fully integrated human beings, and thus help to evolve a complete human civilization for which the world is ripe and waiting. This is the most outstanding contribution of Swami Vivekanand to human thought today. This synthetic vision of his finds lucid expression in a brief but comprehensive testament of his Vedantic conviction:

"Each soul is potentially divine." The goal (of life) is to manifest this divinity within by controlling nature external (through physical sciences, technology, and socio-political processes) and internal (through ethical, aesthetic, and religious processes).

Do this either by work, or worship, or psychic control, or philosophy – by one, or more or all of these – and be free.

This is the whole of religion. Doctrines, or dogmas, or rituals, or books, or temples, or forms are but secondary details."[3]

Western Thought on the Thinking Process

If we wish to know various Western views about nature and functions of mind we need over here a brief survey of important views of some noted philosophers and psychologists, that may be roughly grouped into the following four categories:

The first type is what is commonly referred to as the *spiritual substance* theory. According to this view, mind is a non-bodily entity which is always identical with itself and which acts as the unifying bond of momentary conscious experiences, such as acts of thinking and willing and feeling, by "having" them as functions of itself; it is the permanent "substratum" to which these experiences belong, in which they inhere, and which thus unifies them into one system. This view is associated particularly with the names of Plato among the ancients and Descartes among the moderns.

The second type of theory is that which conceives mind as identical with the organization of conscious experiences, as the time transcending yet time including unity of such experiences. According to this view, mind is not a spiritual substance which stands over against particular conscious experiences as different from them; it is, rather, precisely such experiences organized into meaningful wholes. This view springs in principle from Kant; but it was modified in more or less significant ways by Hegel and his followers, who changed Kant's formal statement of it. It is known by different names, three of the most common being "transcendental", "organic", and "personalistic". We shall speak of it henceforward as the *organic theory of mind.*

The third type is the view of mind as an aggregate or collection of experiences, non-bodily in nature and connected only by certain laws of association. According to this view, there is no spiritual bond of unity among conscious experiences, whether conceived as a spiritual substance or as an inclusive unity of them; on the contrary, there are only sundry experiences haphazardly joined by habit and custom. If you could exhaustively enumerate all of the experiences of a given individual from birth to death in their various more or less accidental arrangements relatively to each other; you would then have compassed the totality and adequately described his mind as conceived by this theory. *Actualism* is the name sometimes attached to this theory, and we shall refer to it by the name which is perhaps as convenient as any. In the history of philosophy the theory is, of course, chiefly represented by Hume.

Finally, there is the general type of theory which virtually denies that there are any conscious experiences at all, or at least in anything more than a Pickwickian sense. According to this theory, all experiences of willing, feeling, thinking are merely bodily responses to environmental conditions; and the unity among such experiences their organizational structure, is completely explicable in terms of the neuromuscular system. For it, mind is behaviour and the principle of unity is the behaving organism. This view is sometimes supposed to be of recent origin, and is called *behaviorism;* in principle, however, it is of ancient lineage, some of its tenets at least finding advocacy in the atomism of Democritus.[4a]

Thinking and Neuro-Linguistic Programming (NLP)

Thoughts and Physiology are intimately connected. What and how we think affects our body and our body affects our thoughts. The world we create in our mind is real for the body and *vice versa.*[4b]

For example, stooping, slumping and sighing are likely to trigger depressing thoughts while standing up, breathing deeply and smiling evoke good feelings. Health is both physical and mental and the effects of each cross the boundary of the other. Cleaning up one's internal state could have a very beneficial effect on one's physical state.

Neuro-Linguistic Programming (NLP) conforms to this logic. 'Neuro' means the nervous system through which our experience is processed, i.e. Neurological system of five senses. Linguistic is about language and other non-verbal communications that influence us and others around us, e.g. pictures, sounds, feelings, taste, smell, words. "Programming" is the ability to discover and use the programmes that we run (our communication to ourselves and others) in our neurological system to achieve the desired results, in other words, NLP means how to use the language of the mind to consistently achieve specific and desired outcomes.

NLP believes that we do not perceive the world the way it really is but construct a model of it according to our beliefs, interests, upbringing, pre-occupations and experiences. This model of the world is a way of existing in the world. It is a way of walking, way of talking, of how we relate to others and ourselves and how we respond to stress. NLP believes in not giving the right model of the world but in enriching the one you have. It teaches you how to make a difference and get what you want, whatever your goal may be.

Six Levels

According to NLP there are six different levels that control and influence what we are. The first level is the *environment,* your surroundings and the people you are with. Internal environment is the air we breathe and the food we eat. Social environment are the friends, family and colleagues we interact with. Good relations with the people in our environment are crucial for good health. Loneliness, isolation and poor inter-personal relationships are a definite health hazard.

The second level of *behaviour* includes our thoughts as well as actions. NLP shows us practical methods so we can work on this level.

The third level is *capability*. Capability is behaviour practised so often, it becomes consistent and automatic. This is also the level of 'strategies' habitual ways of thinking and responding. Through habits we form our own strategies for dealing with stress, becoming angry, forming relationships etc. Depression and pessimism are results of habitual ways of thinking. NLP at this level helps us to form thinking strategies so we experience less stress and are more in control.

The fourth level is *belief and values*. Beliefs are commands we act upon. They determine how we see ourselves, how we react to others and to situations and what we understand of our experiences. If a heart patient believes his illness is due to factors he cannot change and has no control over such as worry stress and overwork his progress to recovery will be very slow. Now if he was to believe that he is in control of his life and possesses a very strong inner desire to get well, if he will recover much faster. Certain beliefs can be toxic – hostility, depression and feelings of helplessness – all stem from beliefs about ourselves and the world and can harm our health considerably. Values are what is important to us, e.g. success, harmony, love, health, self-reliance and power. Our values motivate our behaviour. Is there a skill you need to learn but don't consider important? If you don't value it, you will never be motivated enough to learn it. Do you consider smoking bad and you wish to give it up? Unless you value health you may not find the will to do it.

A person may know what to do (behaviour) and even know how to do it (capability) but still does not do it because he is not willing to make a difference (belief). The fifth level is *identity. Identity* is your sense of yourself, the beliefs and values you have that define who you are. I am healthy person is an identity statement that has a great impact on your health. It is important not to take criticism of behaviour at an identity level. One must remember that criticism of 'what you do' is an identity statement that has a great impact on your health. It is important not to take criticism of behaviour at an identity level. One must remember that criticism of 'what you do' is not criticism of you. One of the most important ways to reduce health threatening stress is to make a clear distinction between what you do and who you are. The final level is beyond identity or the *spiritual level* – your connection to others and to that which is more than your identity.

NLP also believes that people, places, sights and sound can change our state automatically. These are known as 'anchors'. An anchor in NLP is any sight, sound or touch that triggers a state. We form anchors by making links and associations, e.g. the voice of a person we love always puts us in a good state. So the voice becomes an anchor for us to feel good. Some anchors have the power to induce a negative state – snakes do that to many people. Sometimes as in phobias, one intense experience can create an anchor immediately. One brain reacts to an anchor whether we see or experience it or just imagine it. According to NLP one way to change the state one finds oneself in is to change one's breathing pattern. Physical movement is another way – go for a walk, exercise etc. NLP teaches the way to change negative anchors to positive ones by changing the association pattern and magically transform your state of mind.

Thus we see that belief and reverence these to are the arch sources for healthy mind and positive thinking. Spiritually speaking these two are the precious gifts of the Almighty. Those are really blessed ones, who have these two. The great saint poet Tulsidas has identified these two with the Lord Shankar and Parvati respectively. Saluting these two he says: "I bow down to the Goddess Parvati and the Lord Shankar who are the embodiment of reverence and belief respectively.

Materialistic View

Materialist thinkers describe thought as a function of brain only without attaching any sting to spirit or consciousness. They take it as a product of matter only. Democritus, a Greek atomist, regards mind as material in nature, being composed of fine, smooth and nimble atoms, Epicurus, another Greek materialist, regards matter, as the substratum of soul, mind and thought, which are its mere accidents. Hobbes (1588-1679) reduces thought to motion of the brain. He defines soul or spirit as brain action or nervous substances. Motion produced in the body is conducted by nerves to the brain, and felt as sensation. Sensation is a modification of the motion of the brain. These are forms of equative materialism, which identifies mind with matter, and thought with motion. John Toland (1670-1721) regards *thought is a function of the brain, as taste is a function of the tongue.* Matter is an active substance. It is unconscious in itself but becomes conscious in the brain only. Holbach (1723-1789) regards mind as a nervous substance, and thought as a function of the brain. Cabanis (1757-1808) regards body and mind as identical in nature. The mind is the body endowed with consciousness. The body thinks, feels and wills. *Thought is a secretion of the brain, as bile is a secretion of the liver.* Or, *thought is a function of the brain, as digestion is a function of the stomach.* Julien Offrey De La Mettrie (1709-1751) regards mental processes as effects of nervous or cerebral processes. These are forms of casual materialism. Modern materialism regards consciousness as an epiphenomenon of the brain or matter. Just as flashes of light are struck out by friction of a grinding machine, so the light of consciousness is generated by intense friction of the ganglionic cells. According to epiphenomenalism, mind is an epiphenomenon, a phenomenon of a secondary importance only. It is a byproduct or an offshoot of brain activity. It is caused by the brain, and cannot exert any influence upon the brain. It cannot act upon the brain, and control the body. It is a halo dancing about the brain-cells as Bergson puts it poetically.

Medieval Thought

Medieval thought patterns, which are at times identified with feudal patterns, have indeed strong in the Orient throughout what is thought of as the modern period in the West (roughly the seventeenth and eighteenth centuries) especially in highly religious areas. Generally speaking, many religious seats have remained as medieval in their behaviour as in their manner of valuation. According to Hajime Nakamura the medieval ways of valuation can be characterised by the following features :

(1) The absolute authority of traditional religions was admitted by people in general who were under their strict control. Traditional symbols were stereotyped for a long period.
(2) Consequently, in the realm of social relations and in representing scientific evaluations of the world religious orders were extremely influential.
(3) The absolute sacredness of religious scriptures were stressed. Scholarship was no more than the deduction from and elucidation of, the fundamental dogmas of religions. Learning was in the main, scholastic. Free thinking was not permitted, heretics were punished, skepticism was abhorred.
(4) The tendency of thought was, generally, other worldly. Religious life was regarded as noble, secular life as vile and mean.
(5) As for social structure, a feudalistic hierarchy of status was accepted by the common people and was enforced by authority.
(6) Cultural life was limited to the upper classes; common people hardly participated in it.

Religious Character of Indian Thought

Indians are basically religious people. Their all activities including the daily routines also have a religious touch right from a sweeping of the house to the preparation of a pyre for the dead body they observe some or the other religious norms. Man is not supposed to be the highest in God's creation. The Hindus believe in the existence of super human beings also, and since they are very much higher than man spiritually, they evoke our awe and admiration. The scriptures tell us to be considerate to our kith and kin not only in their life but also to remember them with gratitude even when they have passed away.

It will not be out of place to mention here that charity movement in the west began at a later date. Indians were the first to establish the spiritual and social tradition of public welfare service. The great epics like Ramayana and Mahabharata are replete with such examples where the kings showed their express concern towards pubic welfare and charity which existed before many centuries of the Christ, whereas in the west we find no establishments for the relief of the sick. Hospitals were founded until the reign of Constantine (A.D. 306-37). A law of Justimian (A.D. 527-62) included hospitals for the first time among the ecclesiastical institutions.[6]

Hazime Nakamura has rightly said: "Indian natural sciences too were strongly influenced by the religious thought. The ancient Indians wrote many books on mathematics, astronomy, medicine, and other sciences, and other scientific works were stimulated further after the Greek and the Roman sciences were introduced. Here it is noteworthy that almost all these Indian books of science open with words of admiration for and faith in Gods. The Greek sciences made real progress only after they had shaken off the fetters of theology. The Indian sciences, on the contrary, grew as a subsidiary study to aid the study of the Vedas. Among the natural sciences astronomy was first acknowledged as an independent field of study. From an early time, the orthodox Brahmanists regarded Astronomy (*Jyotish*) highly as one of the six subsidiary studies of the Vedas. They needed astronomical knowledge to hold religious ceremonies on the exact dates given in the secred codes. And for this purpose they began with the observation of the relation among the sun, the moon and the fixed stars; thus the study of the twenty-eight constellations occupied an essential part of their astronomy. It is natural that their science of the heavenly bodies had from the beginning a very strong hue of astrology and that its later development was inseparably related to this art of divination. The growth of mathematics in India was paralleled by that of Astronomy. Mathematics, too, developed chiefly to meet ritualistic needs. The ancient Indians had their alchemy and this also bore a strong religious colouring. The naturalistic philosophy of the Vaisheshik supposed "the invisible power (*adrishta*) to explain the movements of the atoms. And with the lapse of time, they came to attach religious significance to this power."[7]

Counsels of Kao-yao

According to Kao-yao there are in all nine virtues to be discovered in a man-at-his-best. They are:

- affability combined with dignity
- mildness combined with firmness
- bluntness combined with respectfulness
- aptness for government combined with reverent caution
- docility combined with boldness
- straightforwardness combined with gentleness
- an easy negligence combined with discrimination
- boldness combined with sincerity, and
- valour combined with righteousness.

Highlighting the impact of these virtues on the personality of the individuals and the society at large he says: "When these qualities are displayed and that continuously, have we not the good officer? When there is a daily display of three of these virtues their possessor could early and late regulate and brighten the clan of which he was made chief. When there is a daily severe and reverent cultivation of six of them, their possessor could brilliantly conduct the affairs of the state with which he was invested. When such men are all received and advanced, the possessors of those nine virtues will be employed in the public service."[8]

The message conveyed by Kao-yao in the passage above is that in order to maintain social life clean and transparent the public servants has to take initiative since the values or virtues are filtered downward. The very inspiration and motivation should filter down from the top, then only there will be congenial atmosphere for nurturing a good work-culture.

In the introduction of his famous book "Ways of Thinking of Eastern People" Hajime Nakamura has outlined certain characteristics of Eastern and Western people which may interest the readers and as such we are putting forth here in a summarised manner:

"It is often said that the peoples of the East are intuitive and accordingly not systematic or orderly in grasping things, by contrast the Westerners are said to be postulational or logical and that they try to grasp things systematically and by orderly planning. Indeed, the ways of thinking of the Chinese or the Japanese may be characterised as intuitive. But in case of the Indian this label is hardly to apply. For example, the intericate arguments of Abhidharma literature are logical and can never be called intuitive. There is no need to refer to the difficult literature of theology in order to point out how far removed from intuitive grasp is that complicated, fantastic, and strange set of sentiments symboliged in Indian paintings and sculptures. Indian art urges us to form a complicated association of iedas, and leads the spectator into a strange, fantastic atmosphere.

Secondly, it is often asserted that the ways of thinking of the Eastern peoples are synthesis, and that of the Westerners analytic. The Chinese word, for instance, gives us the impression that it is synthetic, but it is more properly set in a stage prior to analysis of linguistic or psychological phenomena. We cannot say that only Westerners have a tendency to be analytical. For example, Indian grammar was more advanced in the analysis of words and phrases, but very weak in synthetic construction of sentences while, on the other hand, Greek Grammar has left an excellent achievement concerning syntax which deals with the synthetic field of words and phrases. Therefore, it is unjustifiable to characterise the ways of thinking of the Eastern people simple as synthetic."[9]

Metaphysical Thought

Due to the misconceptual notion of Indian metaphysics or due to their ignorance many Western scholars have undervalued the moral and spiritual depth of Indian thought. In 19th century one Mr. William Archer, in his "Jem d'esprit" assailed the whole life and culture of India and even lumped together all her greatest achievements, philosophy, religion, poetry, painting, sculpture, Upanishads,

Mahabharata, Ramayana in one wholesale condemnation as a repulsive mass of unspeakable barbarism. In answer to this Sir John Woodroffe, a great Indologist, wrote an important book titled as "Is India Civilized?" because he thought that even an attack of this ignorant kind ought not to be neglected. According to Aurobindo "he (John Woodroffe) took it as a particularly useful type in general kind, first, because it raised the question from the rationalistic and not from the Christian and missionary stand point and again, because it betrayed the grosser underlying motives of all such attacks…his purpose was to disclose the conflict of European and Asiatic culture and, in greater prominence, the distinct meaning and value of Indian Civilization, the peril it now runs and the calamity its destruction would be to the world."[10]

There is and old saying that all great men think alike, which is applicable to the thinking of all the thinkers of the ancient world, may it be East or West. Our great sages of India, like Veda Vyas, Valmiki, Angira, Kashyap etc. Mahavir, Buddha, or the Christ etc. have recorded their thought in various ways and forms which resemble with each other in terms of content, theme etc. At times we find very astonishing similarities among their thoughts. T.W. Rhys Davids has rightly remarked on the theme: "I can find no evidence whatever of any actual and direct communication of any of these ideas from the East to the West. Where the Gospel narratives resemble the Buddhist one, they seem to me to have been independently developed on the shores of the Mediterranean and in the valley of the Ganges. The similarities of ideas are evidenced not only of any borrowing from the one side or the other, but similar feelings engendered in men's minds by similar experience… The lessons drawn from the study of early Buddhism may be found useful for the true apprehension of early Christianity as the Vedas are useful for the true appreciation of classical mythology."[11]

Omission of Thought

Thought no doubt, is very important for the individual and society as well. Here it will not be out of place to quote J. Krishnamurthy who has an angle with a difference, when he says:

- "The death of thought is life eternal."
- "When the mind purges itself of all thought, only then there is the silence of creation."
- "Thought is continuous movement in time; this movement cannot enclose within itself a state of being which is not of time."

This is what Zen Buddhism also enjoins: "Blessed is the one who has emptied himself." Of course, for self-realisation purgation of all sorts of thought becomes essential. But when the one is in the flow of the world, on this stage of the world he has to perform various types of roles, has to share different types of responsibilities. Here comes the importance of *Niskam Karma Yoga* (Yoga of disinterested actions). A man may do hundreds of works for himself or for others; but when attachment will not be there a man will stop thinking about their fruits, results, future etc. which may be good or bad, positive or negative, beneficial or harmful. Doing so he will not be involved in any sort of thought. But to bring about an excellence in his action, to perform his duties in a better way, or to distinguish himself from others he has to think about the idea for the object connected. If we take this type of thinking also as an action, that should also be unattached. Unfolding the secret of *Karmyoga* Gita says:

"In this path of disinterested action a beginning made is not lost (the seed is not destroyed) and there is no fear of contrary results (due to omissions). Therefore, even an ounce of practice of this (Yoga of disinterested action) rids the Sadhaka of great fear (viz. that of birth and death)."[12]

Here the word 'Swalp' (little) is very important because it sounds the practical angle of Yoga of disinterested action. Perfection in this Yoga is very difficult. Latencies of past sins, evils like egoism, attachment, sense of possession etc. and contact with objects of the senses as well as with erring souls and people devoted to sense-enjoyment arrest our progress, no doubt, but whatever advance made on the path of disinterested action is not lost. For, there is no reason why an action performed without reference to its fruits and without attachment and with a balanced mind, according to the behests of God, should be lost. Only an action done with a particular object in view comes to an end after it has yielded the desired result.

A philosopher like Plotinus also felt the need of empty mind for self-realisation or God-realisation. He says : "To attain the God, we must ascend to the highest state and fixing our gaze thereon, lay aside the garments we donned when descending here below, just as in the Mysteries, those who are admitted to penetrate into the inner recesses of the sanctuary, after having purified themselves, lay aside every garment and advance stark marked."[13]

This idea of laying aside the garment of thought and being naked is quite old one as envisaged in our scriptures and subsequently persuaded and advocated by our great saints and devotees like Valmiki, Jyaneshwar, Tulsidas etc. Once Swamy Vivekanand said to Nivedita, "Learn to recognize the Mother as instinctively in evil, terror, sorrow, and annihilation, as in that which makes for sweetness and joy. Fools put a garland of flowers around Thy neck, O Mother, and then start back in terror and call thee 'The merciful'.... Meditate on death. Worship the Terrible. One by the worship of the Terrible can the Terrible itself be overcome and Immortality gained. There could be bliss in torture too.... The Mother Herself is Brahman. Even Her curse is blessing. The heart must become a cremation ground – pride, selfishness, desire, all burnt to ashes. Then and then alone, will the Mother come."[14]

Thus burning of desires etc. to ashes is a form of emptying the heart as well as mind, a pathway to self-realisation. J. Krishnamurthy put it other way round in the following words : "We are always with something, with a problem, with a book, with a person and when we are alone, our thoughts are with us. To be alone, naked, is essential."

Struggle for Thought

Thinkers come and go but their thoughts remain for which they have to struggle a lot during their lifetime. In Human History no new thread of thought was well received. On the contrary they had to lay down their lives for the survival of their thoughts,

Conningham says:

"The battle has been fought on widely diverse fronts, and the forces involved render the conflict an ineradicable characteristic of cultural evolution. The deaths of Socreates of Athens, Jesus of Nazareth, Giordano Bruno of Rome, Girolamo Savonarola of Florence, and hundreds of others whose intellectual integrity brought them at last to martyrdom bear tragic testimony both to its scope and to its perpetuity. Whoever ventures to set his own point of view in antagonism to the traditional, in whatever field, ventures greatly; and one or the other must go down in the struggle. But the struggle cannot be brought to an end; the very nature of the contending forces is such that they are inherently antagonistic and the conflict is therefore an unending one since neither force can in the end be utterly suppressed."[15] G. Watts Conningham, further adds:

"Thus there develops a conflict between the individual and his group, between his own meanings and the traditional ones of the group-mind. And it is precisely this conflict which gives rise to the problem of freedom of thought and action. So long as there is no such conflict there can be no problem of free thought, this is, individual thought, for the very simple reason that then there is, strictly speaking, no "individual thought" at all so long as the individual thinks precisely as the group thinks, there is no one to raise the query he has a right thus to think. But just as soon as differences among points of view emerge within the group, so soon are traditional ways of acting and believing placed in jeopardy; and at once there arises the all important problems of right of the individual to set up his own point of view in antagonism to that of the group."[16]

With the advancement of the civilization of the groups the problem of freedom of thought became more in vogue. At the primitive stages a man was rather innocent of this problem, as he used to follow customary activities and accept traditional belief. Without thinking, which was but natural on the part of a primitive man. In a country like China there has been complete thought control as exercised by government machinery as a policy matter, in spite of tremendous advancement in the field of science and technology.

New Pathways

Due to its vitals Eastern Thought has survived through the centuries and its future is also not disheartening. Twenty-first century is likely to be the century of synthesis J.C. Kapur predicts:

"New and beautiful pathways are being carved through the intricacies of concepts and symbolism in the latest advances in the physical science and the mystical traditions of the East. Many intellectuals are weaving together the relatively less understood behind the linguistic, ritualistic and environmental diversity and the wide divergencies in the patterns of concern in the Hindu, Buddhist, Taoist and Zen Buddhist systems and many of their totalities are termed as *Eastern Thought*. This eastern thought may make a significant contribution, establishing cross-currents in hitherto parallel streams of thought and may well provide new perspectives in unfolding the deeper mysteries of the physical sciences and our comprehension of the universe."[17]

REFERENCES

1. यज्जाग्रतो दूरमुदैति दैवं तदु सुप्तस्य तथैवेति ।
दूरङ्गमं ज्योतिषां ज्योतिरेकं तन्मे मनः शिवसंकल्पमस्तु ॥
येन कर्माण्यपसो मनीषिणो यज्ञे कृण्वन्ति विदथेषु धीराः ।
यदपूर्वं यक्षमन्तः प्रजानां तन्मे मनः शिवसंकल्पमस्तु ॥

— *Yajurveda* 34.1-2

2. Swami Ranganathananda, *Religion and Science*, pp. 1.32-33.
3. C.W.S.V., Vol. I, 11th edition, p.124.
4a. G. Watts Cunningham, *Problems of Philosophy*, pp. 262-63.
4b. आहारशुद्धौ सत्त्वशुद्धिः सत्त्वशुद्धौ ध्रुवा मतिः ।

— Upanishadic Saying

5. Hajime Nakamura, *A Comparative History of Ideas*, p. 477.
6. Vincent A., Smith, *Early History of India* (Oxford, 1994),p. 301, note 1.
7. Hajime Nakamura, *Ways of Thinking of Eastern People*, p.160.

8. The Living Thoughts of Confucious, pp.127-28.
9. *Ways of Thinking of Eastern Peoples*, pp.13-14.
10. Shri Aurobindo, *Foundation of Indian Culture*, p.1.
11. T.W. Rhys Davids, *Lectures*, pp.151-52.
12. नेहाभिक्रमनाशोऽस्ति प्रत्यवायो न विद्यते।
    स्वल्पमप्य धर्मस्य त्रायते महतो भयात्॥
    — Bhagavadgita, II.40
13. Plotinus, *Enneads*, I, Vi, 6.
14. Quoted from the Life of Vivekanand, by Romain Rolland, p.141.
15. G. Watts Cunningham, *Problems of Philosophy*, p. 164.
16. *Ibid.*, p. 155.
17. J.C. Kapur, *India – Uncommitted Society*, p.50.

3

EASTERN CONCEPT OF MAN

> "The Asian view of man is not very much different from the ancient European view of man. I do not believe in the pseudo science of national or continental psychology which affirms that all Asians are this and all Europeans are that. The history of any people is slightly more complicated than these sweeping statements would suggest. As a matter of fact, the Asian and the European peoples had common beginnings and developed from relatively independent views and acquired features which marked from each other."
>
> — Dr. S. Rādhākrishnan

Biologically speaking a man belongs to the category of 'homosapiens', which sets him apart from other species. That is very humanistic psychology differs from other psychologies. The former views a man not solely as a biological organism; but as a person, a symbolic entity, capable of pondering his existence, setting goals, refining his life-style by using his conscience and reasoning power.

Vitalism Vs. Mechanism

There have been too many philosophies to account for relation between life and matter. One is vitalism and another is mechanism.

Vitalism is a philosophy which assumes that life is made possible by some unique, eternal, supernatural force incomprehensible by experimentation. Living organisms are, therefore, considered as non-living matter plus the life giving force which is neither physical nor chemical, this force is termed as Psyche by Aristotle, "the inner principle of action" by Kant, the "universal reason" by Hegel, etc. In Hindu philosophy and other religions it is known as the 'atman' (soul) or the divine spark. The vitalistic view of life prevailed among biologists until seventeenth century.

The growth of the doctrine that Brahman is the inner controller in all the parts and forces of nature and of mankind as the atman thereof, and that all the effects of the universe are the results of his commands. This idea gave rise to a theistic current or thought in which *Brahman* is held as standing aloof as God and controlling the world.

It is by his ordaining, it is said, that the sun and moon are held together, and the sky and earth stand held together (Brhadaranyak Upanishad III. 8–1) God and soul are distinguished again as following:

Two bright feathered bosom friends
Flit around one and the same tree;
One of them tastes the sweet berries,
The other without eating merely gages down.

— Svetasvetara Up. IV-6

Mechanism is a philosophy that assumes that life can be explained entirely in chemical and physical terms. In this philosophy there is no need to invoke the supernatural force to understand life. Adherents of these two philosophies have debated for the last several hundred years and would continue to do so because the topic is of great interest to man.

Humanistic Tradition

Vyas, Buddha, Ashoka, Patanjali, Shankarāchārya, Chandidas, Akbar, Rāmkrishna, Vivekānanda, Aurobindo and Gandhi etc. emphasised one or other aspect of Indian personality according to the state of society and the needs of time. But such emergence always commenced the processes of regeneration and reorientation not through an aggressive communication system but through human contact, through word of mouth straight to the hearts of the people In the East, particularly in the Indian subcontinent there had been a long tradition of humanistic thinkers, who had a man in very high esteem; but Krishna Dvaipayan Vyas, compiler of Mahabharat, a great epic of India, has outsmarted all the thinkers of past as well as the future by saying that "A man is the best of all the creations, there is no object or idea better than man."[2]

Though we find similar sayings about a man from Protogores to Carl Marx and from Gautam to Gandhi; but Vyas stands as the foremost thinker as far as the assessment of real worth of an individual and unity of mankind is concerned.

Here we are reminded of Socrates death-bed statement: *"I am not Athenian or a Greek but a citizen of a world."* To think onself a part of the whole, offshoot of the cosmic soul and observe the tenet of universal brotherhood has been the thinking of the Eastern man from the time immemorial. Unilateral intellectualism leading to self-centred tendency had never been his ideal, as he believed in transformation of soul. Dr. Rādhākrishnan says, "man is more than sum of his appearances. When Crito asks 'In what way shall we bury you, Socrates?' Socrates answers, "In anyway you like, but first catch me, the real me. Be of good cheer, my dear Crito, and says that you are burying my body only, and do with that whatever is usual and what you think best."[3]

In spite of all scientific advances and speculations of our Western Philosophers we could not escape the fact of unity of the Mankind. The two modern philosophers who most consistently reject the Eastern notion of transformation of soul and the concept of reincarnation, Hume and William James have totally rejected the notion of self-identical Soul-substance. There are many other threads and fibres of Western as well as Westernized thinking which do not tally with the Eastern thought. A.N. Whitehead observes that "The platonic and Christian doctrine of soul, the Epicurean doctrine of a Concilium of subtle atoms, the Cartesian doctrine of Thinking substance, the Humanitarian doctrine of rights of man, the general common sense of civilized mankind – these doctrines between them dominate the whole span of Western Thought."[4]

Spiritual Being

As compared to spirit matter has been a negligible substance in the East. This advocacy of spirit and designing the lifestyle accordingly made an European man obviously a spiritualistic. According to Dr. Rādhākrishnan "The Indian thinkers do not oppose nature to spirit. When the natural life of a man comes to itself, his spiritual being becomes manifest. Man's final growth rests with himself. His future is not solely determined, like that of other animals by his biological past. It is controlled by his own plans for the universe. Man is not an insignificant speck in a depersonalized universe. When we overlook the inward subjectivity of man, lose ourselves in the world, we confuse being with having, we flounder in possessions as in dark, suffocating bog, wasting our energies, not an life, but on things. Instead of using our houses, our wealth, and our other possessions, we let them possess and use us…[5] Adi Shankarāchārya, noted founder and great exponent of Monistic school of Indian Philosophy has already warned us of this very phenomenon of consumerism. He says that because of Avidya (devoid of knowledge) man, instead of consuming the things, allows consumables to consume him.[6] There is no end to one's materialistic desires. The more they are accomplished, the more speedily they emerge and a man hankering after desires swiftly moves from one point to another just like the monkey who jumps from one branch to another for plucking more and more fruits.[7] Dhammapada further adds "River is very mirth-giving and as such it is liked very much by one and all; but those who are completely drowned in its flow of mirth how can they suffer from ailments, old age etc."[8]

Jain canons also assess man's worthiness or unworthiness by his acts only. Uttaraddhyayan Sutra clearly declares 'by having shaven one's head one does not become shramana, simply by chanting the holy syllable "Om" one does not become Brahman. Only by having taken refuse into the woods one does not become muni (sage). Only by wearing valkal cloth (made out of bark of particular tree) one does not become an ascetic'.[9] In the same vein Confucious says "When substance overbalances refinement, crude ıess results. When refinement overbalances substance, there is superficiality. When refinement substance are balanced one has great man."[10]

Further he adds:

- Look as the means which a man employs, consider his motives, observe his pleasure. A man simply cannot conceal himself."[11]
- First he sets good example, then he invites others to follow it.[12]
- At fifteen I thought only of study, at thirty I began playing my role, at forty I was sure of myself, at fifty I was conscious of my position in the universe, at sixty I was no longer argumentative, and now at seventy I can follow my heart's desire without violating custom.[13]
- Today when the people call a man filial they mean that he is supporting his parents. But he does as much for his dogs and horses. If he does not show respect for his parents, how is he differentiating between them and the animals.[14]

Available historical evidence shows that the Harappa and Mohenjodaro civilization was the earliest of Indian civilisation which was followed by the Vedic Age including the age of the Upanishads. However, as no literature relating to the age of Harappa and Mohenjodaro is forthcoming to give us a clue about the philosophy and the concept of man in vogue in those bygone days, our consideration can begin with the Vedas. It would also be a futile exercise for our purpose to enter into the controversy that continues to baffle the historians about the origin of the Aryans and whether they existed prior to the Dravidians or coexisted with them and so on, for the purpose of our consideration is confined to the main theme of the concept of man as expounded in the Vedas and the literature in the subsequent ages. Thus our discussion begins with the Vedas so far as the conception of man is concerned.

The primary question is ...what is the Veda, after all? Etymologically it is derived from the root *Vid* which means to know. In other words Veda implies the storehouse of secret knowledge. Answering the primary question it may be said that the Vedas are compilations of hymns called Riks or Mantras or Sanhitas seen by the Rishis or Sages and there are four such compilations. The Riks recited in praise of the gods are collected andcompiled as the Rik

Veda. The mantras meant exclusively for ritualistic functions are found in the Yujurveda. Some hymns are primarily for singing and find a place in the Samaveda. The hymns in the Atharva Veda are meant for the black arts and acquiring a control and victory over enemies.

Again each of the Vedas is divided into four parts—the *Samhitas,* the *Brāhmans,* the *Āranyakas* and the *Upanishads*. The Samhitas are the riks or Mantras included in the Vedas. The Brahmanas explain both in prose and in verse the details of the rituals to be performed during the sacrificial ceremonies. The philosophical discussions and speculations and spiritual revelations as important conclusions are contained in the *Āranyakas* and the Upanishads. In short the Vedas are a record and a compilation of the esoteric truths about god, man and the manifested world as revealed to the Rishis.

The most striking feature of the Vedas is its hymns and the sacrifices by way of invocation to the different gods like *Agni, Varuna, Mitra, Indra, the Aswinis, Surya, Vayu, Brihaspati, the Ribhus, Vishnu, Rudra, Soma and the goddesses like Aditi, Sarawati, Ila, Bharati, Sarama,* etc. The worship of these gods and goddesses has led the Western scholars to conclude that the Aryans are a race of barbarians trying to propitiate a set of malevolent nature gods of whom they were terribly afraid and on whose mercy depended their protection and prosperity. But Indian scholars rightly point out that the Vedic Rishis shrouded the secret knowledge of the highest spiritual realisations with naturalistic forms for the common man and left the deeper interpretations for the contemplation and realisation of the thoughtful. In their opinion *Agni* symbolises the Divine will Force, or the Illumined will *Indra* the giver, *Surya, Savitri*... the Creator and the Increaser, *Brihaspati* power of the soul, *Vishnu* the all pervading godhead, *Soma* lord of Delight and Immortality, cows for light, horse for power, ghrta for thought or mind and so on. In a word the terms used in the Vedas are all symbolic and carry double connotations one outward and ritualistic for the ordinary and the other deeper and spiritual for the seeking souls. These godheads whom the Aryans worshipped represented to them the different powers and personalities of the Supreme or the Absolute who is one and Indivisible, yet who has manifested Itself as the many. Thus the

Aryans, who appeared to believe in polytheism, were truly monists in their approach to the Almighty, or rather it can be said the monism and polytheism prevailed among them simultaneously. They were aware that God is one and Absolute and yet he has expressed himself in infinite forms in the world of phenomena.

Cosmos in the Vedas

The Vedas in their characteristic esoteric way also speak of the phenomenal world coming into existence. This is clearly brought out in the Purusha Sukta which finds repeatedly in all the four Vedas in view of its importance. This Sukta speaks of the Supreme Reality on the one hand and the cosmic manifestation on the other. It reads : "Thousand headed is the Supreme Being, thousand eyed, thousand footed, embracing the earth all around. He yet exceeds it by a span."[15]

Here thousand is not a numerical figure, it signifies infinity, *ananta*. Indicating the Supreme as Infinite the last part of the mantra says that He is even beyond that. Then it says :

"From Him was born the Cosmic Egg and from that the person. Born, He reached beyond the earth, behind as well as before."

Such is the declaration of the Hymn about the Supreme Divine Being and His cosmic creation. Then it says: "With sacrifice the Gods worshipped the Supreme embodied in the Cosmic Person." This implies that the Supreme offered his own Body in sacrifice and the creation is the result. All the diverse manifestations of life and sub-life are the products of this self-sacrifice, the supreme holocaust of the Supreme Person.[16]

Then the Rishi of the Hymn declares :

"Coming out of the waters and too of the sap of Earth, He was above the creators. Twashtr, the celestial architect comes designing His form, of that Supreme Person was the Universe first born. I know the Great being of the hue of the Sun beyond the reach of Darkness. He who knows Him thus becomes immortal here; there is no way else for release."

Beauty and opulance are Thy wives; Day and Night Thy sides; the constellations thy form. The Aswins are Thy form. The Aswins are Thy wide mouth. Grant this our desire Here; grant the Yonder;

grant us All."[17]

Thus, the Hymn confirms that this manifested world is as much real as the Spreme Brahman. What is manifested here is the Divine Reality. What Form and Name is assumed in the manifestation is as Real as the reality that is shaped into the Form and name. This in essence is the Truth and Knowledge of the Veda and it is this truth and knowledge that we find extended in the subsequent scriptures – the Upanishads, the Tantras and the Gita.

Man in the Vedas

It should be clear from the above discussion that man in the Vedas is not different from the divine reality, individually and socially. The individual as well as the universe in which he lives are both a manifestation of the Supreme Reality, essentially and substantially. The following quotation from the Rig Veda establishes the principle:

"Who has perceived this Truth occult, that the Child gives being the Mothers by the workings of his nature? An Offspring of many waters, he comes forth from them a seer possessed of his whole law of nature. Manifested, he comes forth from them a seer possessed of his whole law of nature. Manifested, he grows in their lap of crookedness and becomes high, beautiful and glorious."[18]

Explaining the above Sri Aurobindo writes, "We see that these Waters are... closely connected with the clarity and the honey, - *ghrtasya yonau sravatte madhunam, scotanti dhara madhuno ghrtasya:* they flow to the Truth, they are themselves source of the Truth, they flow in the unobstructed and shoreless vast as well as here upon earth."[19]

Thus, the mantras stand to mean that man is a child of Truth and Force and Delight, but in the manifested universe everything is distorted or has become crooked and man, through a process of evolution, grows into original divinity which he essentially is and becomes high, beautiful and glorious. Thus, the Vedas have always seen man as divine in his birth and divine in his fulfilment. There is nothing else than divine about him.

Man, the Individual

The Vedas consider Man superior to the gods he worships. They proclaim that his destiny lies within his own powers and he can realise his won destiny through Karma and Yajna (work and sacrifice), as the gods are pleased with both and offer boons according to sacrifices, for the gods are no more than the powers of their won personality and seated in their own being. The Aryans, at least in the early Vedic period, did not think of other worldliness or realising heaven beyond the world of human existence. They always hoped to realise both *purushartha* and *paramartha* (material affluence and spiritual perfection) here on earth during their own life-time of hundred years which everyone aspired to live.

The *purushartha* is described to consist of *artha* (wealth), *kama* (desires), *dharma* (religion) and *moksha* (liberation). The Srutis mention only the first two, and the latter two were added during the early and later Upanishadic age. This implies that the Vedic rishis perceived all their fulfilment in *artha* and *kama* but at the same time it has to be remembered that they never lost themselve. They enjoyed everything with a sense of detachment for the delight of existence which the rishi of the Isha Upanishad latter proclaimed as *tena tyaktena bhunjithah*, renouncing thou shall enjoy. It is also to be mentioned there that *artha* or wealth does not imply material prosperity only, it implied *Sri* and included an alround prosperity. Similarly *kama* also includes not only the fulfilment of worldly desires but also *dharma*, that which steadily leads to integral progress and *moksha*, the ultimate union with the Supreme Reality. The Vedic rishis never discriminated between the material and the spiritual, both being the two dimensions of the same truth.

Man, the Social Being

The Vedas (as much as the Upanishads) had a well defined concept of the society and the position of the Individual therein. They divided the members of the society into four classes according to the nature of work assigned to them in the society for its proper sustenance – the *Brahmins* or teachers, the *kshatriyas* or warriors, the vaisyas or the businessmen and *Sudras* or the producers and cultivators (similar class system also existed in the European society in the Greek and Roman civilisations). The brahmins were engaged in self-study, contemplation and imparting knowledge to others. The kshatriyas were expected to protect others from external invasion and internal destruction. The *Vaisyas* were mainly concerned with exchange of goods and maintain property. The duty and the function of the Sudras were to cultivate, produce things of the day to day requirements of mundane life and thus render service to the society. But it has to be noted here that this classification was neither very rigid nor based on birth but related to the inherent nature (*swabhava*) and selfbound duty (*swadharma*) of an individual. Thus a kshatriya became brahmin and a Brahmarishi while brahmins like Parsurāma and Drona were continuously engaged in battles and warfares. Thus the castes were flexible with possibilities for migration from one to another.

The migration was further strengthened by intercaste marriages which was permissible in the Vedic days. A brahmin could marry a brahmin, a *kshatriya* or even a vaisya girl, a kshatriya could marry a girl of his own caste or of vaisya or sudra and so on. It has to be noted that no caste was considered to be superior or inferior, for, every work was considered, necessary and useful, as such the work of brahmin was as much important as that of a kshatriya or a vaisya or a sudra. It is only at a later stage the sense of superiority and inferiority creeped in as a result of brahminical domination leading to an ultimate degeneration and dissolution of the system. In the nearly Vedic days brahmin was believed to have been born of the forehead of Brahman, the kshatriya from the shoulders, the vaisya from the heart and the sudra from the feet. The *Purusha Sukta* of Rig Veda and while Yajur Veda reads, *"brahmanosya mukhamaseet vahurajnnyah kritah, urutadasyayad – vaisya padabhyam sudro ajayata."* There was nothing wrong about the belief as long as it was symbolic, for the head is the seat of knowledge and the sole function of the brahmin was acquisition and imparting of knowledge. Similarly the shoulders are the seat of power, the heart the seat of love and the legs stood for service and these symbols very well fitted to the different castes associated with them. The difficulty arose only when the head was considered to be superior to the other limbs which was wrong, for the body depends on all its parts for its functioning and survival. The more important thing to be noted in this connection is that the Veda considers all castes in the society to be divine origin as such no caste can be considered to be superior to the other. The society runs smoothly due to the contribution of all its members.

Thus, in conclusion, it may be stated that the Vedic concept of Brahman and Self, man and society stands out in clearest terms with no ambiguity and is hailed as high and vulnerable in the modern times as in the Vedic days. Transcendentally, the Brahman is the absolute, the one without a second, the Supreme Purusha with a thousand (innumerable) heads, a thousand eyes and thousand feet. Phenomenally He is the universe and cosmos manifesting in all beings. From Him man takes birth and to Him he returns, the society is an extension of his different dimensions and power. He is all and there is nothing beyond him.

Man in the Upanishads

The Upanishads claim a unique position in Indian philosophy, there can be no two opinions on the contributions of the Upanishads to the field of knowledge. Pointing out the importance of the Upanishads Sri Aurobindo writes: "...the sears of ancient India had, in their experiments and efforts at spiritual training and the conquest of the body, perfected a discovery which in its importance to the future of human knowledge adwarfts the divinations of Newton and Gallilio, even the discovery of the inductive and experimental method in Science was not more momentous..."

But what are these Upanishads? The answer comes from Prof. Sharma. He says: "The Upanishads are the revelations vouchsafed not to single prophet but to the sears of a whole age, which is one of the most brilliant in the annals of mankind. They are inspired utterances, the results not of a logical but of a poetic approach to Reality."[20]

The Upanishads are also known as veda-anta, the conclusion of the Vedas or in other words, the last word, the crown and summit of the Vedas.

Supreme Reality in the Upanishads

In his essay titled 'Philosophy of the Upanishads', Sri Aurobindo brings out clearly the nature of the Reality as revealed to the Upanishadic Rishis. He says, "the idea of transcendental Unity, Oneness and Stability behind all the flux and variety of phenomenal life is the basal idea of the Upanishads: this is the pivot of all Indian metaphysics, the sum and goal of our spiritual experience."[21] Sri Aurobindo proceeds to point out that the Upanishadic seers, through their process and method of Yoga came to three crowning realisations about the Reality.

In the first place they beheld a Unity and stability behind all phenomenal appearances. This reality, they declared, is the Nityo'.....*nityānām,* the One Eternal in the many transient, something Absolute and transcendent of all even of Time, Space and Causality.

The second discovery of the Upanishadic seers was that the transcendent absolute self of things was also the Self of all living beings, *cetanāscetanānām,* the One Consciousness in many consciousnesses or the One Intelligence working behind all the myriad forms of the intelligence (and non-intelligence).

Thirdly, they realised that there is an identity between the Transcendental Self in the individual as well as the Self in the Universe or Universal Self. In other words the true individual Self, the Universal Self and the Transcendental Self are one and the same, this stupendous truth found expression in the two famous formulas of the Vedanta – *'so'ham',* (He am I) and *'aham brahma asmi',* (I am Brahman, the Eternal).

Sri Aurobindo considers these four grand truths – *"nitya nityanam", "cetanaschetana", so "ham" and "aham brahmasmi"* – the four mighty pillars on which the whole edifice of Upanishadic philosophy stands.

Man, the Individual in the Upanishads

As mentioned earlier the Vedas considered man superior to the gods, for, when the different gods are capable of the specific powers vested with them, it is within man's reach to realise the Supreme Reality.

The Taittiriya Upanishad brings out the possibility in the clearest terms. The *Bhriguvalli* of the Upanishad points out now Bhrigu, son of Varuna came unto his father and prayed him to teach him about the Brahman. Varuna advised his son to acquire the knowledge of the Eternal through meditation. Bhrigu after, successive concentrations of his thought came to know of Brahman in successive revelations,[22] first : anna or food (or body) as brahman (*annam brahmeti*), secondly, prana (or life) as brahman *(prananam brahmeti)*, thirdly, manas (mind) as brahman *(manah brahmeti)*, fourthly, vijnana (wisdom) as brahman *(vijnānam brahmeti)*. In other words this would mean that the human personality consists of five aspects or sheaths, namely body, life, mind, wisdom and bliss. Explained in a different way, man in his childhood is only body conscious, concentrating on the bodily needs. As he grows up he becomes conscious of his life enjoyments. As he grows further in age, the mind or the thinking process becomes more predominant. Further development of the personality brings in maturity and clarity of understanding about himself and the universe. When man is a fully developed being he is nothing but a blissful being merged in the universal and the Eternal.

The Mandukya Upanishad explains the individual self in a different way. It points out that all this Universe as much the individual self is the Eternal Brahman and the self is fourfold, or man lives in four states of consciousness – the wakeful, the dreaming, the perfect sleeping and the featureless beyond the three.

The first is the wakeful self Jagruti known as Vaiswanara, the Universal Male, or the gross material self. In this state of consciousness man is filled with impressions derived directly from the objects presented to the senses. This is the self of sense perfections.

The second is the self of Dream or dream consciousness *(swapna)* in which the senses are quiescent and so the impressions are not derived directly from the objects but from the images stored in the memory. Here the subject is only indirectly dependent on the object, this self is called the *taijasa,* the inhabitant in luminous mind or inner intelligence or the subtle self and enjoys things in a subtle way.

The third relates to the state of dreamless sleep *(susupti)* in which not only the senses but also the mind is quiescent. This state is the causal self known as *prajna*, the Lord of wisdom, or the Womb of the Universe or the inner Soul, the Omniscient. In this state of consciousness the self is blissful in which the subject is practically, though not entirely, free from the object. Of course, the consciousness may at any moment come back to the dream to the wakeful state.

And finally there is the fourth State of *turiya* in which the subject is permanently free from the principle of objectivity and in which one has the positive experience of the liberated spirit; this is the state of Om, the Atman or Eternal Brahman whom the Upanishad describes as:

"Letterless is the fourth, the incommunicable, the end of phenomena, the Good, the One other than whom there is no other: thus is Om. He that knows is the Self and enters by his self into the Self, he that knows, he that knows."[23]

It may be observed here that the individual self as described in the Taittriya and the Mandukya Upanishads have a similarity in conception as indicated below:

Mandukya	State of Self-consciousness	Taittiriya
1.Walking State	Subjective Self fully under influence of objective senses	Anna (Matter of physical + partly Prana (vital)
2. Dream State	Subjective Self free from direct objective sensory experiences but under influence of memory of sense experiences	Partly Prana and partly mental (lower or mechanical mind)
3. Susupti or Dreamless State	Sunjective Self completely free from objective influence	Vijana or Prajna (Pure knowledge or wisdom)
4. Turiya State	Indentification with Brahmic Consciousness	Ananda or Bliss

Thus the Upanishads conceive man, the individual in five aspects or four states of being. Sri Aurobindo's concept of man has a great similarity with that of the Upanishads.

Man, the Social Being

The concept of society as in the Vedic days with the four castes continued through the Upanishads as well, but the caste system which was more flexible and based on the *swabhava* and *swadharma* of the individual during the earlier period had become rather rigid by the age of the Upanishads. In this regard we are reminded of the story of Jabala, the son of a *Sudrani* who went to Rishi Gautama for acquiring knowledge. When he (Jabala) was asked who his father was, he replied that he did not know. Gautama who normally did not accept any disciples other than Brahmins could come to know that Jabala who was a truthful could not be born of any father other than a Brahmin and accepted him as his disciple after renaming his as Satyakama Jabala. This shows how adherence to Truth and search after knowledge was more important than the caste system in the Upanishadic days. The basis for the caste system in the ancient days has already been discussed under the Vedas. In those days no caste was considered inferior to the others, each caste being great in its own function. Social degeneration began long after the Upanishadic age when birth into a family, and not intrinsic nature, became the criteria for determining the caste.

Man, the Divine Being

As in the Vedas, so in the Upanishads, man is considered as a divine being, a manifestation of the divine reality. The Upanishads are replete with expressions like *'soahm'* (I am That), *'Aham brahmasmi'* (I am the brahman), *'Tattwamsi'* (Thou art That) etc.

As indicated earlier the transcendent Self in man is identically the same as the transcendent self in the universe and this identity is the one great key to the knowledge of the absolute Brahman. Two assertions ensue from the above mentioned statement, viz. Identity is a fact in the reality of things and difference is a fact in the appearance of things. The difference which begins in the world of causality widens in the layer of subtle matter. Thus, we observe the completest identity of Supreme Self with man and the widest difference as twin facts of the one Truth (identity).

The different levels of identity at different levels of matter are better explained by the conceptions of mind at these levels. The basal conception for Mind as conditioned by gross matter is Dualistic, the knower here is and must be different from the known. However, the identity between them is self (hence realised and known) by the supreme sympathy of love and faith as the Lord and his beloved. Similarly, the basal conception for mind in the subtle universe is Dualo-monistic, the knower is not quite different from the known, he is like and of the same substance, but inferior, small and dependent, his sense of the oneness may account to similarity and co-substantiality but not to coincidence and perfect identity. The individual here comes to realise certain unity with the great whole, he is enlarged and aggrandized into a part of the Universal Self, but the sense of identity is not complete or cannot be complete.

As the individual self rises in its evolution and enters the universe of causal matter the media and methods of knowledge begin to disappear. Mind comes into almost direct relations with its source and the difference between the individual and the Supreme Self is greatly attenuated. The knower is aware that he is coeval and co-existent with the Supreme Self, he is aware of a sense of Omnipresence, he is on the other side of phenomena and can see the Universe at will with him and without him. Yet he is not necessarily realised the Supreme as himself, but such realisation is now without his grasp. The basal perception for mind in this Universe is Monism with a difference, but the crowning perception of Monism becomes possible.

But the last and final stage of Identification comes when the individual self rises in the process of evolution and enters into full realisation with the Supreme Self and ceases to be the individual self, becomes again the eternal an absolute Brahman. This identification is known as the *Laya* or Utter Absorption of Hinduism, the highest nirvana or extinction from phenomena of the Upanishads or the Buddhistic metaphysics. This is in brief the process of evolution or the upward movement of the individual self as brought out by the Upanishads and that is the divine destiny of man.

Thus we see that man is divine in his origin, apparently undivine in the middle, but again the same divine self at the end. Hence the Upanishads proclaim:

"He is unborn, he is everlasting, he is ancient and semptiiternal;

he is not slain in the slaying of the body." (Katha Up. 1.2.18). Eternal is man.

Man, in the Gita

Among all the Indian scriptures the Gita is the most popular, and yet it is the most baffling, every action and inaction, violence and non-violence, action and knowledge, *pravrtti* and *nivrtti* find sanction from it. It has served as a guide to all the Acharyas from Shankara to Sri Aurobindo.

What was the occasion for the pronouncement of the Gita? Viewed most materially and superficially it was the battlefield of Kurukshetra where the Kauravas and Pandavas stood ready to fight with each other to establish their respective rights over the kingdom which each party claimed for itself. In a subtle sense the fight was between two ideals – dharma and adharma, legality and illegality, order and chaps. Above all it was a time when the perception of the rishis as contained in the Vedas and Upanishads had dwindled into insignificance and darkness, and desires and vital enjoyment or bhoga had taken precedence over Tyaga or abandonment. The Time Spirit had necessitated the pronouncement of the Gita.

Supreme Reality in the Gita

Chapters eight, eleven, twelve and fifteen expound the concept of the Supreme Reality in the Gita. Explaining this concept from chapter XV of the Gita Sri Aurobindo points out that the Gita takes not a monistic or a dualistic, but a synthetic and integral view of the Reality. He writes:

"There is a spirit at work in the world that is one in innumerable appearances. It is the developer of birth and action... the constituting reality of all this stir in time and space, it is itself. Time and Space and Circumstances... it is the gods and men and creatures and things and forces and qualities and quantities and powers and presences... this single self-existent spiritual entity, the one, the Eternal. But we see obviously at work before us, is not the Eternal and his conscious Shakti, but a Nature which in the blind stress of her operation is ignorant and limiting play… The inherent power in her…is the *Kshara,* the Universal Soul, the spirit in the mutability of cosmic phenomenon and becoming one with Immutable and the Supreme. …" But then there is another spirit of whom we become aware and who is none of those things, but self and self only. This spirit is eternal, always the same, never changed or affected by the Manifestation… It is the self of all and yet unmoved, indifferent, intangible…. This spirit is timeless though we see it in Time; it is unextended in space…. This is the *Akshara,* the immutable in the mutable, the immobile in the mobile, the imperishable in things perishable.

"The *Kshara* spirit visible to us as all natural existence and the totality of all exitences moves and acts pervadingly in the immobile and eternal *Akshara*… This Akshara is the self higher than the Buddhi – it exceeds even the highest subjective principle of Nature in our beings – These two then are the two spirits we see in the world; one emerges in front in its action. The other remains behind it steadfast in that perpetual silence from which the action comes and in which all actions cease and disappear into timeless being, Nirvana. *Dvavimam purusam loke ksharas caksara evaca.*[24]

The Gita does not stop at this, it finds in its supreme vision of the Purushottama the solution for this cosmic illusion. For the truth of the Kshara and the Akshara are contained in the Purushottama who is both and yet transcends them. *Uttamah puruses tvanyah paramatme tyudahrtan, yo lokatryam, avisya bibhartya-vyaya isvarah* (But other than these two is the highest spirit called the Supreme Self, who entered the three worlds and upbears them, the imperishable Lord).[25]

The Gita further points out that the Supreme is even beyond his supreme abode paramadharma. It reads: *Yatra no bhasyate surya no sasanka no pavakah, yadgatwa no nivkartante taddhamam paramam mama*[26] which means, the sun shines there not, neither moon nor fire, reaching there none returns; that is my supreme abode."

Thus the Gita's concept of the reality boils down to one expression, *Surya Vasudeva iti* (All that we perceive is Vasudeva) which is replica of the Upanishadic concept, *Sarva Khalvidam brahma* or *All this is Brahman.*

Man, the Individual

It is an eternal portion of Me that becomes the Jiva in a world of Jivas[27] says the Lord in the Gita, explaining the Statement Sri Aurobindo writes: "It means that each soul, each being in its spiritual reality is the very Divine, however, partial its actual manifestation of him in Nature. And it also means...that each manifesting spirit, each of the many, is an eternal individual, and eternal unborn undying power of the one Existence.... The individual spirit exists and ever existed beyond in the Eternal, for it is itself everlasting, *sanatana*....

This eternal individual is not other than or anyway really separate from the divine Purusha. "It is the Lord himself, the Ishwara by virtue of the eternal multiplicity of his oneness."[28] *(Ishwara sarvabhutanam hridese Arjuna tisthati* – says the Gita).

Thus we see that according to the Gita the individual is a portion of the Divine struggling in the world with his ego and triple nature, but once he can withdraw from his outer nature and live in his inner self he can change into divine nature which in his true self.

But as the changes are Law of Nature, a man undergoes various changes in his life-span sometimes due to misconceptual notion of progress, sometimes due to sheer greed and ego. According to Dean Inge – "The theory of progress and the theory of decadence are equally natural, and have in fact been held concurrently whenever men have speculated about their origin, their present condition and then future prospects".[29] Thus consequently a man becomes a combination of divinity and demonity together. It is only the difference in degree which makes a man good or evil. According to K.M Munshi, "The divine element in man is the Fundamental Aspiration which yearns for light, love, beauty, bliss, joy, freedom and calm Because of this, he is not an atom moved by Physio-Chemical Laws not merely a unit of life, like an amoeba; not a bundle of instinctive reactions, like an animal, not even a thinking machine as he believes himself to be. Because of it, he is a spark of divinity whose destiny leads towards God."[30]

Similarly Gita[31] describes demoniacal instincts of a man which include hypocrisy, arrogance, pride, anger, harshness and ignorance etc. These are called negative values also. Men cherishing such type of values are not able to distinguish between good and bad. They do not know what is right activity and what is right cessation of activity. Therefore, the possess neither purity (internal or external) no good conduct nor truth. Divine values are regarded as conducive to liberation, whereas negative or demoniacal values are supposed to be conducive to bondage. According to A.C. Bhaktivedanta Swami Prabhupada:

"There are various theories regarding consciousness. Here (XIII 29-34) Bhagvadgita gives the example of the sun and sunshine. As the sun is situated in one place but is illuminating the whole universe, so a small particle of spirit soul, although situated in the heart of the body, is illuminating the whole body by consciousness. Therefore, the consciousness is the proof of the presence of the sun. When the soul is present in the body, there is consciousness all over the body, and as soon as soul has passed from the body there is no more consciousness. This can be easily understood by any intelligent man. Therefore, the consciousness is the proof of the presence of the sun. Therefore, consciousness is not a product of combinations of matter. It is the symptom of the living entity. Although qualitatively one with the supreme consciousness, the consciousness of one particular body does not share that of another body. But the Supersouls, which is situated in all bodies as the friend of all individual souls, is conscious of all bodies. That is the difference between supreme consciousness and individual consciousness."[32]

In the introduction[33] to his own volume on Gita Prabhupada observes that a living being in the mundane world has four defects:

1. He is sure to commit mistakes.
2. He is sure to be illusioned.
3. He has a tendency to cheat.
4. His senses are imperfect.

According to the Eastern notion of personality a man is not what he does, but what he was and what he "is" now. To 'be' is nobler than to 'do'. To be truly 'oneself' is a higher service than serving others. The consecration of self to the task of attaining higher selfhood is far nobler than acts which do not spring from the process. Surprisingly enough the same thinking we find in ancient Chinese books. On the bathing-tub of T'ang, the following words were engraved – "If you can one day renovate yourself, do so from day to day. Yea, let there be daily renovation."[34]

Confucious says that there are few men in the world, who love and at the same time know the bad qualities of the object of their love, or who hate and yet know the excellences of the object of their hatred. Hence, it is said, in the common adage. "A man does not know the wickedness of his son; he does not know the richness of his growing corn. This is what is meant by saying that if the person be not cultivated, a man cannot regulate his family."[35] That is why Krishna says in Gita :–

"The Yogi is higher than the Ascetic. He soares above the seers who knows. Higher than those who work too, is he. Therefore, Arjuna, be thou a Yogi."[36]

The Gita throughout emphasizes on refinement of human nature for cultivation of the intrinsic values like the good, the truth, the beauty and so on. It also provides a scheme of training and of social synthesis by which every human being can rise higher. Thus the pathway of Yoga is opened to everybody.

Man, the Social Being

The message of the Gita to man as a Social being is very often misunderstood. It appears to many that the Gita recommends the renunciation of the all worldly duties and take to 'sanyasa' as early as possible. Such an interpretation of the teachings of the Gita is far from the truth. It is a fact that the Gita speaks of Sanyas Yoga, but it also speaks of Karma Yoga, Jnana Yoga and Dhyana Yoga etc. and the integral message as conveyed through all the chapters has to be truly appreciated.

The secret of the Gita is essentially the secret of action. Pointing this out Sri Aurobindo writes, "The secret of action", so we might summarise the message of the Gita, - the word of its divine Teacher, "is one with the secret of all life and existence". Existence is not merely a machinery of Nature, a wheel of law in which the soul is entangled for a moment or for ages; it is a constant manifestation of the Spirit. Life is not for the sake of life alone, but for God, and the living soul of man is an eternal portion of the Godhead. Action is for self-findings, for self-realisation and not only for its own and apparent fruits of the moment or the future.[37]

For self-realisation through action the Gita suggests three important steps. Every action involves three aspects – the act, the doer or subject and the result. It has already been indicated that liberation does not comes through abandonment of action but renunciation of the desire motivating the action. This comes through the renunciation of the attachment first to the result, secondly, to the work and finally to the doer.

The secret of work lies in this line of the Gita – *Sve Sve karmanyabhiratah samsiddhi labhate narah,* which means 'Devote each to his own duty, man attains the highest perfection.' This statement linked up with the earlier quotations would mean that as the caste system is based on the nature and sense of duty of a man, no caste is higher than the other and a person born into any caste has the possibility of attaining his perfection by performing his duties sincerely, the Brahmanas through the practice of knowledge, the Kshatriya through his heroism, the Vaisya through his love and the Sudra through his work and service and each path leads to the Supreme.

Man, the Divine Being

There is no need to point out that according to the Gita, man is divine, in essence and in substance. The whole of the Gita (as much as the Vedas and the Upanishads) points to and establishes this one truth. This is particularly brought out in Chapter 13, *kshetra kshetrajna vibhage yoga,* of the Gita. The Blessed Lord says: "This body, O Kaunteya, is called kshetra, the field he who knows it is called kshetrajna by the sages."

And know Me as the "Kshetrajna in all Kshetras, O Bharata." In simple words it means that in man dwells the Kshetrajna or the Lord and his body is the abode for the Lord. As mentioned earlier the Gita also says, *Iswara sarvabhutanam hrdesherjuna tisthati'* which means 'God dwells in the heart of every creature.'[38]

Thus the secret of the Gita can be summarised in a few sentences: Its take an integral view of the Reality who is Purusottama, the Supreme Person, and above Kshara, the mutable and Akshara, the Immutable and even above his Paramadharma, his highest abode. He is present in the Universe as Vasudeva and creature as his true self. Man, shrouded by his ego and his triple lower nature is not conscious of this reality, but once he is conscious of it, he can transcend his lower nature and rise to his higher nature and realise the Supreme Self through a triune path of divine-work, divine-knowledge and divine-love which consists of abandonment of desire in all its shades and forms.

Man in the Tantras

What is the Tantra

Explaining the meaning and concept of "Tantra" Sri Aurobindo writes: "There still exists in India a remarkable Yogic system which is in its nature synthetic and starts from a great central principle of Nature, great dynamic force of Nature; it is a yoga apart, not a synthesis of other schools. This system is the way of the Tantra".[39]

Sri Aurobindo points out:

"Tantric discipline is in its nature a synthesis. It has seized on the large universal truth that there are two poles of being whose essential unity is the secret of existence, Brahman and Shakti, 'Spirit and Nature, and that Nature is power of the spirit or rather is spirit as power. To raise nature in man into manifest power of spirit is its method and it is the whole nature that it gathers up for spiritual conversion....In two directions it enlarges by its synthetic turn the province of the Yogic method. First, it lays its hand firmly on many of the main springs of the human quality, desire, action and it subjects them to an intensive discipline with the soul's mastery of its motives as a first aim and their elevation to a diviner spiritual level as its final utility. Again it includes in its object of Yoga not only liberation

(*Mukti*), which is the one all mastering preoccupation of the specific systems, but a cosmic enjoyment *(bhukti)* of the power of Spirit, which the others may take incidentally on the way, in part, causally, but avoid making a motive or object. It is a bolder and larger system."[40]

Man, the Individual

In Siva Tantra (also known as Saivism of which Kashmiri Saivism is the oldest) man is the Jiva and an embodiment of Siva. The Jiva is none else than Siva Himself shrouded in Ignorance. "Siva cloaked in the body is Jiva, uncloaked he is the supreme Siva"[41] says the Tantra. *(Sarira Kancukitah Sivo, Jivo niskancukah Parasivah).* The Jiva through several births and through a process of self-analysis is able to cast away the cloak of ignorance and realise its identity with Siva; the Supreme Reality. Once the mist of ignorance melts away the Jiva emerges as Siva or it realises its identity with the Divine Reality.

Parasiva or chaitanya is the Absolute consciousness or the Supreme Reality in the Tantras. He is the one without a second.

Man, the Social Being

The Tantra recognises that men are in different states of development and classifies them according to their nature being governed by Tamas, Rajas or Sattva. Men are broadly classified into three categories – *pasubhava* (animal type), *virabhava* (hero type) and *divyabhava* (godly type). The Tantra believes that a person even in the lowest type can progress and rise to the highest type by his own efforts or Sadhana. Thus the Tantra does not pitch itself so high as the Veda or the Vedanta in its demands. It believes that a person can begin in whatever stage or state he may be and it is positively hopeful about man's possibilities and destiny.

The Tantra places its highest regard on all women, for according to it, all men are emanations of the Divine Mother, and women are the Mother Herself. Thus to look upon all women with high esteem is a contribution of the Tantra tradition. It is only after the coming of the foreigners that women were cosidered things to be enjoyed *bhogyavastu*.

In fine, the Tantra considers both the individual and the society as an embodiment of Shiva Shakti; the delight of the Divine Mother can permeate and pervade as much in the society as in the individual.

Man, the Divine Being

It would have been clear to the reader by now that the Tantra in continuity and conformity with the Indian tradition treats man essentially as divine clothed in ignorance and he can attain his original divinity by becoming more and more conscious of it, aspiring for it, working for it, in short, living for it. In this concept of man as a divine being all are included, none are expected, not even the sudra or the chandala. The ultimate destiny of man, the Jiva, is parasiva, the Supreme Reality, in all its aspects – *Chidananda*.

The Vishnu – Tantra and the Shakti - Tantra takes a similar view of man and the society.

Man in the Epics

Though the Brahmins, Kshatriyas and Vaisyas were permitted to study the Vedas, their secret knowledge was accessible only to a selected few. Hence the epics were written to educate the common man and to meet his religious and spiritual needs. The lodest epics are as old as the Vedas and the Upanishads. As the epics were meant to expound the esoteric knowledge in a popular way for the ordinary men who were not expected to take to life in seclusion (*vanaprastha* or *sanyasa*) but attain self-realisation leading the life of a householder, the doctrines and principles were presented in a simple way for their easy understanding and practice. Thus, the epics did not contain deep revelations as in the Vedas or high philosophy as in the Vedanta but included stories of day to day life and contained all the teachings as in the ancient scriptures. The epics continue to guide the conduct of the common man as much today as in the days of the *Ramayana* and the *Mahabharata*.

The teachings contained in the epics stressed mostly on the

karmamārga and *bhaktimārga* and sometimes on the *Jnanamārga*. In karmamarga or the way of the works the grahastha was expected to perform all the duties enjoined to him towards gods, ancestors, sages and other members in the society (elders, brahmins, guests, cows and other domestic animals etc.) with a sense detachment to the fruits (results) and as an offering to God who is seated in his own heart, in the hearts of others and pervading the universe. *Bhaktimārga* or the way of devotion laid greater stress on the devotional aspect and surrender to the divine who usually took the form of a personal deity like Siva or Vishnu or Durga (Divine Mother) etc. *Jnanamārga* proceeded on the basis of a sincere quest after the nature of Brahman and Reality, the nature of the soul or self and how to realise the identification of the individual self with the supreme self. In other words it was in the path of dispelling ignorance through self-analysis and meditation.

The oldest epics are the *Ramayana* and the *Mahabharata*. Valmiki, the poet of *Ramayana* lived prior to Vasistha who was a Vedic Rishi. Thus *Ramayana* is believed to have been composed prior to the Vedas. The eighteen puranas (in Sanskrit) are believed to have been composed during the Gupta Vakataka Age, i.e. from fourth to sixth centuries A.D. It is known that all the epics have an overtone of morality, performance of duties and discharge of social obligations through which one can attain the heaven in a world beyond. This moral ideal was meant to be emulated by the common man.

Man in Buddhism and Jainism

It is popularly believed that Buddhism and Jainism rose in opposition to Hinduism, this is far from the truth. There was no Hinduism in those days there was only Ārya Dharma and both Buddhism and Jainism were Āryadharamas inasmuch as both Gautama and Mahavira were born as Āryans, lived as Āryans and died as Āryans and both of them had a great respect for the word "Ārya" which meant for them "Noble" or "Sublime" and both of them have used the word profusely in their teaching. Their voices were only against *"Anārya Justam"*, that had crept into the Āryadharma at the time.

Thus they can be taken as social and religious reformers and not as opponents of the Āryadharma, also known as Sanatana Dharma, the religion which has no beginning.

As for that, there is no religion on the earth the teachings of which cannot be traced into the eternal voice of the Sanatana Dharma, but that is not a matter for our present discussion. But suffice it to say that the teachings of both the religions, Buddhism and Jainism, have their origin in the Āryadharma and the ideas and principles propounded in both are more in common to these in the orthodox religion, the difference being a matter of degree of shade and stress. No wonder that Buddha had been accepted and worshipped as an incarnation of Lord Vishnu.

Comparision

The deal common to both the orthodox and hetrodox religions (Vedic and Buddhistic) was the spiritual realisation of identity with the Atman or Brahman in the former and Nirvana in the latter both being a state of bliss attained through a freedom from ignorance and bondage to the mundane world. The orthodox insisted on leading the worldly life, the life of *Grhastha,* for the society according to the Vedic religion which was cosmic and consisted of four elements – gods, ancestors, sages and ordinary men and a *grhastha* had duties to all the four. But for a Buddhist the world is an illusion, *aleeka* and *anitya,* transitory and non-existent and hence the only duty of an individual is to himself – to cut the gordian knot through self analysis and realise the state of *nirvana*, *Sunya* according to the *Madhyamikas* or according to the *Vijnanavadins*. The methods for such realisation is to rise above *Karma* or complete renunciation whereas for the orthodoxites the freedom from action is to be realised by performance of *karma* or duties and not by their renunciation.

The other features common to both are that both the orthodox and the hetrodox admit the existence of gods (though the latter do not accept the existence of a Supreme god) *Karma* and *Karmaphala* (action and its results) transmigration and rebirth and the final redemption from the birth and death.

Man, the Individual

According to Jainism the world is divided into two categories Jiva or the spirit or soul or atman of the orthodox school and ajiva or matter. The Jiva in its pure state is unbound, omniscient and nearly infinite. The ajiva or matter is of various kinds – time, space, motion, rest and atoms – all are substances. Even *Karma* is conceived as material substances.

Man is the Jiva bound by ajiva or matter assuming a gross physical body. Due to Avidya or ignorance karma enters into it and binds it to the world of action. In other words the Jiva bound by Karma constitutes man. The Jiva takes birth again and again in different forms and castes according to the action performed in previous lives. Karma binds man to the world through false knowledge *(Mithya darshana),* incontinence *(avirati),* negligence *(pramada),* passion *(kasaya)* or anger, egoity, deceitfulness and greed and action (yoga used in the sense of taking karma from alround). It is for the human individual to cut himself off from the chain of karma and attain salvation.

Buddhism, however, views the human being similar to the Upanishads but not believe in anything, like self, soul or atman. According to it man in his essential nature is nirvana, a state of bliss – *Sunya* according to the *madhyamikas* and *vijnana* according to the *vijinanavadins.* He is also a pudagala, a psychological person, which is somehow formed through ignorance and when it is analysed away, the original nirvana is realised. The pudagala or the psychophysical personality consists of five aggregates or skandhas, viz. *Rupaskandha* (the aggregate of matter), *vedanāskandha* (the aggregate of feelings and emotions), *Samjnaskandha* (the aggregate of ideas), *Samskaraskandha* (the aggregare of instincts, impressions and propensities) and *vijnanaskandha* (the aggregate of consciousness).

To explain the formation of the pudagala Buddhism brings in the theory of causal occasionalism or *pratity-samutpada* which says that the cause is only an occasion for the appearance of the effect, it does not enter the effect. In other words it means that everything in this world is monetary; the cause, therefore, being monetary, cannot continue to exist in the effect. The effect is a different entity. Yet the effect can come into being only with reference to the cause. Hence the cause is necessary, but it acts only as the occasion for the effect to appear.

This theory of causal occasionalism is clearly brought out in the four great Aryan truths *(Arya chatustaya)* propounded by the Buddha. They are *Dukha, Dukha Samudaya, Dukha Nirodha* and *Dukha Nirodha gamini pratipadā*. This implies that world is a suffering, there is a cause for the suffering, the suffering can be prevented and there is a way for preventing it or the way leading to the freedom from suffering. Buddha explains how human life is replete with suffering – to be born is suffering, decay is suffering, disease is suffering, death is suffering, to be joined with things which one does not like is suffering, so also to be separated from things one loves is suffering, and so on. As for the cause of suffering, Buddha points to the sensual pleasures. *Trishna,* the desire and seeking after the satisfaction of the senses more and more. The third truth consists in overcoming the causes of suffering and this is done through the Madhyamika pantha or the *majjhimamārga* and expounded as the fourth.

Buddhism indicates the twelve links leading to the causation of the world; these are Ignorance *(Avidya),* Impressions or Instincts *(Samskaras),* Initial consciousness *(Vijanana),* body-mind *(Namarupa)* senses, sense contact, sense experience, Thirst (*Trishna*), clinging (to objects) Tendency to be Born, Rebirth and Old Age and Death.

Similarly the noble eightfold path or the Arya Astangika consists in *Samyaka Drsti* or *Right Views, Samyaka Sankalpa* or right action, *Samyaka Ajiva* or right means of livelihood, *Samyaka Vyayama* or right effort, *Samyaka Sruti* or right-mindfulness and *Samyaka Samadhi* or right concentration of mind.

Jainism, however, confines the virtues to only three – right view, right knowledge and right conduct. The last includes *Ahimsa* (non-violence), *Satya,* (Truthfulness), *Asteya* (non-Stealing), *Brahmacharya* (celebacy) and *Aparigraha* (non-acceptance of gifts).

Thus the Buddhistic concept of man is one anatma (without a soul or self), anitya or non-permanent and full of Dukha or Sorrow.

Man, essentially nirvana, but shrouded by Karma through ignorance thinks himself to be the psycho-physical personality and passes through suffering until he is able to come out of it through self-analysis and the Arya Astangika and realise the pure state of Nirvana. Karma or worldly activities are a hindrance to such realisation and therefore, to be got over. Hence Buddhism and Jainism reject the Veda as it stresses on the worldly actions and sacrifices. While Veda stresses on all the three margas – *Karmamārga, Jnanamārga* and *Bhaktimārga.* Buddhism and Jainism stress only on *Jnanamārga* and reject other two. Thus the aim and method of the hetrodox religions are only partial and not integral.

Man, the Social Being

Buddhism and Jainism have little concern for society and social life. As mentioned earlier the world is non-permanent and transitory according to both. Buddhistic and Jain society was confined to the monastic Sangha and obtaining alms from the general public. The hetrodox religions were not opposed to the caste system of the orthodox order but preached that a person belonged to a particular caste not by virtue of his birth by the nature of work and duties he performs. The gates of the monasteries are flung open to all irrespective of their caste and sex. While the members of the ordinary society who are interested in the doctrines of the hetrodox religion are advised to practise the principles as much as possible the monks had no duties to gods, ancestors or sages as in the orthodox society but were required to practise the eight great virtues as a means to realise nirvana. As the two religions did not take into cognisance the social and political needs of the country, they became alienated from the society and soon had to seek refuge in countries other than that of their origin.

Man, the Divine Being

The concept of man being a manifestation or representative of the divine was not admitted by either Buddhism or by Jainism. For both the soul or the self did not exist. Their concern was to get rid of sorrow by analysing away the psycho-physical personality in case of Buddhism and Ajiva in case of Jainism. Attaining mukti or nirvana, i.e. redemption from human miseries was the only concern of man.

But Sri Aurobindo points out, "Buddha, it must be remembered, refused always to discuss what was beyond the world. But from the little he said it would appear that he was aware of a permanent beyond equivalent to the Vedantic Para-Brahman, but which he was quite unwilling to describe. The denial of anything, beyond the world except a negative state of *Nirvana* was a later teaching, not Buddha's. From this it would appear that Buddhistic philosophy was not wholly nihilistic originally and the Sunya concept was only a later development."

In conclusion it may be said that Buddhism and Jainism are only two daughters of the Vedic Sanatana Dharma and the concept of man that they present is not as much cosmic and global as their mother's and is confined to a limited view of life and its fulfilment which may have been relevant and worthwhile to the needs of the society at that time but does not hold valid to the needs of the future man who aspires to be integral in every way.

Man in the Medieval Age

After Buddha and Mahavira many thought currents have inundated the soil of India, but they were not very much deviated from the main stream of the Vedas and the Upanishads. These thoughts can seldom be considered as new philosophies, they were only new interpretations with different shades and stresses. Thus, the Sankhya-yoga, Advaita Vedanta, Vishistadvaita come under this category. As these are only repetitions of the Vedantic philosophy, no detailed discussion on them is entered into. A brief indication of these philosophies is given below:

Sankhya-yoga

Kapila and Patanjali were the founder-exponents of the Sankhya-yoga system. Sankhya signifies relising the Ultimate through knowledge and reflection, while Yoga signifies a realisation through a steady, consistent and persistent meditation. The Sankhya-yoga system revolves round a pluralistic (fundamentally dualistic) realism. It recognises that objects exist independent of the mind which perceives the objects.

Purusha and *Prakriti* are the two co-present and co-equal realities of the system. Purusha is the principle of pure consciousness, the soul, the self, the spirit, the subject and the knower. It is also the transcendental consciousness which is neither the cause nor the effect of anything. The Prakriti is uncaused, eternal and all-pervading and is constituted by the three *gunas* (nature) with the help of which she creates the cosmos. The essential message of the system is that man has to realise the futility of secular values and seek the spiritual freedom of the *Purusha* by transcending *Prakriti*.

Advaita Vedanta

Acharya Shankara is the founder of the Advaita Vedanta philosophy which states that *Brahman* or the Pure Consciousness is the Ultimate Reality which is devoid of all attributes and not categories of the intellect. According to Shankara *Brahman Satyam Jaganmithyā* or Brahman is only Real, the cosmos which is only an appearance is unreal. The individual soul is *Atman* and different from the Brahman. The world is a creation of Maya or illusion. The individual on account of Avidya distinguished himself from Brahman and mistakes this world of multiplicity to be real. For all practical purposes Shankara comes very near to Buddha and Mahavira for he denies the reality and existence of the world and recommends an escape from it by casting away the ignorance and illusion of maya and realising oneself as Brahman through self-analysis, introspection and renunciation.

Vishistadvaita

The system of Vishistadvaita ensues from Ramanuja who qualifies the Monism or Advaita of Shankara. This philosophy of Vishistadvaitavada considers the Absolute as a concrete whole or vishista consisting of unrelated and interdependent subordinates` known as *Viseshanas* and the Immanent and controlling Spirit known as *Vishesy.* The Absolute is this whole, he is the Immanent, the inner controller, the Supreme Real who holds together in unity the dependent matter and individual soul as his body. Thus Ramanuja recognises *achit* (matter), *chit* (soul) and *Brahman* (god) as the three realities. Though all are real, the former two are subordinate to God. In relation to God they are his attributes. They are the body of God and God is their soul.

According to Ramanuja God is the material and instrumental cause of the world. The universe is latent in God and is also equally manifested in him. He is unaffected by the imperfections of the finites. He is *Antaryami* or the immanent soul of the universe, Narayana, the creator, preserver and destroyer of the worlds, the Avatar descending in human and animal forms to restore Dharma and finally the deity installed in the temples to be worshipped by his devotees. Thus the relation between God and man is very intimate, for man and his soul are the body of God. Karma is the cause of bondage and man can realise his divine personality through devotion and worship.

Man in Modern Thought

The discussion on the concept of man cannot be complete without a reference to the modern thinkers of the East of whom Swami Dayananda, Swami Vivekananda, Rabindra Nath Tagore and Mahatma Gandhi, prior to Sri Aurobindo were the great luminaries of the nineteenth and the twentieth century. Of course, they were not philosophers in the sense that Buddha, Shankara and Ramanuja were, but they had their own influence in the thought process of the country. They were primarily nationalists and their contribution towards social reform was a part of their nationalism and this was based on the religious and spiritual heritage of the country. Each according to his own nature interpreted the heritage and enriched the thought process in his own way. It would not be too much to say that present India owes its resurgence to these thinkers. As these modern thinkers were not system builders, their contribution to the field of thought are presented in a general way.

Swami Dayananda Saraswati (1824–1883)

"Among the great company of remarkable figures that will appeal to the eyes of posterity, at the head of Indian Renaissance, one stands out by himself with peculiar and solitary distinctness, one unique in his type as he is unique in his work... a great cascade of pure, vigorous and fertilising water gushing out from its strength as a very formation of life and health to the valley. Such is the impression created on my mind by Dayananda" says Sri Aurobindo.[43] Swami Dayananda, an ardent defender of Hinduism, preached the infallibility of the Vedas, instilled a superiority complex among Indians, founded the Arya Samaj and remains till today a figure of whom many are critical but none could deny his regour and impact.

As a thinker Swami Dayananda had a philosophical base though he was no system builder. For him god is the source of all knowledge and the only medium of acquiring knowledge. God is all truth, all knowing, all beautitude, almighty, just, merciful, unbegotten, infinite, changeless, without a beginning, incomparable, omnipresent and the maker, supporter and the lord of all creation. To him all worships are due. Dayananda believes in three essentials – God, Soul and Prakriti as the prime elements. The most ardent assertion of Dayananda is that the Vedas are the repository of all true knowledge, and the social evils like caste, child marriage, satee, etc., were later interpolations. He would refuse all opposition to the Vedic ideas contained in later scriptures. He rejects infallibility of the Gurus. He has revived the original "Karma Veda" or theory of Karma. Accordingly an individual is to continue doing good deeds throughout his life so that he could reap the benefit thereof in his next birth. He calls upon individuals not to be satisfied with one's own good but to contribute to social and spiritual upliftment of the whole mankind. He attaches the theory of incarnation and declares idol-worship not being sanctioned by the Vedas. He rejects the idea of world as Maya or illusion, for him, it was shrinking of one's duty. For him the true test of every religion is its effect upon conduct. He believes that everyone has an equal claim to receive the highest form of education. He would not agree with distinction of caste, status or sex. He considers the original four-fold division of caste to be valid and that in its origin it was occupational, based on capability and not on birth. Similarly he supports monogamy. He is against dowry. He introduces 'Suddhi' Kriya by which Hindus can be allowed to return to their faith from other religions. He believes in *'Sangathan'* or organisation to give shape to his religious and philosophical outlook.

Swami Dayananda was a revivalist in matters of religion as much of education. His ideas and ideals of education have been spelt out in his 'Satyaratha Prakash' in which he suggests the establishment of *Gurukulashram* on lines of Ashrams of the Vedic rishis where the student or brahmachari acquired knowledge away from his parents. He did not live to see his own ideas taking shape. It was Swami Shradhananda who established the first Gurukulashram at Kangri which is now functioning as an autonomous institution deemed to be a university. Presently more than fifty Gurukulashrams are understood to be functioning in the country.

Swami Vivekananda (1863–1902)

Vivekananda's influence, including on contemporary India, can hardly be over-emphasised. From Tilak to Sri Aurobindo, from Gandhi to Subhas Bose, every generation of leaders of Indian Freedom Struggles were all drunk with his magic potion. Vivekananda's success as a spiritual mission of India, his wide acceptance in the West coupled with his charm, made him a unique figure in India in his lifetime. In the sense he was one of the first to assume a larger than life image among Renaissance thinkers. With the grace of Ramakrishna Paramahansa, one who had realised God through all religions, Vivekananda had Nirbikalpa Samadhi, an experience of God through a Supercosmic trance. Yet he was asked by Ramakrishna to devote this realisastion for the nation and mankind as a whole and not for himself. Vivekananda established Ramakrishna Mission to give shape to these dreams.

To speak of Vivekananda's metaphysics, like most of his contemporary counterparts, he was no system builder even though he was quite coherent in his thought. Basically he advocates monism of the Upanishads but denies the Sankrite Mayavada or the cosmos as an illusion. For him religion is the idea which is raising the brute unto man and man, unto God. He wants man to transcend his brutal qualities and rise to divinity, godhead with virtue and righteousness as the key. He projected *Sat-Chit-Ananda*—Truth, Realisation and Knowledge and Bliss as the ultimate. He rejects utilitarianism, individualism and materialism and preaches individual salvation and realisation be made to serve a universal divine realisation. He is sangha oriented but wants men to realise the divine within. His concept of divinity has a human aspect too, the ideal of 'service to man is service to God' appeals to him strongly. Besides this service aspect, like most other thinkers he would not outrightly reject the caste system. But he wants the system to be free from social disadvantage to any group or the supremacy of the priests.

According to Swami Vivekananda 'Education is the manifestation of perfection already in man'. Thus he believes that man is potentially perfect and he has only to manifest it. Conforming this contention he writes:

"No perfection is going to be attained. You are already free and perfect. What are these ideas of religion and God and searching for the hereafter?... It is god within your ownself that is propelling you to seek for Him, to realise Him,... He for whom you have been seeking all the world over... is nearest of the near, is your ownself, the reality of your life, body and soul. This is our own nature, assert it. Not to become pure, you are pure already, you are not to be perfect, you are that already."

Thus according to Swamiji, "Each soul is potentially divine. The goal is to manifest this divinity within, by controlling nature, external and internal."[45]

Rabindra Nath Tagore (1561–1941)

As Sri Aurobindo was a poet first and a poet last so was Rabindranath an artist first and an artist last and artist in the true sense of the term. He was born as an artist, lived as an artist and died as an artist. He was a poet, a story writer, a dramatist, a musician, composer and producer of dance-dramas and a painter par excellence. He has created new traditions in all his artistic creations, his music goes by the name of Rabindra Sangeet. He was the first Indian to win the Nobel prize for his immortal creation, the *Gitanjali* in 1913. He was again the first Indian to introduce a new system of education by converting the Shantiniketan (abode of peace) established by his father at Bolopur, a village north of Calcutta into a school which ultimately developed into the Viswabharati, an international university, now functioning as a central university. His interest in education was much deeper and wider with the aim of coming in relation with men and nature. His concept of man and education and social service was as much artistic as his own personality.

Rabindranath does not profound a philosophical system of his own, however, he had his own way of looking at life and man. He was well-versed in the teachings of the Vedas and the Upanishads. For him the Supreme is All-Blissful and the cosmos and the individual as manifestation of the blissful aspect of the Supreme Reality. Everything in the world is harmonious and beautiful. Man's life is a saga of discovering and establishing this harmony between his own personality and the Universal person and the Supreme Person. Harmony, beauty and bliss or *ananda* are the key notes of his philosophy and approach to life.

Tagore's ideal of education is consistent with his ideal of life. About life he says, "It is the duty of every human being to master, at least to some extent, not only the language of intellect, but also that personality which is the language of art. It is a great world of reality for man,... vast and profound,... this growing of this own creative nature. This the world of art."[46] It is the vast and the infinite, the bhouma, that one should seek in life. Hence he says, "...the vision of the infinite in all forms of creation, in the human relationship of love to feel it in the air we breathe, in the light in which we open our eyes, in the water in which we bathe, in the earth on which we live and die."

As in life so with education that Rabindranath sought. He writes: "The highest mission of education is to help us realise the inner principle of unity of all knowledge and all the activities of our social and spiritual being."[47] Thus for Tagore true education meant the realisation of unity and harmony of the human life with all existence.

Tagore sees education as the harmonisation of human nature with universal nature. In other words Tagore views education as the process of evolving new patterns of life culminating in the realisation of Universal Man.

Mahatma Gandhi (1869 – 1948)

Mohandas Karamchand Gandhi, popularly known as Mahatma Gandhi is perhaps the most popular figure of the present century in modern India. Though many nationalists a prior to him and initiated the Freedom Movement in the country. It was Mahatma Gandhi who was destined to lead the nation to its Independence. He was essentially a politician, a social worker and a social reformer, but his contributions towards the educational development of the country was original and turned a new chapter in the history of the Indian nation.

For Gandhiji 'God is Truth and Truth is God'. He writes in Harijan (in 1935) :

> "God is Truth, but god is many other things also. That is why I say Truth is God.... Only remember that Truth is not one of the many qualities that we name. It is the living embodiment of God, it is the only Life, and I identify Truth with the fullest life, and that is how it becomes a concrete thing, for God is His whole creation, the whole Existence, and service of all that exists... Truth... is service to God."

Thus Gandhiji always tries to adhere to Truth in all his activities and tread on the path of Truth and he titles his autobiography as 'My Experiment with Truth.' He also believes that 'Service to man is service to God, and was one with Swami Vivekananda that God comes to the poor through the morsel of his food. Hence he tried to devote himself to the upliftment of the downtrodden whom he gave the exalted name of Harijan. Another ideal the fervently cherished in his political life was that non-violence which went hand in hand with *Swadeshi*, *Swaraj* and Boycott. While Swaraj was the ideal, non-violence was the method for him. Non-violence for him did not mean just abstinence from killing, it was a positive and powerful ideal suited for carrying forward the Freedom Movement under the prevalent conditions of the country.

Coming to Gandhiji's educational ideal we see that he took the etymological meaning of education. For him education means to bring out the best in the child and man, his body, and mind and spirit. This implies that education for Gandhiji is not something poured from outside (in the form of information usually mistaken for knowledge) but a process of bringing out or bringing forth. Secondly, the best (perfection in the words of Swamiji) is already there in the human being (child or adult) and this has to be helped to come out (manifest, as Swamiji prefers to put it). Thirdly, education has to take care of all the three dimensions of the human personality... physical, mental and spiritual. For this Gandhiji's thinks of the harmony and co-ordination of three His... the head, the hand and the heart, correlation in the keynote in Gandhiji's system of education which goes by the name of Basic National Education or the Wardha Scheme which got an independent treatment as an experimental system for about three decades and was integrated with the main stream during the sixties.

Gandhiji was a Karmayogi, he believed in work and service, emancipation of the poor and for which he experimented with life and education the basis of which was Truth identical with God. His experiments with basic education shall continue to create interest among educators for years to come.

Confucian Thought

The following thoughts pertaining the two qualities of 'Superior man' and 'Inferior man' have been taken from the book titled as "*The Wisdom of China and India*" by Lin Yutang (Modern Library New York, 1955). For the convenience of the readers page numbers are given in the brackets.

Confucious said, 'The superior man understands with is right, the inferior man understands what will sell.'

Confucious said, 'The superior man loves his soul, the inferior man loves his property. The superior man always remembers how he was punished for his mistakes, the inferior man always remembers what presents he got.'

Confucious said, 'The superior man is liberal towards others' opinions. But does not completely agree with them, the inferior man completely agrees with others' opinions, but is not liberal towards them.'

Confucious said, 'The superior man is firm, but does not fight, he mixes easily with others, but does not form cliques.'

Confucious said, 'The superior man blames himself, the inferior man blames others.'

Confucious said, 'The superior man is easy to serve, but difficult to please, for he can be pleased by what is right, and he uses men according to their individual abilities. The inferior man is difficult to serve, but easy to please, for you can please him (by catering to his weaknesses) without necessarily being right, and when he comes to using men, he demands perfection.'

Confucious said, 'You can put a superior man in an important position with large discretionary powers, but cannot give him a nice little job, you can give an inferior nice little job, but you cannot put him in an important position with great discretionary powers.'

Confucious said, 'The superior man is broad-minded towards all men and not a partisan, the inferior man is a partisan, but not broad-minded towards all.'

Confucious and his followers had to go for days without food in Ch'en and some of his followers fell ill and were confined to bed. Tselu came to Confucious in low Spirits and asked, 'Does the superior man also land in difficulties? Confucious said, 'Yes, the superior man also sometimes find himself in difficulties, but when an inferior man finds himself in difficulties, he is likely to do anything.'

Confucious said, 'The superior man attends to the spiritual things and not to his livelihood. You let him cultivate a farm, and he will be starved, but if you let him attend to his studies, he will find riches in it. The superior man does not worry about his poverty but worries about the spiritual things.'

Confucious said, 'The superior man is always candid and at ease (with himself or others), the inferior man is always worried about something.'

Confucious said, 'The superior man develops upwards, the inferior man develops downwards.'

Confucious said, 'The superior man is dignified and at ease, but not proud, the inferior man is proud, but not dignified.'

Confucious said, 'The superior man keeps to the standard of right, but does not necessarily keep his promise.'

Szema Niu asked Confucious about being a gentleman, and Confucious replied, 'A gentleman has no worry and no fear.' Does having no worry and no fear them constitute a gentleman? Confucious said, 'If he looks within himself and is sure that he had done right, what does he have to fear or worry about?'

Confucious said, 'The superior man goes through his life without any preconceived course of action or any taboo. He merely decides for the moment what is the right thing to do.'

Confucious said, 'The superior man doesn't insist on good food and good lodging. He is attentive to his duties and careful in his speech, and he finds a great man and follows him as his guide. Such a person may be called a lover of learning.'

Confucious said, 'A scholar who intends to follow the truth and is ashamed of his poor dress and poor food is not worth talking to.'

Confucious said, 'A scholar who is in love with living conforts is not worthy to be called a scholar.'

Confucious said, 'A man who serves his king and three times finds his advice rejected and still does not leave the country, is hanging on to his post for the sake of the salary. Even though he says that it is not the salary that attracts him, I won't believe him.'

Confucious said, 'A gentleman is ashamed that his words are better than his deeds.'

Confucious said, 'A gentleman is careful about three things: In his youth, when his blood is strong, he is careful about sex. When he is grown up, and his blood is full, he is old and his blood is getting thinner, he is careful about money.'

(A young man loves women, a middle-aged man loves struggle, and an old man loves money.)

Guide the people with governmental measures and control or regulate them by the threat or punishment, and the people will try to keep out of jail, but will have no sense of honour or shame. Guide the people by virtue and control or regulate them by it (moral discipline), and the people will have a sense of honour and respect.

When the ruler himself does what is right, he will have influence over the people without giving commands, and when the ruler himself does not do what is right, all his commands will be of no avail.

With the right men, the growth of good government is as rapid as the growth of vegetation is in the right soil. Indeed, good government is like a fast-growing plant. The conduct of government, therefore, depends upon the men. The right men are obtained by the ruler's personal character. To cultivate his personal character, the ruler must use the moral law. To cultivate the moral law, the ruler must use the moral sense.

Therefore, it is necessary for a man of the governing class to set about regulating his personal conduct and character. In considering how to regulate his personal conduct and character, it is necessary for to do his duties towards those nearly related to him. In considering how to do his duties towards those nearly related to him, it is necessary for him to understand the nature and organization of human society, it is necessary for him to understand the laws of God.

Summary

The concept of Reality as much of man runs essentially identical in all the Indian Scriptures…the Vedas, the Upanishads, the Gita and the Tantras.

In the first three scriptures as the absolute is One and Individual beyond Time, Space, Causality. In the Vedas he is the Supreme Purusha worshipped by the sages in different names like Agni, Indra, Mitra, Varuna, Vishnu, Brihaspati, Aditi, Ila, Saraswati, etc. In the Upanishads He is the Sachchidananda or Brahman, and in the Gita He is Purushottama, above the Mutable and Immutable and even his supreme abode, Paramadhama.

The Tantra is as old as the Vedas and it is a practical yogic science. It lays stress on Prikriti or the Nature-Soul and realisation here on Earth and not in a Supra-cosmic heaven. According to the

Tantra Siva cloaked in the body is Jiva and uncloaked he is Parasiva who is the Supreme Reality. The Jiva can at any moment throw away its sheath of ignorance and becomes parasiva again through a process of evolution. Realisation of Ananda or Bliss is the essence of Tantricism. In all the scriptures the phenomenal world or the cosmos is a manifestation of the Supreme Reality. The Vishnu-Tantra and the Shakti-Tantra present a similar concept of man and society.

The Epics, some of them as old as the Vedas, came to be written to expound the deeper truth of the Vedas in a simple form for the understanding of the common people. They lay stress on the performance of the religious rites and duties towards parents, forefathers, sages and gods, and observance of social and moral rules of conduct. The aim of life is to realise happiness in the heaven, a supracosmic existence.

Jainism considers man as the Jiva bound by Ajiva or matter. Karma binds man to the world through false knowledge. The human individuals has to cut himself off from the chain of Karma and attain salvation.

Buddhism is similar to Jainism indentifying the reality of the world and accepts the Upanishadic concept of the individual being a soul. It, however, does not accept the existence of God or any Absolute Reality and considers nirvana in the Sunya or vijnana as the ultimate distiny and goal of human life. It prescribes the eight-fold middle path as the means for this realisation.

There was a revival of the study of the Vedas, the Upanishads and the Gita during the modern period and hence modern Indian thought closely resembles the ancient thought with difference in the stress on various aspects. For Dayananda the Veda is the repository of all Knowledge. Swami Vivekananada considers man as already perfect, he is only to manifest his protection in his daily life. While Rabindra Nath insists on a unity and harmony between individual nature, cosmic nature and Supreme Nature, Gandhiji considers "God as Truth and Truth as God" and stress on a perfect correlation between the head, the heart and the hand to bring out the best in the child and man.

Thus we see that the Eastern concept of man right from the earliest period stands out in the clearest term is hailed quite high and vulnerable. Human dignity was maintained at all cost. The flower of humanity blossomed in its all fragrance and elegance so intensively and vehemently that the West also could not remain unaffected and unescaped.

The Club of Rome's "Limit to Growth"[48] and Alvin Toffler's "Future Shock"[49] and scores of similar works gave well-deserved shock treatment to victims of the consumerist hypnosis. Through a devastating attack on human greed, carelessness and sense of irresponsibility towards the environment. Rachel Carson crossed the line of single dimensional development in "The Silent Spring"[50] and added one more dimension to the blind-folded reach of humans for an illusion they call the future. Toffler warns a man of throw-away culture again and again. He opines: "We develop a throw-away mentality to match our throw-away products. This mentality produces, among other things, a set of radically altered values with respect to property. But the spread of disposability through the society also implies decreased duration in man-thing relationship."[51]

Progressive unification of mankind, intensification of finally, movement towards the convergent structure of evolution as it seeks out its cosmic centre.[52] Teilhard's approach thus transcends ordinary technological approaches, placing in human hands a key to the next stage of the cosmic process. He said: "The sense of man believes in the magnificent future of the tangible world and the Gospel seems to despite it.... And between the gospels of many orders and the sense of man there is at present a deep rift."[53]

It needs mention here that the approach of the East has been apostolic as far as perception of mankind is concerned. Let's conclude this topic with statement of the philosopher Kao who compares man's nature with water and says – "Man's nature is like water whirling round in a corner. Open a passage for it to the east, and it will flow to the east. Open a passage for it to the west, and it will flow to the west. Man's nature is indifferent to good and evil, just as the water is indifferent to the east and west."[54] Here we are recalled of the similar saying about a man by Lao, traditionally called profounder of Taoism –

Man at his best, like water

Serves as he goes along
Like water he seeks his own level
The common level of life.[55]

In fact, the natural phenomenon which the Taoists saw as bearing the closest resemblance to Tao itself was water. They were struck by the way it would support objects and carry them effortlessly on its tide. The Chinese characters for swimmer, diciphered, mean literally "one who knows the nature of water". Similarly one who knows that it will sustain him if he will only stop his thrashing and flialing and trust it to buoy and carry him gently forward –

Those who flow as life flows know
They need no other force
They feel no wear, they feel no tear
They need no mending, no repair.[56]

REFERENCES

1. Dr. S. Radhakrishnan. *Religion and Culture*, p.109.
2. न हि शप्तः प्रतिशपामि
   किंचित् दमं द्वारं ह्यमृतस्येह वेद्मि।
   गुह्यं ब्रह्म तदिदं ब्रवीमि
   न हि मानुषाच्छ्रेष्ठतरं हि किंचित्।
   — Mahabharata, Shanti Parvan 176.120
3. *Religion and Culture*, p.111.
4. A.N. Whitehead, *Adventures of Ideas*, p.217.
5. *Religion and Culture*, p.112.
6. भोगाः न भुक्ताः वयमेव भुक्तास्तपो न तप्तं वयमेव तप्ताः ।
   कालो न यातो वयमेव यातास्तृष्णा न जीर्णा वयमेव जीर्णाः।
   — Vairagya Shatak-7

   (The worldly pleasures have not been devoured, no religious austerities have gone through; but we ourselves have become scorched, time is not gone (being ever-present and infinite), but it is we who are gone (because of approaching death). Desire is not reduced in force, though we ourselves are reduced to senility.)
7. मनुजस्स पमत्त चारिनो
   तण्हा वड्ढति मालुवा विय
   सो पलवेति हुराहुरं
   फलमिच्छं व वन्हि वानरो ।

— Dhammapad, Tanha Vagga 24-334

8. सरितानि सिनेहितानि च
सोमनस्सानि भवन्ति जन्तुनो
ते सोत-सिता सुखेसिनो
ते वे जाति-जरूपगा नरा ॥

— *Ibid.*, Verse 341

9. न वि मुंडिएण समणो न ओंकारेण वंभणो ।
न मुनि रण्णवासेन कुसचीरेण न तावसो ॥

— Utaradhyayan Sutra 25/31

10. James R. Ware, *Sayings of Confucious*, p.47.
11. *Ibid.* II.10.
12. *Ibid.* II.13.
13. *Ibid.* II.14.
14. *Ibid.* II.7.
15. Pundit, M.P., *Studies in the Tantra and the Veda*, pp.107-11.
16. *Ibid.*
17. Sri Aurobindo's Translation, *SABCL*, V. 10, p.108.
18. *Ibid.*, p.114.
19. Sri Aurobindo, *SABCL*, V.12, p.14.
20. Sharma, D.S., *The Upanishad : An Anthology, Introduction.*
21. Sri Aurobindo, *SABCL*, V.12, p.1.
22. *The Taitiriya Upanishad*, Sri Aurobindo's Translation.
23. *Ibid.*
24. Sri Aurobindo, *SABCL*, V.12, pp.422-27.
25. *Ibid.*, p.427.
26. *Ibid.*, p.426.
27. *Ibid.*, p.430.
28. *Ibid.*, pp.431-321.
29. *Five Essays of Dean Inge*, p.65.
30. K.K. Munshi, *Bhagvadgita asnd Modern Life*, p.203.
31. *Gita* XVI 4, 6.
32. Bhaktivedanta Prabhupada, *Bhagvadgita*; As It is, pp.216-17.
33. *Ibid.*, Introduction p.XXVI.
34. Alfred Doeblin, *Living Thought of Confucious*, p.41.
35. *Ibid.*, p.44.
36. तपस्विभ्योऽधिको योगी ज्ञानिभ्योऽपि मतोऽधिकः।
कर्मिभ्यश्चाधिको योगी तस्माद्योगी भवार्जुन॥

— Gita VI-46

37. Shri Aurobindo, *SABCL*, Vol. 12, p.553.
38. *The Gita*, 18-61.
39. Pundit, M.P., *Shri Aurobindo on Tantra*, p.1.
40. *Ibid.*, p.4.
41. Pundit, M.P., *Bases of Tantra Sadhana*, p.5.
42. Sri Aurobindo, *SABCL*, V.22, p.62.
43. Sri Aurobindo, *SABCL*, V.16, p.331.
44. *Complete works of Swami Vivekananda*, V.2, p.82.
45. Swami Vivekananda, *The Vedanta Philosophy*, p.39.
46. Cinkner, W.M., *The Hindu Personality in Education*, p.37.
47. *Ibid.*
48. Teilhard de Chardin, *Future of Man*, London, Collins, 1964.
49. Alvin Toffler, *Future Shock*, New York, Random House, 1970.
50. Rachel Carson, *The Silent Spring*, Greenwich, Connecticut, Faweett Publ., 1962.
51. *Future Shock*, p.57.
52. *Towards the Future*, p.9.
53. *Ibid.*, p.26.
54. Alfred Doeblin, *Confucious*, p.85.
55. Quoted from Huston Smith's '*The Religions of a Man*', p.191.
56. *Ibid.*, pp.190-91.

4

KARMITE LAWS

"Karma is nothing but the will of the spirit in action, consequence nothing but the creation of will. What is in the will of being, expresses itself in Karma and consequence. When the will is limited in mind, Karma appears as bondage and a limitation, consequence as a reaction or an imposition. But when the will of Being is infinite in the spirit, Karma and consequence become instead the joy of creative spirit, the construction of the eternal mechanist, the word and drama of the eternal poet. This lesser, bound, seemingly, separate evolution is only a step in the free self-creation of the spirit from its own illimitable Ananda. This is behind all we are and do; to hide it from mind and bring it slowly forward into the front of existence and action is the present play of self with Nature."

— Sri Aurobindo,
The Problem of Rebirth, p. 113.

Karma is one of those fundamental concepts in Hinduism around which a host of other valuation crystalize, such as reincarnation, other worldliness, renunciation, cosmic illusion etc. *Karma* automatically enters into all of them; it reinforces them and makes them hang together. K.W. Kapp[1] identifies *Karma* with the iron law of retribution which works itself out over not one but several lives by spreading action over several incarnations and by tracing its good and evil consequences through several "heavens". *Karma* encourages other-worldliness. By linking action with inescapable retribution it promotes renunciation of action and its fruits. By positing *Karma* as cosmic regularity it emphasizes the interconnectedness of the cosmic process and individual life and promotes a desire for *Moksha* or freedom.

Jain and Buddhist View

The Indian Jains and Buddhists also held the *Doctrine of Karma,* that man suffers from the fruits of their own deeds. According to Sutra – Kritanga (I, 2, I) "In this world living beings suffer individually for their deeds; for the deed they have done themselves, they obtain punishment, and will not got over it before they have felt it… Notwithstanding their pleasures and relations, all men must suffer in due time and the fruit of their work; as a coconut detaching itself from its stalk falls down, so life will end when its time is spent. Even a very learned or virtuous man, or a priest or an ascetic, will be severely punished for his deed when he is given to actions of deceit… therefore *a wise and worthy man should be careful,* ceasing from sin and being entirely happy. The virtuous heroes of faith have chosen the great road, the right and certain path to perfection." In this very vein Confucious has very rightly opined: "Deeds are roots and fortunes are the fruits."

Man is not so helpless that his entire existence is to be left to the blind chance only. In our scripture he is called the maker of his own fortunes. His future depends upon his good or bad Karma (action). Dr. Radhakrishnan has rightly observed: "Karma literally means action; deed. All acts produce their effects which are recorded both in the organism and the environment. Their physical effects may be short-lived but their moral effects (*samskar*) are worked into the character of the self. Every single thought, word and deed enter into the living chain of causes which makes what we are. Our life is not at the mercy of blind chance or capricious fate. The conception is not peculiar to the Oriental creeds. The Christian Scriptures refer to it. *'Be not deceived; God is not mocked: for whatsoever a man soweth, that shall he also reap'*. Jesus is reported to have said on the Mount, *'Judge not that ye be not judged, for which what judgement ye judge, ye shall be judged, and with what measure ye mete, it shall be measured to you again.'*[2]

The Buddhist interpretation is of an unbroken continuum of life from the limitless past to limitless future. In that life, each person has created a karmic account as a result of past actions. There is a certain amount of latitude; since the way the person lives at present can alter the karmic load his life has borne from the past. The late Arnold Toynbee interestingly compared the human karmic situation to a banking account in which entries are always being made in the debit and credit column to alter the balance, which is the fate of the individual life at given moment. Buddhists believe that what Dr. Toynbee called balance-sheet continue in effect after death and into coming lives. The following passages of Dhammapada confirms the above statement:

"All that we are in the result of what we have thought: it is founded on our thought, it is made-up of our thoughts. If a man speaks or acts with an evil thought, pain follows him, as the wheel follows the foot of the ox that draws the carriage."[3] In the same vein further it adds, "All that we are is the result of what we have thought: it is founded on our thoughts, it is made-up of our thoughts. If a man speaks or acts with a pure thought, happiness follows him, like a shadow that never leaves him."[4] According to Dr. C.D. Sharma, *Theory of Karma*, like a few other important theories, is based on the doctrine of Dependent Origination *(Pratitya-samutpada)*. He says, "The theory of Karma is based on this (doctrine of Dependent Origination), being an implication of the law of causation. Our present life is due to the impressions of the Karmas of the past life and will shape our future life. Ignorance and Karma go on determining each other in a vicious circle."[5]

St. Augustine who was largely a platonist, says, that "Not God but man is responsible for his moral fall. Much earlier Lord Buddha declared: "One's own actions (deeds) are the root cause of one's happiness or sorrow. High or low birth, poverty or richness – are the fruits of one's deeds."[6] It is also said – "It is the cycle of one's actions which makes a man moving in the flow of the world. When one's actions, good or evil, positive or negative, are fully matured they start yielding the corresponding fruits. The actions are the cause of man's birth and rebirth.[7]

Hindu View

In Valmiki Ramayana the doctrine of Karma and the concept of reward after death are so well argued for the first time in the post-Vedic poetry. Evidently, Hanuman had realised and owned this philosophy of life, and had impressed Rama for attainments in these spheres of thought. Rama's final refutation of Bali's accusation of Rama's shooting at Bali, instead of boldly calling on him for a fight, is, in a way, the earliest instance on record of a behaviour of a hero acting upto the immaculate traditions of Karma Yoga in the family of Ikshavaku. Rama declares here that it was not possible for every man to assess the merit of an indispensable strategy of an action.

In Gita[8] Lord Krishna also declares that it was difficult for a man to understand the impact of momentum of an action. Every man was not competent to judge what was absolutely right to be performed and what was absolutely wrong to be avoided. Lord Krishna further says: "One who sees inaction in action and action in inaction, is intelligent among men, and he is in the transcendental position, although engaged in all sorts of activities."[9]

Commenting on this Shloka (IV.18) Bhaktivedant Swami says

> "A person acting in Krishna consciousness is naturally free from the resultant action of work. His activities are all performed for Krishna, and therefore he does not enjoy or suffer any of the effects of work. Consequently, he is intelligent in human society, even though he is engaged in all sorts of activities for Krishna. Akarma means without reaction to work. The impersonalist ceases fruitive activities out of fear, so that resultant action may not be a stumbling block on the path of self-realization, whereas the personalist knows rightly his position as the eternal servitor of the Supreme Personality of Godhead. Therefore, he engages himself in the activities of Krishna consciousness. Because everything is done for

Krishna, he enjoys only transcendental happiness in the discharge of this service. Those who are engaged in this process are without desire for personal sense gratification. The sense of eternal servitorship to Krishna makes one immune to all the reactionary elements of work."[10]

In its ingredients the *doctrine of karma* has many similar points of the Western thought. Pelagius says: "Grace of God means the aid which God gives to the faithful, or by creating a good natural constitution for some men, or, by the law of God revealed to men with regard to what he ought or ought not to do, or, may mean in clearing the reason of some men which reason gets darkened by sin. Pelagius grants that some heathen like Plato, Buddha and others have become redeemed soul because God had given them a good constitution of soul." He further adds that grace is given according to one's merits, it would not be consistent with God's justice to give it to all sinners.[11] In Bhagvadgita Lord Krishna declares his promise: "I grant bliss to men as per their sense of devotion and dependence upon me."[12] God's grace can be expected through karma only not simply sitting idle. H.W. Longfellow, therefore, rightly advises:

Trust no future however pleasant:
Let the dead past bury its head.
Act-act in the living present
Heart within and God O'erhead.

Comparison

We should not mourn over the past as it would come back again; but we should try to improve upon the present as it is ours. Upanishads also inspire us to act to meet the shadowy future without fear and manly heart – *Charaiveti Charaiveti*. Ramanuja's doctrine of grace in Vaishnavism is very close to that of Pelagius, a contemporary of St. Augustine. Pelagious denied the doctrine of "Original sin", predestination and grace crystally. Bible also declares: "Every sinner has his future and every saint has his past". Therefore, one should not be biased on the basis of our surface perfection. Whatever is perceived with physical eyes is always not true. Bryan Wilson has tried to compare the Eastern and Western view on the doctrine of Karma. He says:

"Man always seeks an explanation for his circumstances, and often what he has not able to explain by reference to empirical observation (or what he has not been prepared to accept as the consequence of his own doing) he has explained as due to supernatural causes. In the Christian case, he has sometimes regarded his fate as *the will of God* and particular events as *acts of God* – a phrase still used in English law for otherwise inexplicable accidents. In Buddhism, the notion of Karma represents a more significant element of personal responsibility, but since the cause of present circumstances lies in earlier lives that he cannot recall, the individual's immediate sense of responsibility is somewhat muted. Perhaps the idea of Karma operates effectively in giving people warning, in the shape of present sufferings, of what they might be laying up for themselves in the future if they fail to conform to the moral demands of the present. In this sense Karma might be represented as a socially functional agency of control, or as a way of inducing men to cultivate self-control.

Although the idea of *karma* embraces powerful intimations of determinism, this type of theodicy clearly admits the operation of free will, if not as the influence decisively affecting the present, as least as a powerful agency in the determination of the future. What is, is already settled; what will be (in future lives) men may yet influence. Thus the debilitating effect of total fatalism is escaped, even though the individual may absolve himself from immediate and present responsibility for his current sufferings. The rewards of moral conduct now are envisaged as something that will be realized only in – possibly remote – future lives (and indeed, since there is no continuing consciousness between lives, the differences in the interval between cause and effect is both incalculable and inconsequential).

Sociologically, karma operates over an apparently longer interval than is envisaged in the traditional Christian conception of reward and punishment for sins in some immediate post mortem circumstance. Whether the threat of hell-fire has been more effective as an agency of social control than the prospect of creating bad effects in future lives, is not easy to assess. Christians were once powerful affected by fear of hell and hopes of heaven. Perhaps those emotions were strongest and, because they were subjected most effectively to control, the effect greatest during the period of early Calvinism and in the Puritan and Pietist movements that followed. At that time men began to look for immediate consequences of moral and immoral acts in the course of their actual earthly lives, at least by way of intimations of their post mortem prospects. The strength of self-control of the emotions that were attached to these utterly serious concerns led to a new type of effective regulation of conduct in society. The growing individualism the period entailed that men should take on responsibility for their own consciences. Since they had more opportunity for individual action and were less bound by local traditional custom, which had kept men safe within the confines of conventional morality, their concern with sin and rectitude was intensified.

"The philosophical implication in the *doctrine of karma* is thus not one that is altogether alien to the thinking of Western peoples – namely, that there should be a balance between cause and effect, between one's dispositions towards good and evil, and the consequences that follow from such dispositions. Despite their differences, Buddhism and Western philosophy embrace not dissimilar moral economy. There appears to be an implicit attraction in the natural justice of a cause-and-effect programme, even though the time-span of the Buddhist conception of things and the discontinuity of individual identity are difficult elements to comprehend for minds wholly formed in the Western tradition."[13]

Krishna Dvaipayana Vyas says in Stri Parvan of Mahabharata:

> It is karma that brings joy or sorrow
> Willing or unwilling. We live by our karma.

Observe the potter shaping his pots:

> Some break on the Wheel,

Some crack after removed from the wheel
Some spoil when wet, some when dry,
Some burst while being fired,
Some after removal from kiln,
Some shatter in use.......
So some of us die in the womb,
Some immediately after birth,
Some a day later,
Some a fortnight later, some a month,
Some after one year, some after two,
Some in youth. Some in middle age, some old.
Their karma determines it all.[15]

Views of Bhartrihari

In his beautiful verses Bhartrihari has sung the glory of human karmas interweaving various mythological references and anecdotes from Indian culture. He says:

"Bow to that karma (past actions) through whose influence the Creator (Brahma) is continuously working like a potter into the interior of the vessel of universe, the protector (Vishnu) is thrown into a series of misfortunes by assuming the well known ten incarnations, the Destroyer (Shiva) is made to beg from door to door with a skull in hand, and the sun is compelled to revolve incessantly into the sky."

"It is not the result of handsome person nor that of his noble birth, nor that of his learning, nor that of his attentive service of his master, but it is only the necessary consequence of man's fortune as made up of his past good and virtuous actions that enabled him to enjoy the pleasures and happiness of this world."[17]

It is only the virtuous actions of the former lives which protect a man from injury and danger when he is thrown into the midst of a dense forest, a raging battlefield, a crowd of enemies, a deep ocean, and a burning fire; or at the time when he is fast asleep, or drunk, or is placed in a dangerous or difficult position.

The idea is that in whatever place and in whatever circumstances one may be placed, the merit accumulated in a previous birth is always with its help.

REFERENCES

1. K.W. Capp, *Hindu Culture, Economic Development and Economic Planning in India*, pp.42-43.
2. Dr. S. Radhakrishnan, *An Idealistic View of Life*, p.218.
3. मनो–पुब्बंगमा धम्मा मनो–सेट्ठा मनोमया
   मनसा च पदुट्ठेन भासति वा करोति वा
   ततो न दु:खमन्वेति चक्कं व वदतो पदं ।

   — Dhammapada
4. मनो – पुब्बंगमा धम्मा मनो – सेट्ठा मनोमया
   मनसा चे पसन्नेन भासति वा करोति वा
   ततो नं दु:खमन्वेति छाया व अनपायिनी ।

   — Dhammapada
5. Dr. C:D. Sharma holds that the doctrine of Dependent Organisation is the Central teaching of the Buddha and his other teachings can be easily deduced from it as corollaries. Besides the Theory of Karma other such corollaries of the said doctrine are – Theory of Momentariness (*Kshan-bhangur-vada*), theory of Noego (*Nairatmya-vada*), the theory that so called matter is unreal, the theory of casual efficiency (*artha-kriya-karitva*) etc., - Dr. C.D. Sharma, *A Critical Survey of Indian Philosophy*, pp.74-75
6. कम्मस्सका माणव सत्ता कम्मदायादा
   कम्मबन्धु कम्मपटिसरणा, कम्मं सत्ते
   विभजति यदिदं हीन – पणीतताया' ति।

   — मज्झिमनिकाय, चुलकम्मविभंग सुत्त
7. कम्मा विपाका वत्तन्ति विपाको कम्मसम्भवो ।
   कम्मा पुनब्भवो होति एवं लोको पवत्तती ।

   — Vibhanga, p.426
8. कर्मणो ह्यपि बोद्धव्यं बोद्धव्यं च विकर्मण: ।
   अकर्मणश्च बोद्धव्यं गहना कर्मणो गति: ।।

   — Bhagvadgita 4.17
9. कर्मव्यकर्म य: पश्पेदकर्मणि च कर्म य: ।
   स बुद्धिमान्मनुष्येषु स युक्त: कृत्स्नकर्मकृत् ।।

   — *Ibid.* 4.18
10. A.C. Swami Bhaktivedanta, *Bhagvadgita As It Is*, pp.76-77.
11. Quoted in 'Critical Survey of Western Philosophy', p.148.
12. यथा मां प्रपद्यन्ते तांस्तथैव भजाम्यहम् ।

    — Bhagvadgita

13. Bryan Wilson and Daisaku Ikeda, *Human Values in a changing World*, p.61.
14. *Ibid.*, p.62.
15. Mahabharata of Vyas, Transcreated by P. Lal, p.301.
16. ब्रह्मा येन कुलालवन्नियमितो ब्रह्माण्ड भाण्डोदरे,
विष्णुर्येन दशावतारगहने क्षिप्तो महासंकटे।
रूद्रो येन कपालपाणिपुटके भिक्षाटनं कारितः,
सूर्यो भ्राम्यति नित्यमेव गगने तस्मै नमः कर्मणे ।।

— Niti Shatak 95

17. नैवाकृतिः फलति नैव कुलं न शीलं,
विद्याडपि नैव न च यत्नकृतापि सेवा।
भाग्यानि पूर्वतपसा खलु संचितानि,
काले फलन्ति पुरुषस्य यथैव वृक्षाः।।

— *Ibid.*, 96

Cf.(a) विनाडपि प्राक्तनं कर्म न दाता कोडपि कस्यचित्
आगर्भाज्जन्तुरश्नाति पूर्वकर्मतरोः फलम् ।।09।।

— Kathasaritsagar, Ratna Prabha
Lambak, Tarang-6

(b) भाग्यं फलति सर्वत्र न च विद्या न च पौरुषम् ।
समुद्रमधनाल्लेभे हरिर्लक्ष्मी हरो विषम् ।।

(c) जन्मजन्मान्तरे शुभमथाप्यशुभं यदेव यैरर्जितं स्वपरिणामवशेन कर्म ।
तथोग्यमेव फलमिष्टमनीप्सितं वा तैः प्रात्यते किमिति शोचसि हेतुहीनम् ।।

— Chandraprabha Charit, Canto III

18. वने रणे शत्रुजलाग्निमध्ये
महर्णवे पर्वतमस्तके च।
सुप्तं प्रमत्तं विषमस्थितं वा,
रक्षन्ति पुण्यानि पुराकृतानि ।।

— *Ibid.*, 97.

5

STATUS OF WOMEN-FOLK

"So too the subjection of women, the propriety of man over the women, was once an axiom of social life and has only in recent times been effectively challenged. So strong was or had become the instinct of this domination in the male animal man, that even religion and philosophy have had to sanction it, very much in the formula in which Milton expressed the height of masculine egoism, 'he for God only, she for God in him'. This idea too is crumbling into the dust, though its remnants still ailing to life by many strong tentacles of old legislation, continued instinct, persistence of traditional ideas, the fiat has gone out against it in the claim of woman to be regarded, she too, as a free individual being."

— Aurobindo[1]

Linton[2] referes the term "status" as the position of an individual in social structure, defined by his/her designated rights and obligations. These rights and obligations, to be justified, have to be made use of by the individual concerned – this is defined as the "role". Thus the "role" that an individual will assume in a social set-up ultimately determines her "status"; the dynamic aspect of "status" is thus the "role" that the individual plays for a woman, which in a culture complex. A person can play more than one role at the same time, some more dominant than others. Broadly speaking a woman has three roles – that of a wife, mother and career woman. In a progressive and balanced society adjustment has to be made and a cohesive balance has to be struck between the three. There is no gainsaying the fact that it is the cultural pattern which determines the position and not legal rights or constitutional guarantees as the acceptability of the society is one of the prominent factors in deciding the position. Unless the role conforms with the prevailing scheme of values, it may not be acceptable and non-acceptability by the society entails a great struggle for a woman, which she has been facing throughout the ages, right from the epic period to the modern time.

Vedic Age

The Vedas also speak of the woman – feminine powers without whom the masculine are not effective for work and formation, for some of the Vedic rites the very presence of woman was very essential. In one of the greatest hymns, the twenty-second of the first Mandal, he (Medhatithi) expressly mentions of the *Patnih Devanam,* the brides of the Strong Ones, who are to be called to extend protection, to breathe a mighty peace, to have their share in the joy of Soma Wine. In one of the hymns of Atharva Veda[3] the husband and wife are called as complementary to each other. The prayer is as below:

> "May the husband and wife be each other's
> complementary.
> The husband a song, the wife a verse,
> the husband a sky, wife the earth. It is in their
> union that offsprings result. Each emotionally fulfils
> the other to completion."

In one of the hymns of Rigveda goddess of learning, Saraswati is invoked in the following manner:

> O, Saraswati, goddess of learning, symbol of purity and source of intellectual powers, with your wisdom, be our inspiration.

Come and participate in our noble deeds.
The whole cosmos is aflame under the impact of your wisdom, without which there will be darkness.
All awakening in the world is only manifestation of your supreme intellectual power.
You are the power behind all achievements of human genius.[4]

In Hindu scriptures we find two extreme types of description of a woman. On one side it is said that a woman does not deserve any freedom and as such she is protected in childhood, youth as well as in old-age by the parents, husband and children respectively. On the other hand she is described as inspirer, complementary to a man, energy supreme, an emblem of Shakti etc. In the difference and divergence of such descriptions the angle and insight of the describer, poet or author counts a lot, as Aurobindo has rightly observed. According to him, "The women of Vyasa and Sophocles have all a family resemblence, all possess a quiet or commanding masculine strength of character which reveals their parentage. Other poets we see succeeding in a single feminine character, often repeating, but failing or not succeeding eminently in the rest. Otherwise women in poetry are generally painted very much from the outside. The poets who have had an instinctive insight into women, can literally be counted on the fingers of one's hand. Shakespeare in this as in other dramatic gifts is splendidly and unapproachably first, or at least only equalled in depth though not in range by Valmiki. Racine has the same gift within his limits and Kalidasa without limits,...."[5]

In Ramayana, the statement of Ravana himself indicates the attitude of Rakshas towards the women-folk. He persuaded Sita at Lanka to accept him as husband. Eloping the married or unmarried woman was common in demonaic culture when Ravana could not succeed to persuade Sita, he ordered demonaic guards to behave harshly with Sita so that she might be compelled to accept his proposal. On this Sita told the Rakshasas about the difference in life-style of demons and Aryans. Refusing completely to accede to the demand of Ravana she said:

"A girl of Manava creed cannot become the wife of a demon. You all may swallow me but I cannot accept Ravana's proposal. My husband may be weak or deprived of Kingdom. He is my master, he is my instructor, I am always thirsty of his love and would ever remain so like a sunshine which remains the follower of the sun."[6]

Besides this Sita enumerated the examples of other ideals like Savitri, Rohini, Damayanti and Anusuya etc. who remained true to their husbands even in miserable moments. On the other hand Shurpanakha the real widowed sister of Ravana approached Rama and Lakshmana with the request to accept her as their wife.

While analysing the 'place of women' Subramania Bharti, an apostle of patriotism, writes thus with pointed force:

"Nations are made at home. And so long as you do not have justice and equality fully practised at home, you cannot expect to see them practised in your public life. Because it is the home life that is the basis of public life. And a man who is a villain at home cannot find himself suddenly transformed into a saint the moment he gets to the councils or to courts of justice."[7]

Deteriorating Trend

Educational development of women as depicted in the Mahabharata that women were not given adequate opportunities for the development of their personalities. While tracing the reasons of backwardness of women in education, we find that their overall social status was mainly responsible for this. Their field was mainly household. They were not supposed to earn the livelihood. In the prevailing social phenomena, they were not safe. There was every fear of atrocities by enemies or abduction by dacoits. Under such circumstances it was not considered wise to send girls to the hermitages located in far-flung forest areas. Therefore, as far as possible, their education was arranged at home only.

According to Altekar[8] education of women prevailed in the Vedic society. But by the time of the Mahabharata the tradition of study of the Vedas by the women-folk was almost extinct. This very phenomena is indicative of the degeneration of the then civilization. It was mostly confirmed opinion of the people that the knowledge of scriptures was not essential for women.

Again security problem seems to be one of the reasons, as said above, for depriving women from the study of the Vedas and allied scriptures. However, in spite of certain restrictions and lack of safety, some women used to study the Vedas. In the Mahabharata many women are said to have learnt by heart many hymns and prayers from the Vedas. Vinata blessed Garuda by reciting Vedic verses. While deserting "Karna" Kunti prayed[9] for his welfare and recited Vedic mantras.

Socio-Religious Status

In the Rigveda[10] it is mentioned that couple, who performs sacrifices and offers prayers with harmonious minds, always becomes happy. It was a common belief that the mental make-up and conduct of a child is influenced by his parentage. Therefore, the right of learning the Vedas and performing Agnihotra was given to women. They deserve initiation (Maunji-Bandhan) also, as Nirvana-Sindhu puts it.[11]

Theoretically the Mahabharata holds that women have the right not only for learning but teaching also. There is good evidence to testify to this notion. There is a reference of Brahmini (female Brahmin) named "Shiva",[12] who studied all the Vedas and having practised penances, attained salvation.

Similarly, there was a Brahmini Siddha[13] who attained the heavenly abode by the virtue of her celebacy and yogic practices. In Shanti Parvan there is a famous episode of Sulbha, who debates with Janaka on various subtle issues of spirituality and introduces herself to Janak.[14]

Formal Vs. Non-Formal Education

In general, girls used to have non-formal education from elder brothers, parents, learned guests, etc. King Drupad had appointed a learned Brahmin to teach statecraft to his son. His daughter

(Draupadi) also learnt Brihaspathi-Artha-Shastra from a learned Brahman at home.[15] Shakuni, the Prince of Gandhar and Gandhari (sister of Shakuni) were both well-versed in the Arthashastra.[16] Though the girls were not sent to hermitages, they were sent to stay with some female members used to live which included the Guru's wife, daughters, etc.[17]

Muni Durwasa, being pleased with the hospitability of Kunti at her father's (Kuntibhog) house, trained her in the effective use of the "Atharva-shiras" mantra.[18] By virtue of this very mantra, it is said, Kunti pleased various gods and got three sons – Yudhishthira, Bhima and Arjuna. Madri followed the footsteps of Kunti and pleased the twingods (Ashwini) and got twin sons – Nakula and Sahdev.

From the above description, it is clear that though the girls were not sent to the hermitages, for princesses and women-folk of hermitages such occasions were not rare when they received knowledge of the Vedas and other scriptures through learned fathers, brothers or other scholarly guests. They also used to develop their knowledge and understanding by listening to the discourses of sages and other scholars from time to time particularly on occasions of certain ceremonies including various sacrifices, etc. In ordinary families also traveller guests used to tell various interesting stories pertaining to the various places they had travelled through. In village "Ekchakra" where the Pandavas lived in disguise with their mother (Kunti), a Brahmin had narrated various interesting stories to Kunti.[19] Shakuntala living in the hermitage of Kanva came to know about her parentage by hearing a conversion between the sage Kanva and a traveller guest.

Women used to take keen interest in narrating and listening to stories. This was not only a source of entertainment for them but also a book of knowledge. Brihannala (named adopted by Arjuna in disguise in the kingdom of Virata) used to narrate various interesting stories and amuse the ladies in the inner apartment of King Virata.

Special Tutors

In affluent families or royal families special tutors were appointed to teach the girls. In the palace of Virata Brihannala was entrusted with the duties of training the females in the fine arts like dance, singing, music, etc.[20]

For this singular evidence available in the Mahabharata it appears that the appointment of male teacher for girls was not appreciated. This is why King Virata got the impotency of Brihannala ensured before assigning him the job. In the joint families the girls used to get practical lessons in various useful matters before their marriage from their father, mother and other elderly women available in the family. Kunti[21] and Gandhari[22] had educated their daughters and also daughters-in-law duties towards members of the family, arts and crafts etc.

The data available in the Mahabharata reveal that the women's education was almost informal. There were no formal agencies of education for them. The attributive used for maid servants of Yudhishthira indicates that they were well-versed in all the 64 arts mentioned in "Kamasutra" and other treatises. They must have learnt these arts informally only. In such informal education, women used to learn all that was required for leading a happy married life, but at times, because of emotionality, they ignored their duties. Because of such non-informal education, they were generally found to be good at heart but they lacked rational temper at times. Being invoked with 'Pativrit Dharma' Gandhari used to have her eyes entied with a piece of cloth (because of her husband was blind). By doing so she neglected duties as a mother. Has she not done so she could have reared her children in a proper manner and cultivated in them the desired social and spiritual values.

In his famous treatise, "Education in Ancient India" Dr. A.S. Altekar rightly observed: "In the heyday of her glory education in India was broad-based." Women and ordinary people were allowed to derive the maximum benefits from it. Although it would not be fair to compare "the scanty remains of a bygone system" with the tremendous advance that the West has made in our times, it can be said that the education during the epic period "developed character and personality. It included civic virtues, introduced a high standard of culture and emphasised the necessity of self-imposed discipline and stern regard for duty."

Ambivalent Attitude

Though the early Indian mind, prone to exaggeration, perhaps overdid the necessity of wifely obedience, her status was not without honour.

> "The wife is half the man,
> the best of friends,
> the root of the three ends of life,
> and of all that will help him in the other world.
>
> "With a wife a man does mighty deeds...
> With a wife a man finds courage.
> A wife is the safest refuge...
>
> "A man aflame with sorrow in his soul,
> or sick with disease, finds comfort in his wife,
> as a man parched with heat
> finds relief in water.
>
> "Even a man in the grip of rage
> will not be harsh to a woman,
> remembering that on her depend
> the joys of love, happiness, and virtue.
>
> "For woman is the everlasting field,
> in which the self is born."[23]

Passages like these, showing the honour and esteem in which women were held, are quite as numerous as those which stress their sub-servience. Everywhere it is stated that a woman should be lovingly cherished, well fed and cared for, and provided with jewellery and luxuries to the limits of her husband's means. She should never be upbraided too severely, for the gods will not accept the sacrifice of the man who beats his wife. The ancient Indian attitude to women was, in fact, ambivalent. She was at once a goddess and a slave a saint and a strumpet.

The latter aspect of her character is frequently brought out in semi-religious and gnomic literature. Women's lust knows no bounds:

"The fire has never too many logs –
 the ocean never too many rivers,
death never too many living souls,
 and fair-eyed woman never too many men."[24]

As in Greece, the higher class Hetaira was an educated woman. The authorities on erotics demand that, as well as in the art immediately essential to her profession, she should be thoroughly trained in "the sixty-four arts". These formed a stock list, which included not only music, dancing and singing, but also acting, the composition of poetry, impromptu and otherwise, flower-arrangement and garland-making, the preparation of perfumes and cosmetics, cooking, dress-making and embroidery, sorcery conjuring and sleight of hand, the composition of ridddles, tongue-twisters and other puzzles, fencing with sword and staff, archery, gymnastics, carpentry and architecture, logic, chemistry, and mineralogy, gardening, training in fighting cocks, partridges and rams, teaching parrots and mynahs to talk, writing in cipher, languages, making artificial flowers, and clay modelling.

It is hardly likely that the 'ganika' did in fact study all the arts of this rather bizarre list, but it shows what was expected of her. If she mastered those arts most suited to her profession a brilliant future awaited her. "A courtesan of a pleasant disposition, beautiful, and otherwise attractive, who has mastered the arts... has the right to a seat honour among men. She will be honoured by the king and praised by the learned, and all will seek her favours and treat her with consideration."[25] The literature of the Middle Ages fully bears out this statement.

Ideal Women

Sita, the heroine of Ramayana, had a number of names, all derivatives. Sita, the principal one of these, came from a Sanskrit root meaning the "furrow left by the plough", in accordance with the Sanskrit grammatic sutra (or aphorism) "Sita Langala padhathi" (i.e. the way the edge of the plough goes is called 'Sita') and is based on a story connected with her origin on earth. Vaidehi, Maithili and Janaki, her other three names, were derived, respectively, from Videha, the name of the country to which she belonged, Mithila, its capital, and Janaka, her foster-father. She was an avatar (or incarnation) of Goddess Lakshmi, the spouse of Lord Vishnu.

Sita is one of the noblest of the feminine character of the Ramayana.

Janaka, the king of Videha Desa (modern Dharbhanga, changed present form of the original Sanskrit word, Dhanurbhanga, District, and adjoining territory in Bihar State) was an ideal monarch His qualities were so pure that he was considered an ascetic among kings and actually used to be referred to very often as Janaka Maharishi. He was childless and was worried on that account. His advisers suggested his performing a yaga (or sacrifice) to appease the Gods, whereupon, pleased by his devotion and austerities, they were certain to bliss him with progeny.

For the performance of a Vedic sacrifice the spot of ground whereupon it was to be performed, had to be carefully selected and ploughed as to rid to it of all extraneous impurities. A certain field was accordingly chosen for the purpose. Normally such preparation of the land through ploughing and the like operations was done by servants. This time, however, King Janaka decided to do all that work himself, so that the Gods might be doubly propitiated and pleased.

The news that the king himself was going to plough the field had spread all over the country. Thousands of people were drawn to the site longing to witness the unique phenomenon of the Royal personage at the plough. They all felt, as if by a premonition, that something strange would happen that day. Their expectation was not to be believed. Hardly had the king's plough turned the soil into a few furrows, when, much to the astonishment of the gathering and the king himself, the edge of the plough hit a hard substance. On examination it was seen to be box. When it was opened, there was found in it a newly-born baby girl of resplendent beauty.

Saying that the Gods had been pleased even before the starting of the sacrifice, the king accepted the baby as his own and gave her to his queen. They named her Sita, because of her having been found in the furrow produced by a plough.

In course of time King Janaka's wife conceived in the normal manner and they had another daughter. This baby was named by them Urmila. Sita and Urmila got on in years and, as days passed by, bloomed into a pair of dazzling beauties.

Among King Janaka's collection of war weapons there was a giant bow which had come into his possession as a present and which had originally belonged to Lord Siva Himself (i.e. Divinity as the destroyers of the Universe). It was hence referred to as the Siva Dhanus. People felt that it would be a mighty feat for anyone to lift and string that great weapon. One day when Sita, Urmila and their companions were playing with a ball, it rolled under that terrible bow and got entangled. No one could extricate it from that position. Sita, however, nonchalantly lifted the bow with her left hand, put it in another position, as though it were just a piece of stick, and released the ball. Janaka had seen this smart performance on the part of the girl from a distance. The thought then occurred to him that he who would wed her and become her partner in life should also be one who could lift and string that bow.

Accordingly, when Sita came of marriageable age, Janaka sent out a proclamation throughout the length and breadth of the land to the effect that a day would be announced for Sita's swayamvara (or choice of her husband) when, from among those assembled for the purpose, whoever, could lift and string the great Siva Dhanus in the armoury of weapons in his palace, would win the hand of the princess.

The appointed day was soon to arrive. In the meantime, however, an incident had occurred which made that day synchronise with the performance of a sacrifice of victory by King Janaka. When Janaka made his intention widely known that Sita would be given in marriage only to one who could lift and string the holy bow of Lord Siva. Sudhanva, the King of a neighbouring territory called Sankasyapuri, got annoyed, because he felt that Sita should become his spouse. That king, therefore, invaded Janaka's territory of Videha Desa. Before setting out with his forces to meet the invader, Janaka performed Puja (or worship) to Lord Siva to propitiate that Divinity and secure His blessings. This done, he marched with his men and joined issue with the aggressor. In a fierce battle that ensued the invading army was routed and put to flight. Sudhanva himself was killed in the fray and Janaka put his own cousin, Kusadhwaja, on the vacant throne of Sanksayapuri. Then and there King Janaka also renewed his proclamation regarding the test to be applied for the choice of husband for Sita. Simultaneously with this he also announced the performance of sacrifice to celebrate his recent victory in battle. This sacrifice and Sita's swaymvara (choice of her husband) were fixed at about the same time.

All the kings of the various *desas* (or countries) into which the continent of India was then divided (traditionally these were fifty-six in number) had, on invitation, gathered in the place of Janaka in Mithila both to see the sacrifice and to try a hand at the contest for winning Sita's hand in marriage. The Rakshasa (or Demon) king of Lanka (the present day Ceylon), Ravana had also arrived. In a corner of the audience were also present two young lads, who had just reached their teens and who were the two sons of king Dasaratha of Ayodhya, the capital of *Kosala Desa.* These were the Princess Rama and Lakshmana. They had been taken there by the sage, Viswamitra, to whom they rendered yeoman service in protecting the latter's sacrifice from the misdeeds of the Rakshasas (or Demon) of the forest.

The sacrifice of victory duly completed, King Janaka had the mighty bow of Siva brought before the assembled audience of royal personages and others. Formally announcing to the audience once again his decision regarding Sita as the stake to be won at the ensuing contest. King Janaka invited them to come forward and participate in the test. The very sight of the august weapon terrified most of the assembled kings. They started excusing themselves on some pretex or other and the scene produced a comic interlude. One of them said that he did not wish to invite the wrath of Lord Siva on his head by tempering with that Divine bow. Another backed out saying that the one wife he already had was enough for him and that there would only be trouble if another wife was added to the household. Some of the prices, who managed somehow to muster sufficient courage to make an attempt, quailed on actually approaching the bow. A few who tried to handle the weapon miserably failed, being not even able to lift the bow, not to mention stringing it. Even the great Ravana proved an ignominious failure and ran away in utter shame and discomfiture. King Janaka was getting worried at seeing that there was not one among that vast assembly who could perform the task set before them successfully. Just then, the sage, Viswamitra, asked Janaka's permission to let Rama, the elder of the two princes from Kosala, who he had brought there, to try a hand, explaining to the King at the same time who they were and in what circumstances they had got themselves associated with the sage. Janaka readily agreed, feeling inwardly elated at the thought that, if the young prince succeeded and became his son-in-law, nothing could give him greater pleasure than getting thereby united in matrimonial alliance with the great King Dasaratha of the Ikshvaku line.

Young Rama went near the bow, lifted it and not only stringed it, but also broke it into two pieces in the attempt. With him it was just veni vidi vici, and that too within the twinkling of an eye. Sita's hand had thus at last been won. There was great natural rejoicing everywhere over the happy event. Even the God's in Heaven showered flowers on the young conquering hero.

Sequeal to the evil counsel of Manthara and unbecoming attitude of Kaikayee Rama was exiled for 14 years. In spite of resistance from Rama Sita resolved to accompany him. She firmly declared, "To go with you wherever you go – this is my only course". She further assured Rama that she can and she will bear forest life and she will not be a source of trouble at all to him. She shall eat fruits and roots like him and shall not lag behind as they (Rama and Lakshmana) walk. She shall endure the sun, rain, wind, hunger etc. without any complaint. Thus she talked at the height of an ideal of an Indian woman, quite befitting to her royal race and her own sublimed character.

During exile once Sita saw a stag with wondrous beauty having skin shining like gold. Sita being enchanted by unique beauty of the stag requested Rama to catch it for her. Though Rama knew that it was a trick being played by Rakshas, he, on insistence by Sita, had to set out in pursuit of the deer. It was actually Mareech, in the disguise of the deer, who soon changed back to the original form with a shot of Rama's arrow and cried "Ah Lakshmana, Ah Sita". Taking this as Rama's cry Sita forced Lakshmana to set out in search of her husband. Lakshman obeyed her, but quite unwillingly. Meanwhile Ravana, in the disguise of an ascetic, abducted Sita. On the way Jatayu, an old bird, tried to save Sita; but in vain. The gallant bird could not save Sita and laid his life fighting with mighty Ravana. Ravana carried Sita and kept her in 'Ashoka Vatika'.

Rama, in alliance with Sugreeva, a close friend and devotee, could trace out the whereabouts of Sita. Sampati, beloved brother of Jatayu, informed Angad that he had seen Ravana carrying Sita to Lanka, a city built by Maya, father of Mandodari. Being inspired by Jambuvan, Hanuman approached the coast of Lanka, met Sita in 'Ashoka Vatika' and consoled her conveying the message of Rama. He also gave Rama's signet ring to Sita. Sita was consoled but also pained by the thought that Rama had not forgotten her, but was thinking of her, grieving and searching for her. This shows her love and dedication towards Rama.

Sita was endowed with a practical wisdom in state-craft worth to her royal race. When Hanuman proposed to carry her on his back, she flatly refused the proposal saying: "If you snatch me away stealthily from Rakshasas it would be no credit to the valour of my lord. The honour of the Kshatriya race demands that he should come and fight and vanquish Ravana and redeem me as prize of victory."

After abducting Sita, Ravana adopted various ways to compel Sita to surrender. But she was quite firm and never yielded to him. Sita's joy was beyond words when Ravana was killed by Rama. Sita was taken respectfully to the Rama's camp in a palanquin. Seeing Rama Sita's face beamed with joy, but seeing her Rama was not happy, he spoke, "I have slain my enemy and have recovered you now. I have done my duty as a Kshatriya. But you have lived for a year in a stranger's house. It is not proper that, I should take you back now." Thus Sita had to prove her untainted virtue by throwing herself into a lighted pyre and then coming out of it uninjured. At length Rama accepted Sita. They returned to Ayodhya and ascended the throne. But the suspicions of the subject fell on Sita. They doubted her untainted character. For fear of the people Ram had to send Sita to exile, when he was in family way.

Valmiki received her at Chitrakuta, and there her two sons Lava and Kusha, were born. Valmiki composed the poem of the Ramayana and taught them to repeat and thus years were passed.

After some years, through Lava and Kusha, Rama got united with Sita before he performed Ashvamedha sacrifice. But Sita's tragedy did not end here. When Sita reached Ayodhya, people again started to criticize Rama since their suspicion could not be allayed. Rama could not put up with this embarrassing situation. Seeing the pitiable condition of Rama the earth, which had given birth to Sita, yawned and received its long suffering child.

Some scholars take Sita as a mythological figure; but for millions of Hindu Sita is a real human character, a pattern of female virtue and female self-abnegation. She is regarded as the noblest creation of human imagination. Sita's gentleness, virtues, uncomplaining and unconditional devotion and unconquerable love for her lord, were more than human, her sufferings and woes too were more than usually fall to the lot of women. Even to this day for Hindu women, Sita is a model of character, she would like to emulate and to strive after. Thus Sita was one of the shining gems amongst the princess of ancient India.

Tara, a wife of Baali, was a wise and brave lady. She had foresight regarding Rama's divinity and saw Vishnu in him. That is why is tried her best to restrain Baali from taking dual with Sugreeva for second time. Her counsel to Baali on this occasion was as following:

"I am afraid there is a deep game. Your brother was defeated and disgraced and ran for dear life and concealed himself for safety. Now he has returned and raises his noise. Your brother is not such a fool as to challenge you again so soon after the punishment you inflicted on him unless he was assured of help and protection from an invincible ally or tried prowess. Did you not observe that his very roar of challenge had a new note of confidence in it? I shall tell you what I heard from Angada who had it from our scouts who range the forests. Two princes of unrivalled valour, Rama and

Lakshmana, have come from Ayodhya and Sugreeva has secured the promise of their assistance. After all, my lord, your brother is virtuous and brave. Why should you hate him? Who in the world is closer to us than he? He will be your devoted servant and strong ally. It is best to forget the past and make it up with Sugreeva. My dear Lord, listen to my words."

This is an indicative of her virtue and foresightedness. But Baali did not give any heed to her advice. He lost his reason because of excessive wrath and fell in the trap of death. At length, he was killed by Rama. After the death of the king (Baali) there was panic and chaos in Kishkindha. Tara, seeing all this, set aside her own lamentation and put courage in her husband's subjects saying "Till this day you walked before the king to battle! Why then do you flee in fear now. There is no danger for you. Rama killed Baali only to make Sugreeva King. Your lives are in no danger; you will only have a different ruler; that is all. You need not fly or fear." This shows her wit and presence of mind. She was a queen of a hero in real sense. When Rama approached to console her, she said to Rama without any sign of malice on her face – "With the weapon with which, O Warrior, you killed my husband, kill me too and enable me to join him. Even in heaven, he will not be happy without me. Do not fear that it would be a sin. It will be a meritorious act to unite husband and wife. This will cleanse your sin, your treacherous slaying of my husband.

Kaikeyee was the youngest queen of Dasharatha and mother of Bharata. Basically she was very noble and kind hearted lady. She was well-versed in theoretical knowledge of warcraft. Once Dasharatha, on Indra's request, went to his help when the latter waged war against powerful demon-king Shambara. In battle when Dasharatha got wounded and lose consiouness she drove his chariot skilfully out of battlefield, carefully removed the darts from his body and revived him. Thus saving the life of her husband she proved her worth as a queen of gallant Dasharatha. She loved Bharata; but she equally loved Rama and other sons of Kaushalya and Sumitra.

When Manthara, her pet maid-servant, informed her about coronation of Rama, she was overwhelmed with joy, like the rest of the thousand. She aptly awarded also Manthara for communicating such a good news. Manthara went on poisioning her mind but she did not allow her advances. She said "Manthara, have you not known and rejoiced in Rama's truthfulness, right conduct and humanity? He is elder prince and he gets kingdom. Bharata will get it one day after. What is wrong with all this? Here Manthara caught the point to trap her net. Very croockedly she pointed out that after Rama's succession there will be no chance for Bharata because eldest son succeeds eldest son and not the younger brother as per the rule of succession. She also said that Rama's succession may cause a danger to Bharata's life. Now fear entered in the mind of Kaikeyee. She used for two fatal boons—coronation of Bharata instead of Rama and 14 years' exile of Rama. Rama, in order to keep the promise of his father and keep intact the glory of *Raghukula,* accepted both the boons in the befitting manner without showing any resistance or sign of disappointment. But these boons proved to be very fatal for the King Dasharatha. He could not bear the shock of the separation of his most beloved son, Rama. Soon after his departure along with Lakshmana and Sita, to the forest, Dasharatha breathed his last.

When Bharata came to know the crookedness and treachery of her mother he totally disapproved her course of action and showed utter hatred to his mother. Seeing the real face of Bharata Kaikeyee also repented upon her meanness. She also accompanied Bharata to the forest-side to get back Rama; but of no avail. Ultimately Bharata came back and ruled Ayodhya on behalf of Rama. Being at Nandigram he led a life of an ascetic and carried out all royal business with excellent sense of detachment.

Savari, disciple of the sage Mantanga, living in a heritage situated on the bank of Pampa lake. After the death of her guru Mantanga, Savari waited in the heritage being blessed by him with the boon that she will be able to have *darshan* of Rama over there only. She welcomed them (Rama, Lakshmana and Sita) and offered water to wash their feet. She then presented the berry fruits, which she had gathered specially for them.

She was staunch devotee of Rama. She told him that she wished to depart from that life long ago; but the rishis told her that she was destined to have attained the supreme bliss she kindled a fire and, entering into it, ascended to heaven.

When Vanaras set out in search of Sita, in a secluded cave they saw an aged ascetic lady *(Sanyasini)* practising penances. She was Swayamprabha, a close friend of Hema, a daughter of Vishwakarma who was an architect divine. Being inducted by Lord Vishnu Swayamprabha was practising severe penances for darshana of Rama. At length her desire was fulfilled and she was blessed by Rama and instructed to go to *Badarikashram,* where being engaged in penances she attained salvation. During her stay in the cave she helped vanaras to reach sea-shore and further their great mission, i.e. search of Sita.

Unwed Mothers

Contraceptions, conceptions and abortions annually humiliate, hurt or kill hundreds of thousands of women in our country, a vast majority of whom are Hindus. Immaterial it is whether such deeds or misdeeds are marital or extra-marital, legal or illegal. Do educated Hindu males realise that abortions and contraceptions by far out-number live births? Do they realise that incidents like contraceptions, abortions and live births are anti-women, even though they are carried out by men and for women? Why do such incidents take place at all? Is there any reason to identify contraceptions and abortions with freedom for women? Does the question 'freedom for what?' ever prick the conscience of men who persuade or force women to avoid or to get rid of unwanted conceptions?

Conceptions outside marriage may be (or often are) horrifying experiences for the victims of male sexuality. Stories of children born out of wedlock are legion in Hindu history and yet the unwed mother remains an offence to public opinion. Children born out of non-marital unions live and grow to be baffling anomalies and shameful reminders to the custodian of marital sanctity, apart from turning the helpless mothers into a community of outcastes. Even within marriage a conception or a child birth acquires various implications for women. It may be for one a cherishable experience, an act of self-fulfilment; for another it may be an act of temporary inconvenience or even a symbol of pollution, while for the third it may be a permanent handicap.

As an experience, maternity is unique to woman and as such it is only proper that in matters like conception, contraception and abortion the woman has the last word. Men cannot and must not impose on women their notions of maternity or femininity. It is therefore, obligatory for a society to ensure that there is no coercion of a woman into a sex act so that there is no coercion later on for contraception or abortion. Any sex act which is not based on the emotional involvement of the woman, whether wife or non-wife, must be declared an incidence of rape by law. Husbands, Hindu husbands in particular, should be compelled to realize that any sexual act without the consent of the wife is an act of rape and therefore punishable under the law.

Not many years ago, a Japanese district court sentenced a twenty-six year old husband to two year's imprisonment on the charge of raping his wife (cf. *Hindu* 18 Dec., 1986). If Hindu husbands were to be brought to court on charges of marital rape, millions of them would find themselves behind the bars almost every day of the year. The sexual exploitation of the wife by the husband is so common in our society that one does not need to invoke statistics to prove that husbands are guilty of numerous rapes. Havelock Ellis rightly holds that many more rapes are committed within marriage than outside (cf. Beauvoir, 1953: 162). A Hindu writer says that husbands in general tend to use their wives just as sex objects with no regard to their mood or health (cf. Kapoor, 1974: 34-35). Unless men develop a health their attitude to heterosexual relationships and recognize women's autonomy in matters like maternity, incidents like unwanted conceptions, contraceptions and abortions will continue to plague the generality of women.

Child Marriage

The ancient Hindu institution of what is known as 'child marriage' points to the age-old masculinist philosophy of exploiting and limiting women on all levels. Most authorities on ancient India agree that the ideal age of marriage for girls in those days varied from seven to ten years (cf. Basham, 1967: 167, Shastri, 1969: 87-88 and

Chakladar, 1976: 125-26). The general view in ancient times was that the ideal marriage was a marriage in which the bride was one-third of the age of the groom – so that a man of twenty-four could marry a girl of eight and a man of thirty could marry a girl of ten. A verse in the Mahabharata explicitly states: "A thirty-year old man should marry a girl of ten years called *Nagnika.* Or, a twenty-one year old man should get a girl of seven years" (Bannerji, 1976: 12:29). The Vishnu Purana recommends: "One should marry a girl whose age is one-third of one's own" (cited in Chakladar, 1976: 124). Vatsayana suggests that the bribe should be three to seven years younger than the groom but he also insist that the bride must be a *Nagnika* (cf. *ibid.*, pp. 125-26). The law books warn that if a father does not give his daughter in marriage before her first menstruation, he incurs a sin worse than murder (cf. Basham, 1967: 167). Manu's code, for example, lays down that a father "who gives in marriage a girl of eight goes to heaven, the giver of a girl of nine to Vaikuntha; one who gives his daughter in marriage before she obtains the age of ten attains the heaven of Brahma. But the father of a girl married after puberty goes to hell" (cf. Thomas, 1964: 225). One of the most notorious statements in favour of child-marriage occurs in the *Bhagavata Purana*: "an unmarried girl who menstruates, living in her father's or mother's house, should be regarded as degraded woman; a man commits no sin by carrying her away from the custody of her guardian" (cf. Baig, 1976: 118).

Shakuntala Rao Shastri is not correct in her assertion that child-wives are mentioned for the first time in the Chhandogya Upanishad. Perhaps with the single exception of widow-burning (*Sati*), almost all Hindu customs, practices and views may be traced back of the Vedas. Of course, the Vedas do not insist on child marriage as the only form of marriage for girls; there are mentioned adult wives as well. It is probable that Vedic Aryans recommended child marriage for girls even though they tolerated adult marriage. Ghosha is described as an adult-wife Romasha is spoken of as a child-wife in the *Rig Veda* itself (cf. Chakladar, 1976: 126). It is, however, interesting to note that child-husbands, even boy-husbands, are not mentioned in ancient Hindu texts. The hero of the Ramayana may be solitary example of a boy-husband. Ravana meets Sita to abduct her but he engages her in a pleasant conversation by introducing himself as a mendicant and in the hope that he might as well win her over. It is during this conversation that Sita informs him that at the time of her marriage she was only six years of age while Rama was just thirteen (cf. III: IXX, p. 390).

The rigidity of the scriptural demand that girls must be married at the earliest possible age, in any case before the first menstruation, should be viewed as a concrete example of what might be called *sadistic paedophilia.* We may bear in mind that while the marriage age prescribed for girls varies from seven to ten, that for men varies from twenty-one to thirty. Even the latest Marriage Act prescribes twenty-one as the age for men to marry. As regards men, the ancient Law makers were so generous and forward-looking. They were obnoxious only with regard to women, whether it was marriage or maternity.

The doctrinization of such disparity between Hindu males and females in respect of their desirable age for marriage finds its parallels also in Greece. The Anthenian in Plato's Laws declares that the marriage age for girls "shall be sixteen to twenty years and for a man from thirty to thirty-five years" (p. 785). The main reason for prescribing an earlier age for women than for men to marry was the same as that among ancient Hindus. The necessity that the bride be a "a virgin, coupled with the ancient belief that the young girls were lustful, made early marriage (in Greece) desirable" (Pomeroy, 1975:64). As for the Hindus, Basham observes: "A woman was thought to be naturally libidinous; an unmarried girl attaining puberty would proceed to find a lover, however strictly her parents guarded her" (1967: 168). Imaginary apprehensions like these motivated the custodians of communal morality to make laws that could catch girls young so that they could not defile the family or defame the community. Child marriage was therefore made compulsory for all girls. Such were the views of daughters and sisters held by their noble and enlightened guardians in the golden age of Hindu civilization.

Pointing to the inevitable consequences of child marriage, a scholar has this to say: "Condemned to domestic drudgery, ignorance and premature motherhood, developing in most cases, physical infirmities or deformities, the married woman in respectable households was not fit company for a normal healthy man, and this was in no small measure responsible for the extraordinary high position prostitutes gain in later India and for the hold they obtained even in temples and places of pilgrimages" (Thomas, 1964: 228). Also, as frequent pregnancies and child births rendered these young women, sick, ugly and uncouth, man hated and tortured their wives to spit out the deep-rooted frustrations of their conjugal hopes. The modern Hindu starts gasping for breath when he finds such condemned, helpless and hopeless women glorified both in holy texts and literary masterpieces.

Centuries have come and gone but we are still stayput with our obsolete Law Books. As we Hindus have always steadfastly held on to our 'glorious' past, we have religiously refused to change with the times. The world goes ahead, but we refuse to move forward because, by heredity and nature, we are a backward-looking crab like people. Because we always look back to our illustrious ancestors to illumine our minds and direct our conduct about everything in life, we fail to criticize our heritage. We are probably the only community on earth who can fish out millions from our depleted bank accounts and near-empty purses to watch on portable black-and-white TV sets the antique tales of man and monkeys as picturized. It is no wonder therefore that we still have hundreds of millions of child-wives and child mothers in our midst. The Sharda Act of 1929 had decreed that girls before sixteen could not be married off without their parents risking the rigours of the law and yet a study conducted by Lucknow University in 1971 revealed that in Uttar Pradesh alone 52 per cent of girls were married by the age of fifteen (cf. Mehta, 1970: 20 and Sahai, 1985: XVII). The Marriage Act of 1978 allows a girl to be married only when she is eighteen years of age but a study conducted by the Family Planning Foundation in 1987 showed that 33 per cent girls in Orissa, 38 per cent girls in Uttar Pradesh, 48 per cent in Karnataka and 58 per cent girls in Madhya Pradesh had become married mothers before they were eithteen years of age. These under-eighteen mothers raised the national average of infant mortality rate in India to 105 a thousand, thereby making it one of the highest in the world (cf. *Indian Express* 28 Dec., 1987).

Plight of Widows

Close on the heels of the notorious custom of child-marriage comes the heinous Hindu practice of widow-burning *(sati)*. In a way, widow-burning and child-marriage are the two sides of the same coin. Motivated by the view of feminity, widow-burning has to be analysed in terms of the same scale of values as child-marriage. A girl is to be bound in early childhood to an adult male as her husband, otherwise she will give up her virginity and defile the family. Likewise, a widow must be disposed of along with her dead husband as she has already lost her virginity. As a wife, a woman has to surrender her virginity only to her husband and, having done that, she must remain totally tied down to him ever, that is, both here and hereafter. Only the husband is authorized by Law Books to monopolize his wife's body and soul. A woman not monopolized thus by her husband is impure and sinful. Any Hindu female who has extra-marital sex relations, whether by choice or under compulsion, is a public woman. No other system on earth maintains such a rigid separation between the wife and the prostitute as orthodox Hinduism does. A woman, in its view, is either 'private' or 'public' property. There is no third category. Every woman has to be either a wife or a prostitute for life; the system does not visualize spinsterhood as a possible choice for a woman. But even in the binary division between private and public roles, a woman does not have any option. Whether a girl is going to be a wife or a prostitute is decreed by the male majority. Once decreed to be a wife, a woman must live for the husband and die with the husband because her survival after the husband's death is fraught with hazardous implications. This, in brief, seems to be the crux of the Hindu rationale for burning the dead man's wife on his pyre.

Many ancient people like the Chaldees, Celts, Gauls, Goths, Scythians, Slavs and Thracians buried or burnt a man's widow's, slaves, hearses and other cherished possessions with his corpse in order that he might have all that he loved and needed, in the other world (cf. Basham, 1967: 188, Sengupta, 1974: 97 and Baig, 1976: 19). It is possible that ancient Hindu borrowed this custom from some of these peoples. But there is a basic difference between

Hindu widow-burning on the one hand and widow-burning in these peoples on the other. Widow-burning for most of them was part of their pre-history whereas for Hindus it was part of their post-Vedic history. Vedic Hindus probably did not kill their widows. Then the widow used to be persuaded to marry her husband's younger brother or cousin. This custom was known as 'levirate marriage' (cf. De, 1969: 4-5). It was a common practice that the dead man's younger brother or cousin came to his bereaved widow and proposed: "Rise woman and come to the world living beings. Come, this man near whom thou sleepiest is lifeless, thou has enjoyed the state of being the wife of thy husband, the suitor who took thee by the hand. Come, thou hast now entered upon the wifehood of this the lord who takes thy hand to be the husband and woos thee" (Shastri, 1969: 20-21). Levirate marriage remained in vague for quite some-time. The Arthashastra mentions widow-marriage as prevalent among various castes (cf. Thomas 1964: 73-74). That widows were allowed to survive is evident from the Kamasutra, although by this time they had ceased to enjoy the privilege of remarriage. Widow-burning may have started sometime in the fourth century BC. The earliest datable notice of the immolation of widows occurs in "Greek accounts of Alexander's invasion" (Basham, 1967: 189). Together with child-marriage, it appears to have been firmly established on a large scale during the post-Smriti period. The prohibition of widow-marriage by the Sacred Law was logically followed up by the caste Hindu immolation of widows. Manu represents the consensus of his contemporaries when he declares: "Nowhere is a second husband permitted to respectable women" (V: 162). He clearly lays down that a man may marry after the death of his wife but a wife can never think of another man after the death of her husband (cf. V: 157 & 168). His advice to a surviving widow is: "Until her death let her be patient (of her hardship), self-controlled, and chaste, and strive to fulfil that most excellent duty which (is prescribed) for wives who have one husband only" (V: 158).

According to the Law Books, the highest religious duty of a wife was to see in her husband, alive or dead, her god and her ultimate salvation. Widow-burning followed as a natural corollary of such prescriptions, and in course of time reached menacing proportions. A thirteenth century inscription, for instance, reads: "those who do not bind her (i.e., the widow) and throw her into fire and kill her would get the sin of prostituting their own wives" (Thomas, 1964: 235). Ṣix centuries later, Raja Ram Mohan Roy and his associates claimed in their representation against widow-burning that they had been eyewitnesses to widows have been "forced upon the pire, and they are bound with ropes and pressed with green bamboos, were kept until consumed by the flames" and that those who tried to run away from the flames were "carried back by their relations and burnt to death" (*ibid.*, pp. 295-96). The worst part of this atrocious ritual was that the widow's son (or nearest kin in the absence of son) had to set fire to his living mother tied to his dead father on the funeral pyre (cf. Sengupta, 1974: 70).

Historically speaking, the custom of widow-burning appears to have been practised on a selective basis for a fairly long time from Vyasa to Vatsyayana. The *Mahabharata*, for example, shows that some widows were immolated and some were not. Madri was immolated on Pandu's funeral pyre but Kunti was not. Devaki, Bhadra, Rohini and Madira were burnt with Vasudeva's corpse but his other wives were not. Similarly, Rukmini and seven other queens of Krishna were consigned to the flames along with their dead husband (Krishna) but Satyabhama and the other queens were not (cf. Lal, 1980: 84, 352-353 & 385). As time drew on, immolation of widows became increasingly rigid and regular. It was, however, during the Perso-Arabic period that it acquired the status of a ritual with all the sanctions of the hoary tradition. To prevent her escape from the raging flames, the widow was usually surrounded by men armed with sticks who goaded her to her destination by physical force. Describing his decision to abolish sati by law, William Bentick wrote: "To consent to the consignment, year after year, of husbands of innocent victims to a cruel and ultimately death, when the power exists of preventing it, is a predicament which no conscientious man can contemplate without horror...I should be guilty to little sort of the crime of multiplied murder if I could hesitate in the performance of this solemn obligation" (Thomas, 1964: 263). Sati was not totally abolished immediately after Lord Bentick's Edict, proclaimed on 5 December, 1829. Writing in 1911, Edward Thomson points out: "The number of women burned alive at his funeral had in many states been the criterion of a Prince's success in life. Eighty-four women died with Raja Budh Singh of Bundi, sixty-four with Raja Ajit Singh of Jodhpur, and numbers in the neighbourhood of twenty were usual" (Baig, 1976: 20).

To think about sati to be filled with horror and shame, astonishment and indignation. Sati was, in most cases, the cold blooded and brutal public murder of a lone at helpless widow by the males of the family and locality. All religious or doctrinal rationalizations of this custom are hideous and barbaric. Most Hindu texts contain motivated interpolations and distortions but no distortion is so disasterous and demoralizing as the one which converts a marriage ritual into a death warrant. The Rig Vedic instructions for the widow originally read: "Let the women advance to the altar first" (i.e., *Arohantu Janayo yonim agre*). This line refers to the Vedic custom in accordance with which the widow had to ascend the funeral pyre of her husband only to be led away by his younger brother or cousin for her marriage with him. The post-Vedic Brahmans replaced the last but one letter of the line (i.e., 'r' with 'n' so that 'agre' became 'agne') and it read: "Let the women advance to the womb of fire" (i.e. *Arohantu janayo yonim agne*, cf. Mangalwadi, 1987). The replacement or 'r' with 'n' turned 'to the altar' into 'to the fire' which converted 'widow-marriage' into 'widow-burning'. Max Mullar rightly describes this vicious replacement as "the most flagrant instance of what can be done by an unscrupulous priesthood" (*ibid.*).

It was a rare moment in Hindu history that a crusader like Raja Ram Mohun Roy vowed to fight against this most sinful custom. Started in 1818, his campaign achieved historic success on 5 December, 1829 when Lord Bentick passed his Edict banning widow-burning throughout British India. By 1862 sati was banned throughout India, including the native states. In spite of this, stray incidents of widow burning continued to occur of this, stray incidents of widow burning continued to occur from time to time. Roop Kanwar's consignment to flames on 4 September, 1987 at Deorala in Rajasthan is the most recent public incidence of widow-burning. In spite of incidents like these and a great deal of obscurantism around (cf. *Indian Express*., 13 April, 1988), it would not be wrong to say that widow-burning stopped (almost totally) by 1862 itself.

Once a widow-burning was abolished, the number of widows suddenly shot up. In a few decades the population of widows, including a large number of child-widows, ran into millions. The Widow Marriage Act of 1856 and the Hindu Code Bill of 1954 have not achieved any tangible results. Besides, obscurantist slogans like 'once a widow, always a widow', further add to the ever-increasing widow-population. Looking back over a century and a half, we clearly realize that the legal abolition of widow-burning was one thing, while the legal amelioration of widowhood is quite another. The death of the husband even today means for an average Hindu wife a further worsening of her position in the family.

For a Hindu wife widowhood traditionally means one of three things: immediate death (whether murder or suicide), life long condemnation to segregation and drudgery, and subjection to clandestine sexual exploitation by the males of the family and/or locality. It is possible that in days of old widows at times themselves preferred a painful death to a dreary life of 'hunger, scorn and domestic servitude' (Basham, 1967:190). Forced to refrain from all that was good, healthy and auspicious in life, the widow had to have her head clean shaven as a punishment for her past sins causing the death of her husband in her next life. Presumably large chunks of Hindus believed in the cathartic efficacy of the endless persecution and torture of widows. Always watched by the parents and relatives of her dead lord, lest she broke her vows and imperilled the dead man's spiritual welfare, and shunned as unlucky even by women and servants of the family, the life of the widow was (and is) miserable in the extreme. In the wake of the public uproar against the Deorala outrage, a woman social worker from Rajasthan told a journalist: "At the very moment a dead man's body is removed from the house for cremation, a black sheet is drawn around the widow. For a year she is not to be seen by males or married women. She sits on the floor within this black cubicle, with knees pulled to the chest and the head touching the knees. For ablutions and bath she leaves the cubicle at night. Saltless food is brought to her. Before a meal, she must cry because food is the basis of life, and as a widow she is deemed to have lost her moral right to life her husband's death. She must cry before eating, also express her guilt" (Singh, 1987). Sitting on knees twelve hours a day, forced to live on insipid and scanty food, shunned by people and surrounded by so much condemnation, the widow soon loses her will to have, takes ill and succumbs to death in a few months or years.

The Hindu widow, on the one hand, is ostracized and required to observe a vow of continence and chastity, while on the other, she is often seduced or subjected to sexual exploitation by starving males around. The widow, like the unwed woman, is forced to contraception and abortion. In case she bears children, they are illegitimate and they make her more scornful but not less vulnerable. It is astonishing that the sexual abuse of widows is sometimes recommended or appreciated. The *Kamasutra* describes a widow as a sexual object. As there is no regular marriage for the widow, she is exhorted to ally herself to a seeker after pleasure *(bhogin)* and make the best of her life. Vatsayan's term of such a widow is *punarbhu,* that is, 'a woman allied to a man for second time'. He places the *punarbhu* between a maiden *(kanya)* and a prostitute *(Veshya).* She is just a mistress. She is allowed a degree of freedom unknown to the wife but she is also denied the privileges of wifehood (cf. De, 1969: 97-97 and Chakaldar, 1976: 181-82). How unfortunate it is that most widows are still shunned and sought for wrong reasons and yet they cannot enjoy even the kind of 'acceptability' that was available to Vatsyayana and his contemporaries.

Benevolent Ideas and Institutions

Some organisations came into existence during the last two decades of the 19th century and early 20th century. Sometimes women teachers' conference was held and sometimes at the venue of the Indian National Congress women used to meet separately. But the early organisations and conferences were very limited in their scope and programme and without any definite shape. However, they worked for the general welfare of the women and their importance lies in their beginning of the women's movement in India.

Under the auspices of the Brahmo Samaj the Ladies

Association was founded at Calcutta in 1886 by Swarn Kumari Devi with the object of promoting friendly relation and spirit of service among the Indian women. It also provided for the training of poor girls to become teachers. Pandita Ramabai Sarswati founded *Sharda Sadan* at Poona in 1892 to provide education and employment for women. After sometimes the field of social service was extended and relief was given to the orphans, the destitutes and victims of famine. Like buds opening their petals, the girls began to expand learning to appreciate the cult of service and sacrifice which Ramabai inculcated. In the same year Shri Mahipatram Rupram *Anathashram* was founded at Ahmedabad to help the poor women and the widows. It also gave shelter to the illegitimate children and pregnant women.

Shri Zorostrian Mandal was started at Bombay in 1903 to help the women in general and the Parsi women in particular. It inspired women to become economically independent. It distributed food, milk and medicine among poor Parsi families and also made provision for their education. In 1908 the *Gujarati Hindu Stree Mandal* was started by Shri B.N. Motiwala, one of the important social workers of Bombay. Its objects were to promote contact among Gujarati women to provide them with appropriate education and to raise their status in different fields. The Mandal organised classes in sewing, embroidery, painting, leather work and for training teachers. It taught Gujarathi, Hindi, Sanskrit, English and Music. It had also library for women and children. It also started a young girls' association and published a monthly bulletin.

Ramabai Ranade started *Seva Sadan* at Poona in 1909. It imparted education to the women and gave training in industry, teaching, nursing and midwifery. It also established a hostel. In 1917 it became an independent registered organisation. The names of Ramabai Ranade and Seva Sadan became gradually synonymous.

Mahila Samitis (Women's Institutions) were organised by Saroj Nalin in Bengal in many districts, towns and villages, with a view to imparting education to women. They adopted measures against purdah, early marriage and inspired window remarriage. They enlightened the public on health and sanitation and pleaded for the equal rights of women in franchise and education.

Chiman Bai Maternity and Child Welfare League was established in Baroda in 1914 to take care the health of women. Maharani Chimanbai Udyogalaya was also started to train middle and working class women in some crafts and industries. An organisation was also founded for the sale of manufactured goods on a cooperative basis.

Bhagini Samaj was started at Poona in 1916 to serve the society in general and women and children in particular. Its programme for the welfare of women was very comprehensive. It covered education, social service, propaganda and legal work.

But women felt that necessity or organisation of an all-India character. An humble beginning was made towards the end in 1910 when various women's groups came together and formed Bharat Stri Mahamandal. It was an attempt to weld the women of the different provinces of India into one association. But the conditions not being ripe enough for this, it did not take deep root. But three women's organisations which came into existence later on became very important. Women's India Association (WIA) 1917, National Council of Women in India (NCWI) and All India Women's Conference (AIWC) 1926.

Women's Indian Association 1917–37

Origin: An association was started on the 8 th May, 1917 at Adyar, Madras by Mrs. Dorothy Jinarajadasa, wife of the President of Theosophical Society of Madras and a notable social worker of her time. She was very sincerely assisted by an Irish lady, Mrs. M. Cousins. Another Irish lady Dr. Annie Besant was chosen its first President and she remained on the post continuously for about 17 years till she passed away in 1933, Mrs. Jinarajadasa got the privilege of being its first Secretary. The Association was named as Women's Indian Association. It could have been named as Indian Women's Association also but this title was not chosen because it carried narrow meaning. The title Women's Indian Association was preferred as it was wide in meaning and scope. It had a wider outlook, a large purpose and a deeper understanding ....It was a right ideal not only for all womenhood but for all humanity. The Women's Indian Association was the first organisation whose aim was to be All Indian in scope, to include as members all types of women who were residents in India and to band them together for mutual service and the good of the country.

Aims and Objectives

The aims and objects of this Association were the following:

1. To present to women their responsibilities as daughter's of India.
2. To secure for every girl and boy the right of education through schemes of compulsory primary education, including the teaching of religion.
3. To secure the abolition of child marriages and other social evils.
4. To secure for women the Vote for Municipal and Legislative Councils on the same terms as it was or might be granted to men.
5. To secure adequate representation of women in Municipalities, Taluks, Local Boards, Legislative Councils and Assemblies.
6. To establish equality of rights and opportunities between men and women.
7. To help women to realise that the future of India lies largely in their hands, for as wives and mothers they had the task of the raising, guiding and forming the character of the future rulers of India.
8. To band women into groups for the purpose of self-development and education and for the definite service of others.

The Association began to grow from the very day of its inception. The time was ripe for such an organisation. Within the first year of its existence 33 branches were formed in many towns. The Association has a good record of achievements to its credit within the two decades (1917–37) of its existence. We have to remain satisfied with a brief review of them.

The most important and fundamental work of the Association

was in the sphere of education. But very soon it began to take interest in political sphere also. In 1917, the year which saw the birth of the Association, women's interest in the Home Rule Movement was deeply stirred by the intenment of Dr. Annie Besant who belonged to their own sex. The various branches of the Association took an active part to secure her release.

Home Rule was the talk of the day and this implied extension of franchise. Women's Indian Association was the first organisation in India to make a demand for women's franchise and it succeeded in its mission. It organised a deputation of 14 women to wait upon Mr. Montague, the then Secretary of State for India. He visited India in December, 1917 and the Deputation waited upon him on the 18th December at Madras. Since then the Association, identified itself with the cause of women's franchise and the removal of sex disqualification for the election to all the deliberative bodies. It did not rest until its demand was fulfilled. The franchise committee had denied extension of franchise to women. But the claim was passed by the Women's Indian Association and its allies and the provincial councils were empowered under the Electoral Rules to consider the matter. By 1930 women got franchise in all the provinces of British India. After the attainment of women's franchise the Association began the movement for their representation in the legislative councils. We should also remember that the Association throughout protested against communal representation and reservation.

Three members of the association were elected to the Corporation and one was unanimously elected as an Alder Woman.

The official organ of the Association was *Stridharma* which was started as a quarterly publication but became full-fledged journal within a few years. It was published in more than one language—English, Tamil and Telugu. For about a year (1935-36) Mrs. Cousins was its Editor. It carried the authentic news of the progress of the Indian Women's Movement in India and round the world. There were readers of this magazine in several countries of the world.

By 1923-24, the Association had 51 branches and 1500 membership. They gradually continued to increase. By 1926-27, there were 80 branches and over 4000 members. These branches spread from Cape Camorin in the South to Kashmir in the North. The Association did a lot of useful work in political, social and educational spheres. It took up the cause of moral and social hygiene. It took interest in child welfare work. It expressed satisfaction at the passing of the Child Marriage Restraint Act. During 1931-32 a Sarda Sub-Committee was formed to see the enforcement of the Sarda Act against Child Marriage. It facilitated their entry into legislatures and public offices. Many women were appointed as Honorary Magistrates and many became members of the local bodies. It took interest in the spread of girl education and guiding. It emphasised the introduction of compulsory primary education for girls. It was responsible for the *abolition of Devadasi system* and suppression of immoral traffic in women.

The Association with its branches were active in time of epidemics and distress. They rendered useful service to the needy. The members took an active part in social gatherings, parties, picnics, and other cultural programmes.

The Association also took interest in Adult Education, village uplift and Harijan welfare work. The Association gave a number of scholarships to deserving girls including Harijans. On visit to Madras, Gandhiji was presented a purse for Harijan work. It started and maintained Rescue Homes. An orphanage was started at Mylapore called Avai Home. It was started in 1930 with 10 girls. But during 1931-32, this Home had grown into a multipurpose centre with many sections, creating to more than 800 beneficiaries and had spread its activities on 1 acre land in beautiful suburb of Adyar. The underlying principle of the various activities of the Avai Home Orphanage was to protect all women especially young girls and children not only from the evils of poverty and destitution but also from undesirable associations and surroundings and to educate and to train them to an useful and independent profession.

The Children Aid Society and the Juvenile Court were also established.

Mrs. Sarojini Naidu presided over the 17th Annual function of the Association. Gandhiji visited Madras in December, 1933 and the Association had the privilege of organising the only public meeting of women. In 1933 Dr. Annie Besant died and now Dr. (Mrs.) S.

Muthulakshmi Reddi was elected as its President. She continued on this post for a long time even after the end of the period under review.

Women's Indian Association became the parent of All India Women's Conference which was born in early 1927. It became the vehicle for the expression of the united voice of the Indian womenhood. This was the great pioneering work of the Association.

International Outlook

The Association also developed international outlook and maintained links with various international organisations for some financial help or the other. It sent delegates to attend international conference and also invited outsiders at their own sessions.

The activities of the Women's Indian Association were many and they were expanding each year. Its achievements embraced social, educational and political fields. It was the largest Women's Association in India that had a unitary and all-round programme of work, social, educational and political. It had 72 branches, 23 centres and nearly 4000 members. It has rightly been called the mother of women's organisations in India. By 1937 with the growth of feminine organisations in the country it began to confine its activities to Madras Presidency.

The National Council of Women in India

The National Council of Women in India was formed in 1925 and in the same year it was affiliated to the International Council of Women which was founded in 1888. As a matter of fact it originated as a branch of the latter organisation.

The aims and objectives of the National Council of Women in India were, briefly, to :

1. Promote sympathy of thought and unity of purpose among women in India.
2. Work for the removal of disabilities of women, whether legal, economic or social, and for the promotion of the social, civil

and educational welfare of women and children, ensuring opportunities for their full and free development and advancement.

3. Organise, develop and coordinate the work of its existing councils and branches and such other councils as may hereafter be formed under its auspices or may be accepted by it.
4. Coordinate the activities of other National Organisations in India, whose aims are in conformity with it.
5. And form a link with National Councils in other countries through the International Council of Women.

It had been working along these lines and had also tried to live up to its Motto *do unto others As ye would That they should Do unto you.* In short, it aimed to raise the status of Indian women in all possible ways at home and abroad.

Activities

As one of the pioneering all India organisations, the National Council of Women in India had played a significant role in raising the status of women by working for the removal of various legal and social disabilities from which women suffered for centuries. By mobilising public opinion through seminars, conferences and meetings, the National Council focused attention on many existing problems and those which arose with the march of time, and changed conditions.

The National Council was one of the pioneers in turning the attention of women social workers to village welfare and city labour problems and sponsored a labour conference as early as 1933. It is contributed substantially to the passing of the prostitution Act in Bombay and conducted intensive propaganda in favour of the Sarda Act.

The National Council played an important part in the women's suffrage movement. Jointly with other women's organisations the National Council took a firm stand in favour of unqualified adult franchise for both men and women and opposed reservation of seats on the ground of sex.

Since its inception the National Council has spread education and advocated increase in women's wages and women's inheritance rights, maternity benefits, provision of better facilities for nurses, reforms in women's wards in jails, women police, slum clearance, etc. After the first ten years of work, the Council began to expand into new fields of activity.

Affiliated Council's Branches

The National Council of Women in India was composed of Councils and Branches in almost all the states in India. These were engaged in field activities which included running school libraries, literacy and handicraft classes, child welfare, health hobby and recreation centres, rescue homes, orphanage, clinics, hospitals and hostels.

The National Council holds Triennial Elections and its headquarters rotate with the Presidents. The Official organ of the council is an English language Journal entitled *N.C.W.I. Bulletin*. It has been published from the date of the inception of the council in 1925. It gave news concerning women both at National and international levels. Its members mostly belonged to official and aristocratic classes and they had received English Education.

Thus we see that the principles of gender equality have been basic to Indian thinking. Indian women were accorded a very high status in the Vedic era. We have examples of Maitreya and Gargi, the two females who were well-versed in Vedantic philosophy. The Vedic period extended over 2200-2000 B.C. We also have the glorious example of Rani Laxmibai, a woman who was widowed in her teens, providing leadership to the first liberation movement in India.

The Indian National Congress, the party which led the national liberation struggle for almost six decades adopted gender equality as its quiding principle in its fundamental rights resolution as early as 1931. Mahatma Gandhi, the father of Indian nation, was a champion of women's rights. He always emphasised that "subjugation and exploitation of women was a product of men's vested teachings and women's acceptance of the same." Under his leadership, many women in India stepped out of their homes, perhaps for the first time, and took a very active part in the Indian liberation movement.

Empowerment of Women

The women in India were fortunate enough to get the political rights and civil liberties on an equal footing with men with the adoption of the Constitution on January 26, 1950. The Constitution not only guarantees 'equality before law' and 'equal protection before law', it also empowers the state to adopt positive measures to promote the interests of women in India. The Constitution also guarantees equality of opportunity in public employment and imposes a fundamental duty on every citizen renounce practices derogatory to the dignity of women.

To uphold the Constitutional mandate, the Parliament in India has also enacted various laws from time to time to secure to all its citizens, justice—social, economic and political, liberty of thought—expression, belief, faith and worship, equality of status and opportunity and to promote among them all fraternity, assuring the dignity of the individual and the unity of the nation. It has adopted various legislative measures to counter social discrimination and various forms of violence and atrocities against women. The legal edifice adequately takes care of women and their special needs.

The initial approach of the Government was to focus women as targets of welfare policies in the social sector, in action as far as women's issues were concerned. In the Fifth Plan (1974-78), there was a shift in the Government's approach from 'welfare' to 'development'. In the Sixth Plan, there was a separate chapter on women's development with a definite thrust on health, education and employment. The Seventh Plan aimed at raising their economic and social status and bringing them into the mainstream of national development.

The Eighth Plan (1992-97) realises the need to develop special programmes so that the gains from development in various sectors do not bypass women. We now find a shift from 'development' to 'empowerment' of women. As such, the Government has reflected, articulated and seriously addressed the women's issues from a new perspective. It has adopted many women-specific policies. We also find a progressive increase in the planned outlays during the last 50 years. The outlay for women's needs was Rs. 40 million during the First Plan (1951-56), while it has gone upto approximately Rs.20,000 million during the Eighth Plan.

In 1971, the Government appointed a Committee on the status of women in India which raised certain basic issues about the socialization processes inherent in a hierarchical society, resource and power distribution patterns and cultural values prevailing in India. It stressed the need to transform the *de jure* equality into *de facto* equality. A separate Department of Women and Child Development was set up in 1985 under the newly created Ministry of Human Resource Development. In 1988, the National Perspective Plan for Women was drawn to facilitate mainstreaming of women's issues in government programme and policies. In 1990, the Parliament set up the National Commission for Women to monitor all matters related to constitutional and legal rights conferred on women.

As a signatory to the World Declaration on the Survival, Protection and Development of Children, the Government of India has drawn up an Action Plan for the Girl Child (1991-2000). In a recent legislation, the Government has now banned sex-determination test to prevent female foeticide. The crowning achievements of the current decade have been the 73rd and 74th Constitutional Amendments which guarantee one-third representation to women in all local bodies both in the rural and urban areas and also reserve in one single stroke, one-third of all posts of chairpersons for women. It is expected to be finalised soon. The Government is now planning to set up a National Resource Centre for Women to act as an apex body for promoting and incorporating gender perspective in government programmes and policies.

REFERENCES

1. Shri Aurobindo and the Mother, On women, p.21.
2. R. Linton, *The study of Man*, New York, 1936.
3. अमोऽहमस्मि सा त्वं, सामाहम्
   अस्म्यृक् त्वं, द्यौरहं पृथिवी त्वं

तविह सं भवाव, प्रजामा जनयावहै ।

—Atharva 14.2.71

Compare –

यो भर्ता वासितातुष्टो भर्तुस्तुष्टा च वासिता ।
यस्मिन्नैव कुले सर्वं कल्याणं तत्र वर्तते ।।

—Mahabharata 13.122.17

दम्पत्योः समशीलत्वं धर्मः स्याद्गृहमेधिनः ।

—Mahabharata 13.141.43

4. अहो अर्णः सरस्वती, प्रचेतयति केतुना ।
धियो विश्वा वि राजति ।।

— Rigved 1.3.12

पावका नः सरस्वती वाजेभिर्वाजिनीवती ।
यज्ञं वष्टु धियावसुः ।।

—Rigved 1.3.10

5. Sri Aurobindo and the Mother, on Women, p.15.
6. न मानुषी राक्षसस्य भार्या भवितुमर्हति ।
काम खादत मां सर्वा न करिष्यामि वो वचः ।।
दीनो वा राज्यहीनो वा यो मे भर्ता य मे गुरूः ।
तं नित्यमनुरक्तास्मि यथा सूर्य सुवर्चला ।।

—Ramayana

7. Quoted in "Subramania Bharti" compiled by Prema Nand Kumar, p. 122.
8. Dr. A.S. Altekar, *Position of Women in Ancient India*, p.10.
9. स्वस्ति तेऽस्त्यन्तरिक्षेभ्यश्च पार्थिवेभ्यश्च पुत्रक ।
दिवेभ्यश्च भूतेभ्यस्तथा तोयचराश्च ये ।।

— Mahabharata, Aranyak 292.10-14

10. या दम्पती सुमनसा सुनुत आच धावतः ।
देवासो नित्ययाडशिरा ।

—Rigveda 8.31.51

11. पुराकल्पे तु नारीणां मौञ्जीबन्धनमिष्यते ।
अध्यापनं च वेदानां सावित्रीवाचनं तथा ।।

—Nirnay Sindhu

12. अत्र सिद्धा शिवा नाम ब्राह्मणी वेदपारगा ।
अधीत्य सकलान् वेदान लेभेऽसन्देहमक्षयम् ।।

— Mbh., Udyog. 190.8

13. Mahabharata, Shalya Parvan, 54.6.
14. प्रधानो नाम राजर्षिर्व्यक्त ते श्रोत्रमागतः ।
कुले तस्य समुत्पन्नां सुलभां नाम विद्धि माम् ।।

साहं तस्य कुले जाता भर्तर्यसति मद्विधे ।
विनिता मोक्षधर्मेषु चराम्येका मुनिव्रतम् ।।

—Shanti Parvan 320.82

("I am Sulbha, born in the noble family of the king named Pradhan. Since I could not get a suitable match, I learnt the Vedas and other sacred Scriptures from learned scholars and now I follow Moksha and other sacred vows.")

15. Aranyak, 33.57.
16. जज्ञातेऽर्थविदावुभौ ।

—Adi Parvan 57.94

17. स वसतस्तत्रोपाध्यायस्त्रीभिरहूयोक्तः ।
उपाध्यायिनी ते ऋतुमती । उपाध्यायश्च प्रोषितः ।

— Adi Parvan, 3.89

18. Aranyak 289.20.
19. Adi, 235.6.
20. Virat 2.54.
21. Aranyak 122.32.
22. Ashramvasik 44.54.
23. Adi., 68.40-44.
24. Udyog, 30.6.
25. Kam Sutra 1.3.
26. Based on Women in Hindu Literature by R.P. Sharma, pp. 110-119.

6

RELIGION
An Integral Part of Life

Religion is not a doctrine or principle, but it is a mode of feeling. The shortest definition of religion given by E.B. Taylor is "*the belief in spiritual beings*" and Max Muller calls it "*a mental faculty or disposition which enables man to apprehend the Infinite*". According to Schliermacher, "*The essence of religion consists in feeling, i.e. feeling disconnected from thought on the one hand and morality or aciton on the other. Religion is a warm, intimate, immediate awareness of the infinite in the finite, the Eternal in the temporal, a sense of dependence on the whole.*" He saved religion from barren intellectualism, and mere moralism and revealed it in its mystic inwardness as immediate awareness of God. For Kant religion is "recognition of our duties as divine commandment" and for Mathew Arnold – "Religion is morality, touched with emotions."

Historically speaking religion has such diverse and even contradictory meanings that any attempt to call-out its essential character is very difficult as it has passed through various changes and evolution throughout the ages. Religion is a growing and dynamic subject and therefore it is very difficult to define it. Yet religion has some peculiar characteristics, which are universal. Religion involves a subject and an object and a relation between the two. On the subjective side, it includes all the psychical functions such as feeling, volition and congnition. On the objective side it has reference to a trans-subjective divine Reality. It further involves a living relation of the subject to that trans-subjective objective Reality in worship, fellowship and service. Such relation is controlled by a purpose, such as - the conservation and enhancement of human values both social and the individual ultimately culminating in utter devotional love of the divine Reality for its own sake.

Religious experience is more than a subjective state of consciousness. It points to a trans-subjective immanent spiritual principal wherein value coincide with reality. In religion this perfect world of value is already by anticipation a present realisation. Faith is, no doubt, the substance of things hoped for. But religion is not to be indentified with mere faith in a super-sensible Reality as the seat and source of all values.

Eastern Thought on Religion

"Salutations to that glorious Dharma, as it sustains mankind. Such laws as sustain all, are verily called Dharma."[2]

— Mahabharata[3]

Scores of sages, saints and scholars, Eastern and Western have tried their best to define the religion in order to bring out its essentials. Here we are putting-forth certain views of Eastern sages saints an scholars[1] before we elaborate various aspects of the theme with variety of angles.

"That which brings forth earthly good as well as the supreme good in the form of salvation (Moksha) is Dharma-Kanad.[2]

"That are four-fold indices of Dharma like the Veda, the Smriti, Sadachar and what is pleasing to one's Conscience."

— Manu

"Patience, forgiveness, restraint, unstealing, purity, control over sinse-organs, talent, knowledge, truthfulness and absence of anger— these are ten characteristics of Dharma."

—Manu[4]

"If one is not Man-at his-best, what is the use of knowing the rites? What is the use of knowing about music?"

— Confucious (Saying II)

"Mencious said, "There is a nobility of Heaven, and there is a nobility of man. Benevolence, righteousness, self-consecration, and fidelity, with unwearied joy in these virtues—these constitute the nobility of Heaven... this constitutes nobility of man."

— Confucious (Living Thoughts, p.78)

"If one acts with a vigorous efforts at the law of reciprocity, when he seeks for the relisation of perfect virue, nothing can be closer than his approximation to it."

— Confucious (Living Thoughts, p.79)

"Heaven makes the Laws and general regulations for the life of man; the Government receives and enforces these laws; the executives and people live according to them. There is no place for priestly caste, for the laws of Heaven are not based on any secret dogma; they shape themselves popenly in the form of the phenomena of nature and of human society."

— Confucious

"Dharma stands for the sum-total of religious duties."

— Aitarey Brahman

"Dharma is the eternal truth holding its sway over the world."

— Chanakya, Arthashastra III-1

"God lives neither in wood nor stone, nor in clay. He lives in your inner-feeling (bhava). Thus feeling is the rool of all."

— Chanakya Niti

"Man is identical with a beast so far as food, sleep, fear and sex are concerned; but the additional quality he possesses with him is Dharma. Those who are devoid of a sense of Dharma are veritable beasts."

— Bharatrihari[5]

"O brother, there is no virtue equal to doing good to others, and nothing so mean as to inflict pain on others."

— Tulsidas[6]

The real is in your home within
why wander you from forest to forest;
Go where you will to Kashi or to Mathura,
You will not find Him.

Except in your soul within.

— Kabir

Religion does not consist is mere words...caste is nonsense. Those who love God, love everybody.

— Nanak

Virtue consists in acting
In eradication of four evil qualities namely,
Jelousy, covetousness, anger and evil speech.

—Tiruvalluvar, 39[6]

All souls worship him
who losing his Ego,
gets control of his own soul.

— Tiruvalluvar, 79[7]

"Bhakti to God bears fruits. But this adoration must be accompanied by understanding. The faith of the ignorant has no potency. One must ask for right knowledge first, when saluted God. Commonsense is the starting point of all riches."

— Subramania Bharati[8]

Your name is my penance, my religious gifts,
my pilgrimage, proportion ceremonies,
and chanting of the holy name;
That is my oblution, my observance of the vow, my truth
Karma, Dharma and ritual.
Your name is my Yoga, my sacrifice, contemplation,
family rites and clean rites;
Your name is my thought and practice
and determination and everything,
Tuka says, your name contains all these.[9]

— Tukaram

He who has faith has all, and who lacks faith lacks all. It is faith in the name of the Lord that works wonders, for faith is life and doubt is death.

— Ramakrishna Paramhansa

Man should respect every religion. All religions are true. All religions are good. All religions have vitals to inspire and lead you to the path of divine bliss.

— Kaka Kalelkar

"Your religion teaches you to feel the omnipresence of God and, in spite of this, if you do not have respect and regard for Him, you are not following your religion. If only we could feel the presence of God, we would shudder at telling a lie. Our eyes will blow-out, if we look at lady with evil intentions we should practice in life what we know to be good and true, according to our religion."

— Swami Ram Tirtha

"The highest wisdom in the East holds that it is not the function of our soul to gain God, to utilise him for any special material purpose. All that we can ever aspire to is to become more nad more one with God."

— Ravindranath Tagore[10]

"We should follow the path determined by Shastras and reason, and thereby receives full satisfaction in this world and next". from the foreward to the Bengali translation of Vedanta.

"Perhaps the best method will be not to surrender ourselves completely in the hands of Shastras and reasoning but to illumine the reasoning faculty knowledge of morality by their light and then to depend upon the beneficence of Almighty God" (from the introduction to the English version of the Kenopnishad).

— Raja Ram Mohun Roy

"Let Hinduism concern itself with the salvation of life after death, the concept of God and the Universe. Let individuals be free to form opinions about the trio....But so far as the materialistic and secular aspect is concerned, the Hindus are a nation bound by a common culture, a common history, a common language, a common country, and a common religion."

— Vinayak Damodar Savarkar, Hindutva, pp. 3-4

"Shri Krishna himself says that there is nothing in all the three worlds that the need acquire, and still he acts. He acts because if He did not act, the world will be ruined. If man seeks unity with the Diety, he must necessarily seek unity with the interest of the world also, and work for it. If he does not, then the unity is not perfect, because there is union between two elements out of the three (man and Deity) and the third (the world) is left out. I have thus solved the question for myself and I hold that serving the world, and thus serving. His will, *is the surset way of salvation;* and this way can be followed by remaining in world and not going away from it."

— Bal Gangadhar Tilak, from Geeta-Rahasya

God is one, that is our faith
All rituals we abjure
It is only when religions vanish
The belief is pure

— Mirza Ghalib[11]

"If there is one universal truth in all religions, I place it here, in realising God. Ideals and methods may differ, but that is the central point. There may be a thousand different radii, but they all converage to one centre, and that is the realisation of God, something behind this world of sense, this world of eternal eating and drinking and talking nonsense, this world of false shadows and selfishness. There is that beyond all books, beyond all creeds, beyond the vanities of this world, and it is the realisation of God within yourselfs. A man may believe in all the churches in the world, he may carry in his head all the sacred books ever written, he may baptize himself in all the rivers of the earth; still, if he has no perception of God, I would class him with the rankest atheist."[12]

—Vivekananda

"Each soul is potentially divine.
The goal is to manifest this divinity within by controlling nature, external and internal.
Do this either by work or worship or psychic control or philosophy – by one or more or all of these and be free.
This is the whole of religion. Doctrines or dogmas or rituals or books or temples or forms are but secondary details."[13]

— Vivekananda

"Despondency is not religion, whatever else it may be. By being pleasant always and smiling, it takes you nearer to God, nearer than any prayer."

— Vivekananda

"When religion emphases contemplation, it is to indicate that there are certain inmost sanctities of human life which ought to be preserved. The aim of life is not merely to create an earthly Utopia, but to attain a higher and intenser form of consciousness. The picture of Shiva, Buddha and hundreds of other saints illustrate the truth grasped by Plato, and Aristotle also, that the supreme end of man is contemplation, the freedom and the peace of understanding."[14]

"Every religion has its popes and crusades, idolatry and heresy-hunting. The cards and the game are the same, only the names are different. Men are attacked for affirming what men are attacked for denying. Religious piety seems to destroy all moral sanity and sensitive humanism. It is out to destroy other religions, not for the sake of social betterment or world peace, but because such an act is acceptable to one's own jealous god."[15]

— Dr. S. Radhakrishnan

"Religion reflects both God and man. As religion is a life to be lived, not a theory to be accepted for a belief to be adhered to, it allows scope and validity to varied approaches to the divine; but they are all forms of the supreme."

— Dr. S. Radhakrishnan

"A scientific study of religion reveals two dimensions to every religion, especially to everyone of the highly developed world religions, namely, religion as a socio-political expression and religion as a path to the experience of God, or any value equivalent to it. The first consists of the do's and don'ts of religion and the rules and regulations about food, dress, marriage, and other social disciplines, besides myths and legends and cosmological theories. A science of religions will classify religion in terms such as of their bhakti-yoga, jnana-yoga, raja-yoga and karma-yoga contents. This second dimension consists of the truly spiritual part, with its emphasis on personal morality worship and adoration, and the disciplines designed to ensure the spiritual growth of man. These constitute the essential and invariable and universal core of the religion, while the former from its variable non-essential part, which is also relevant, but only when it does not choke the spirit of the latter."

— Swami Rangnathanand

"Dharma came to mean peculiar duties and privileges for a person as a member of the community, as a member of the varnas or as in a particular stage of life."

— P.V. Kane (History of Dharmashastra)

"Multiplicity of religions has led to much unhappiness and great discord. It is the duty of wise men to find means to end it. May god sow in our minds the seed of true religion that false religions may disappear, and wise men may give-up their hostilities and increase happiness. It is an established fact that five thousand years ago, there was no other religion except the Vedic."

— Swami Dayanand

"It (Hinduism) is not religion but a system. It is not creed but a mode of thought. It allows an amount of individual freedom in thought, the like of which is not known to any other religious system of the world. It gives absolute freedom of worship of every individual, according to his own taste, belief and development."

— Lala Lajpat Rai

"The whole gamut of man's activities today constitutes an indivisible whole. You cannot divide social, political and purely religious work into watertight compartment. It (Religion) provides a moral basis to all other activities, which they would otherwise lack, reducing life to a thing of sound and fury signifying nothing."

— Mahatma Gandhi

"Religion fulfils the spiritual urges of man and channelizes them towards an effort to attain the goal of self or God-realisation. It links the soul of man with the ultimate reality in God and enables man to attain the knowledge of the self which means complete identity with the supreme being."

— Vinoba Bhave

"The world union will be based on spiritual religion of humanity. Spiritual collectivism would subdue social and political chaos of the modern world. A spiritual society alone could build the future richness and good life."

— Sri Aurobindo

Society and Religion

Religion is an integral part of human life. It can only be justified if we accept that religion is the whole man's action. If we study carefully the history of religion we shall find that religion occupies a central place in human life from the dawn of civilisation. The origin of religion has been explained by different theories, in different ways. According to some thinkers the crud form of religion has been said to be associated with many beliefs and superstitions throughout the ages, but its presence in the history of human race cannot be denied. Comte admits that religion embraces the whole of existence and the history of religion resumes the entire history of human development.

In order to discuss the history of man in relation to the history of religion we should also consider the stages in civilisation of culture as a whole. Man's interest is determined by the constant and severe struggle for existence, search for food, need of self-defence against natural perils and the attack of enemies in the savage stage. Thus we observe that the savage could not rise much above material wants. Consequently their religion remained on the same low level; their religious customs were connected with birth, marriage, war and death. It is evident even now that there is a deep emotional response to invisible forces or spirits.

If we make a wide survey of the history of mankind as a whole, (As distinguished from any particular tribe, nation or race), we shall be able to find ample evidence of gradual development of religion throughout the different ages. The historical development of religion begins with the belief in a host of spirit possessing the mysterious power that can be influenced by certain rites, rituals duly performed.

In primitive form of religion fetishism represents retrogression rather than progression. Apart from this degraded form of religion we may regard the religion of the primitive polidaemonism, that is, worship of many spirits. Natural features such a rivers, lakes, birds and snakes were regarded as the location of spirits which are worshipped. Ancestor worship was very widely spread up throughout the savage world. The greater objects of nature for example, the sky, the sun, the moon, the stars and the earth have also evoked in that period.

In course of change in the structure of society with the combination of different tribes, into a different nation either throughout the pressure of fear of common enemy or for a stronger tribe there is a great development of man's mental horizon. Consequently the development in social organisation took place and corresponding to it religion is also developed.

With the development of national religion two important movements are noticeable, viz. the moralisation of gods and movement in the direction of monotheism. Thus it can be said that the history of religion is not only the history of development of our beliefs about our Gods, but also the acts, prayer and sacrifice, devotion and worship for establishing harmonious relation with God.

So far we have been dealing with religion at the stage of its evolution and reached to the development of national religion. Now we shall considered how national religion has paved the way for the universal religion. By universal religion it is said that religion which all men share all over the world, critically speaking there is hardly any universal religion in this sense. Truly though God is one but religions are many. Even then there are three types of religion which may be described as universal religion in the wider sense. They are: Buddhism, Christianism, Islamism.

In this way the historical evolution of religion has made two points clear:

(i) Religion has manifested itself in different forms, for example, crude, futile, ignoable, as well as as noble, idealistic and conducive to human well-being.

(ii) Secondly, through the apparent chaos, rites, beliefs, superstition etc., we can trace the achievements of or progress in religion as a whole. However animism, fetishism and totemism, still prevail in many parts of the world. But the more a country is developed with culture and civilisation the crude faiths have paved the way of a loftier, more rational and spiritual kind. Thus the progress of religion cannot be accounted for in isolation from the other aspects of life but is simultaneous with the progress of social organisation, culture, and civilisation.

Christopher Dawson has rightly remarked:

"We cannot understand the inner form of a society unless we understand its religion. We cannot understand its cultural achievements unless we understand the religious beliefs that lie behind them. In all ages the first creative works of a culture are due to a religious inspiration and dedicated to a religious end. The temples of the Gods are the most enduring works of man. Religion stands at the threshold of all great literatures of the world. Philosophy is its offspring and is a child which constantly returns to its parent."[17]

Here we are not talking about any revealed or formulised religion but a natural religion having humanism as its basic component as Dr. Radhakrishnan had said: "Humanism is a religion secularised." If philosophy is its theory religion is a practical aspect of life in broader sense of the term. Mahatma Gandhi has rightly observed: "The whole gamut of man's activities today constitutes an indivisible whole. You cannot divide social, political and purely religious work into watertight compartments. It (religion) provides a moral basis to all other activities, which they would otherwise lack, reducing life to a thing of sound and fury signifying nothing."[18]

The sixth century B.C. was an age of extraordinary spiritual and mental unrest which inspired many spiritualists and philosophers to find out solutions to the abstruse problems of God and soul, birth and death, and the methods of self-purification to escape from the endless worldly miseries: The religious beliefs of the Harappans and the Aryans led to a variety of beliefs and rituals which laid down the foundations of Hinduism. The growing complexity and the rigors of Vedic practices led to the emergence of Jainism and Buddhism as powerful major religions, while some other schools of philosophy either died out or outlived their utility over time.

Religious Ethics of Confucious

Confucianism is a purely secular system, and its lack of transcendental motives, while probably rendering it better adapted to the requirements of the Chinese race, will doubtless appear to the European to stamp it as unlikely to originate and foster the highest type of character. Prudential motives, the avoidance of extremes, the cultivation of the "mean" that lies between what we understand by sin on the one hand and holiness on the other – in fact, what might be termed a "split-the-difference" kind of morality – differentiates Confucianism from other ethical systems. In spite, however, of this prevailing characteristics, much of its ethical teaching is pure, wise and noble sometimes remarkable for its shrewd and penetrating observation. The sacred books of China make no claim to be considered inspired documents. Its wisdom is content to own its human origin, and makes no vain efforts to scale the heights of the divine.

From the Shu King, or Book of Historical Documents, a few sheaves of thought may be gleaned, such as these. Referring to methods of Government, Yu, a great sage of remote antiquity, gave to a grince the following counsel:

Be cautious. Do not fail to observe the laws and ordinances. Do not find your enjoyment in idleness. Do not go excess in pleasure. In your employment of men of worth, let none come between you and them. Put way evil without hesitation. Do not carry out plans of the wisdom of which you have doubts. Study that all your purposes may be with the light of reason. Do not go against what is right to get the praise of the people. Do not oppose the people's wishes to follow your own desires (*Sacred Books of China*, Vol. I, p. 47).

As early as the eighteenth century B.C. a minister is recorded to have uttered this enlightened sentiment:

There is no invariable model of virtue; a supreme regard to what is good gives the model of it. There is no invariable characteristic of what is good that is to be supremely regarded; it is found where there is a conformity to the uniform conscience. (*Ibid.*, p. 102).

Early and late, never be but earnest. If you do not attend jealously to your small actions, the results will be to affect your virtue in great matters. (*Ibid.*, p. 151).

A small man thinks that small acts of goodness are of no benefits, and does not do them, and that small deeds of evil do not harm, and does not abstain from them. (Yi King, Appendix III. 38).

Virtue small and office high; wisdom small and plans great; strength small and burden heavy: where such conditions exist, it is seldom that they do not end in evil. (*Ibid.*, p.40).

Pride should not be allowed to grow; the desires should not be indulged; the will should not be gratified to the full; pleasure should not be carried to excess. (Li Ki, p. 62).

Virtue, according to the Chinese classics, comprises, five leading principles, or qualities, which are the constituents of human nature – viz., Benevolence, Righteousness, Propriety, Knowledge, and Fidelity. Of these the first is the fundamental quality; Mencius, the greatest of the disciples of Confucious, going so far as to declare that "Benevolence is Man." In the writings of Kwang-Tze, the chief disciple of Lao-Tze, Confucious is recorded to have defined benevolence as "to be in one's inmost heart in kindly sympathy with all things; to love all men; and to allow no selfish thoughts."[19]

Constructs of Hinduism

Unlike the other contemporary religions, the origin of Hinduism cannot be traced to the preachings of any particular Prophet, Saint, Guru, or Avtar. It is, in fact a philosophy developed over ages, an amalgam of a variety of religious beliefs practised by the pre-Aryans, the Aryans and the later Aryan inhabitants of India. The edifice of Hinduism is thus, built largely upon the religious books of the Aryans, viz. the Vedas and Upanishads and the Great Epics of the later period, viz. the Ramayana and the Mahabharata.

The Vedic literature is divided into two parts, viz. Shruti and Smriti. Shruti comprises those books whose content were revealed to the old rishis by God at the beginning of creations. They are the Eternal Truths whose contents cannot be changed. Vedas and the Upanishads belong to this category. The Smriti comprises those books whose contents were thought out by the rishis, remembered by the people, passed on from generation to generation and ultimately reduced to writing. They contain the codes of conduct, rules and regulations, which of course, can be modified according to the changed times. Manu Smriti is one of the more famous books in this category.

The Vedas, which are the most holy books of the Hindus, are believed to have been revealed by God at the beginning of the creation. However, the European scholars believe that the Vedas were composed around 1500 B.C. The Vedas are four in number, the Rig Veda, the Yajur Veda, the Sama Veda and the Atharva Veda; the Rig Veda is the oldest.

The Rig Veda contains richas or hymns in praise of Gods—Indra, Varuna, Agni, etc. and contains 1,028 hymns, which are all beautiful and inspiring. The Yajur Veda contains mantras for performing yajnas and sacrifices. The Sama Veda is the source of the Hindu music and contains hymns and songs taken from and based on Rig Veda. The Atharva Veda contains charms and spells, rites and rituals, songs and incantations for the fulfilment of human desires.

The Upanishads are the scholarly works on Aryan philosophy devoted to the indepth knowledge and discussions and such abtruse subjects as God, soul, matter, birth, death, rebirth, karma, transmigration of soul, salvation. A source of solace, the Upanishads are now read the worldover by the Hindus as well as the non-Hindus, for the magnificence of the philosophy contained in them.

The Puranas which means the older, are the religious books of Hindus which describe the origin of the world, the brave deeds of the Hindus and throw light on the life and history of the later Aryan period. Eighteen in number, the Puranas contain the legends, traditions, rituals and moral codes of the Hindu society. Among the more popular Puranas is the *Bhagwat Purana*.

Ramayana and the *Mahabharata* are the two great epics of the Hindus which have a great bearing on the Hindu way of life. The Ramayana, the older of the two epics, was composed by Maharishi Valmiki and describes the pious life and heroic deeds of Rama. The Mahabharata, composed by Maharishi Ved Vyas, depicts the life and times of the Kauravas and the Pandavas, the Battle of Kurukshetra and the ultimate victory of the good over evil, which also is the theme of Ramayana.

Bhagawad Gita, which forms a part of the Mahabharata, is among the holiest books of Hindu religion. It contains the essence of Hindu philosophy, i.e. the theory of *Karma* and the immortality of soul. It enjoins upon them to do their duty earnestly, without fear and favour and with full trust in God. It seeks to make the man sublime, and it is for the magnificence of its philosophy that Gita has been translated into all the major world languages and read everywhere with respect and esteem.

Analysing the characteristics of Hinduism Dr. Radhakrishnan has rightly observed:

"The Hindu attitude to religion is interesting. While fixed

intellectual beliefs mark of one religion from another, Hinduism sets itself no such limits. Intellect is subordinated to intuition, dogma to experience, outer expression to inward realisation. Religion is not the acceptance of academic abstractions or the celebration of ceremonies, but a kind of life or experience. It is insight into the nature of reality (*darshana*), or experience of reality (*anubhava*). This experience is not an emotional thrill, or a subjective fancy, but is the response of the whole personality, the integrated self to the central reality. Religion is a specific attitude of the self, itself and no other, though it is mixed up generally with intellectual views, aesthetic forms, and moral valuations."[20]

Righteousness and Duty

Righteousness is being used here for "Dharma". The author thinks that religion is not proper synonym for 'Dharma' as analysed in the old scriptures of Hinduism, Jainism or Buddhism. There is a close linkage between 'duty' and 'dharma', so much so that at time 'duty' is used as one of the prominent shades of Dharma'. There is famous saying of Geeta –

"Only duty is thy concern and not the fruit. Don't stand for fruit, nor you should go or inaction."[21]

In the ancient system of Hindus there was a fourfold classification of duties on divisions of society into four Varnas – Brahmin, Kshatriya, Vaishya and Shudra. In Bhagwadgita and other scriptures there duties have also been fixed-up. It can be said a descending trend in the society during post-Vedic period as during Vedic period duties of Varna (caste) were not by birth. Bhagwadgita clearly mentions of this historical fact – "Four Varnas are fixed for human beings according to the quality, nature and ability of person."[22] But later on the lawgivers like Manu etc. established the superiority or inferiority of one Varna with the other for the vested interests of a particular class.

Manu says that for the advancement of the society, the Brahma created the Brahmanas, Kshtriyas, Vaishyas and Shudras from the face, arms, thighs and feet respectively.[23] This passage implies that Brahma is superior to Kshatriya, that Kshatriya is superior to Vaishya and Vaishya is superior to Shudra as face is higher than arms, arms higher than thighs and thighs higher than legs. The same order is indicated in many ancient law-books of the Hindus including Apastamba Dharma Sutra.[24]

Social Institutions

If we investigate into the origin and rationale of those ideas there is no natural superiority or inferiority. Since the potentialities of all the four Varnas are different we cannot compare the one with the other. If the Brahmin is said to be superior in intelligence, other Varnas excell in bodily strength and enduring capacity. For the proper and balanced development of the society all are necessary. Alike intelligence, physical strength, enduring capacity, hard labour etc. are also essential for the desired growth of the society. It is clear that there is no natural superiority or inferiority and that any idea of superiority or inferiority must be artificial created by man only with certain vested interests. Vashistha[25] also enjoins that there Varnas, i.e. Kashatriya, Vaishya and Shudras should remain in the control of the Brahmana. The Brahmana should declare their duties and the kind should enforce them.

In ancient Indian history we have the instances wherein one's Varna was correctly tested by the virtue of one's power of endurance. Once, in the guise of Brahmin, Karna approached Parshuram (preceptor of Acharya Bhisma) in order to learn certain lores in various types of arms. Parshurama accepted him as disciple. One day one poisonous insect inflicted the bite on the thigh of Karna, when his preceptor was resting on the lap of Karna. In spite the severe pain and vehement bleeding from thigh Karna tolerated all this and did not move an inch lest the sleep of his preceptor is disturbed. After sometimes by the touch of the warm blood secreting through Karna's thigh Parsurama awoke immediately and asked Karna, "Who are you? You cannot be Brahmin, Brahmins do not have such great power of endurance." Karna had to reveal the truth to his honourable preceptor.

Thus we can say that four Varnas were designed for progress of the society based on division of Labour but later on many vested interests erect into the Varna-system and the system lost its flexibility. It become so strict and hard that in Ramayana we find a punishment of death for transgressing or violating the provision laid down for particular Varna. Shambuk, being Shudra dared to practice severe penances for certain extraordinary devine bliss and for this he was virtually killed by Lord Rama. That too just to satisfy Brahmins. One Brahmin with a corpse of his child came to the court of Rama and wanted justice in a very agitating mood he said:

"Be happy with your brothers!
But we will be insecure,
For there is no safety for children
In the Kingdom of Ram
Who styles himself a Mahatma ruler
Of the Ikshvaku Dynasty!
Only when raja fails in his duty
Do such heinous things happen:
Crimes flourish
Death comes prematurely
Chaos prevails."[26]

Rama summoned his eight excellent Brahmin advisers, Markandeya, Maudgalya, Vamadeva, Kashyapa, Katyayana, Jabali, Gautam and Narada. He offered them seats and did Anjali.

After the shinning-with-discipline advisers had relaxed, Rama informed them of the accusations of the Brahmin at the gate.

Narada sensed the agitation of Rama and offered this serene advice:

"Listen, King, to the reason
For the child's untimely death,
After which do what you think is right.
In the Krita-yuga,
Brahmins practised tapasya;

Only Brahmins did so;
Having done so, they achieved Brahman
In that yuga,
There were no untimely deaths,
Wisdom was the rule.

In the Treta-yuga,
Kshatriyas practised tapasya;
They were brave, heroic determined
They equalled the Brahmins,
In the Treta-yuga.
The four castes were created,
Brahmins and Kshatriyas practised tapasya,
The Vaishyas traded,
The Shudras offered puja to the first three castes,
Each caste followed its sva-dharma.

In the Dvapara-yuga,
Adharma increased,
Irregularities proliferated,
Vaishyas practised tapasya,
The three castes followed dharma through tapasaya,
But the Shudras, O King,
Were forbidden to do so,
In the Kali-yuga, indeed,
Is possible for a Shudra to do tapasya,
But for him to do so in the Dvapara
It is a grievous crime."[27]

On hearing the plight of his advisers Rama went round all the corners of the country in search of the culprit and lastly found him in a village in southern part of the country. On enquiry of Rama from his dead-downward position, the tapasaya-practiser replied to Rama of noble deeds:

"Illustrious Rama
I was born in a Shudra Womb

I am practising tapasya
To become like a God
Despite my physical body
I am not lying, Ram,
When I say what I desire
To achieve the world of the Gods.
I am Shudra
My Name is Shambuka.[28]

He had hardly finished speaking when Rama unsheathed his flashing sword and cut-off Shambuka's head. By now, it can be confirmly said the 'Uttarkand' of Ramayana is an interpolation of quite later period (IV or V century A.D.) which was made an instrument, among other things, to highlight the supremacy of the previleged class, i.e. Brahmins. This phenomena has been reflected in writings by many noted scholars Eastern as well Western.

In MN. 93 the Buddha supposedly told the young brahmin Ashvalayan, "Thou has heard that in Yona, Kamboja and other (adjacent) frontier regions, there are only two castes: Arya and Dasa. One having been an Arya may become a Dasa, one having been a Dasa may become an Arya. The name Yona (Ionia) for some parts of Afghanistan proves that this passage could not have been written before Alexander's conquest of the Persian empire. The Buddha does not refer to the Rigvedic two-varna system, for there Arya could not become a Dasa; Greek slavery is obviously meant."[29]

What right a man has got to take other man as inferior, or to hate him or torture him? If we got through the passage of history we will find that the atrocities of man were inflicted upon a man on the basis of caste, creed or colour. Our Eastern traditions have no satisfactory answer to this. This phenomena led it to a very poor reputation and the sects like Buddhism and Jainism came into existence. Because of certain conservative tendencies of a few group could not open its windows frankly towards other sects. According to Swamy Vivekananda, "the on great cause of the downfall and degeneration of India was the burning of a wall of custom, whose foundation was hatred of others, round the nation, and the real aim of which in ancient times was to prevent the Hindus from coming in contact with surrounding Buddhist nations. Whatever cloack ancient or modern sophistry may try to throw over it, the inevitable result – the vindication of the moral law, that none can hate others without degenerating himself is that the race that was foremost amongst the ancient races is now a byword, and a scorn among nations."[30] Comparative study of the literature which may be called, 'Indian Cameralism.' In accepting the analogy, it is not forgotten that in analogical reasoning superficial resemblances often mislead. But, they cannot be ignored. What is necessary is that fundamental resemblances and differences should be considered exhaustively.

Dr. Radhakrishnan says, "The Hindu thinkers admit the ineffability of the experience but permit themselves a graduated scale of interpretations from the most 'impersonal' to the most 'personal'. The freedom of interpretation is responsible for what may be called the hospitality of the Hindu. The Hindu tradition by its very breadth seems to be capable of accommodating varied religious conceptions.

Hinduism admits that the unquestionable content of the experience is that about which nothing more can be said. The deeper and more intimate a spiritual experience, the more readily does it dispense with signs and symbols. Deep intuition utterly silent. Through silence we 'confess without confession' that the glory of spiritual life is inexplicable and beyond the reach of speech and mind. It is the great unfathomable musty and words the treacherous."[31]

Chariot of Religion

All our eastern thinkers, saints and poets have conceived it as mandatory that the journey of life can be best and meaningfully accomplished if one possesses some mode of conveyance like value-based religion. Here we would like to refer to a great saint-poet Tulsidas of the medeival age; who has commendably and sincerely reflected the core of Indian thought and cultural tradition in his writings. His monumental work named Ramcharit Manas, popularly called the Ramayana is not only a great literary work but also the exposition of the devotion of the highest order. Scores of scholars, Eastern and Western, including Sir George Grierson and V.A. Smith have bestowed lavish praise on the Ramayana as piece of art and as a work that has modulated religious thought and character of countrymen in India. They have described it as a Bible of Hindus. There is no gainsaying the fact that by his work and by the example of his own life, Goswami Tulsidas played a vital role in the growth and evolution of Bhakti Movement.

During the course of battle between Rama and Ravan at Lanka, Vibhishan, brother of Ravan but follower of Rama was worried that Rama is at a disadvantage against Ravan sittting in his chariot fully equipped with arms on the battle-field. At this moment Rama consoled Vibhishan saying: Listen friend, the chariot which brings victory is different. The wheels of that chariot are bravery and fortitude. Its flags are truth and moral strength. Its horses are force, judgment, self-control and service of fellow-men, tied to the ropes of charity, compassion and equanimity. Devotion is the skilled charioteer, selflessness, the shield, contentment, the sword, charity, the axe, intelligence the mighty bolt the elevated mind, the terrible bow. A heart pure and unruffled, is the quiver, while the arrows are equality, disciplined life and self-control. The impenetrable armour is worship of the teacher and the Brahmins. There are no better weapons for securing victory. My dear friend, for the one who sits in such a chariot, there are no more enemies to be conquered."[32]

In the above-mentioned episode various values enumerated are – bravery, fortitude, truth, judgment, self-control, service, charity, compassion, equanimity, devotion, selflessness, contentment, intelligence etc. which can be called as essential ingredients for any faith or religion on this earth. In one of the Analects Confucious has further condensed these values into five only. Tzu-Chang asked Confucious about humanness.

Confucious said: "He who could put five things into practice everywhere under Heaven would be humane." Tzu-Chang begged to ask what they were and he replied: *Courtesy, generosity, good faith, diligence* and *kindness*. If you behave with courtesy, then you will not be insulted; if you are generous, then you will win the multitude; if you are of good faith, then other men will put their trust in you; if you are diligent, then you will have success and if you are kind, then you will be able to command others.[33]

After a great disastrous war of Mahabharata, Bhishma, on his death-bed of thorns (where he laid himself during his last days) explains and exhorts them: "A fall from compassion is always a moral fall. Just as an elephant's footprints engulfs the footprints of all other animals, compassion engulfs all forms of religion. Immoral thought, word and deed make a person fall from Dharma; therefore a return to Dharma is to be pure again in thought, pure again in word and family pure again in deed. Further he adds:

"Ahimsa is the highest religion,
Ahimsa is the highest discipline.
Ahimsa is the highest penance,
Ahimsa is the highest sacrifice,
Ahimsa is the highest happiness,
Ahimsa is the highest truth,
Gift, ritual, ablution, holy merit—
None is greater than Ahimsa."[34]

On the other hand in Mahabharata it has been said that without violence (*himsa*) no empire can be established, which is true also in its practical sense. There are many other statements, particularly regarding various ethical values, which are contradictory. In this context the Mahabharata can be called a store-house of contradictions.

The great saint Kabir of the medieval age believed that love of God and love of humanity were the fundamental basis of religion and as such according to him there was no religion without bhakti. His poems (*dohas* – a form of Hindi poem) in Hindi look like parables and contain a trenchant criticism of the prevailing beliefs and practices of the age and had a great appeal for the common people. He proclaimed that Rama and Rahim, Krishan and Karim, Mecca and Kashi, idolatry and non-idolatry, Mandir and Mosque, Vandana and Ajan etc. are the universal expression of the same Absolute force. His practical view on value-based religion is depicted in the following poem:

If God be within the Mosque
then to whom does this world belong?
If Rama be within the image, then
who is there to know what happens without?
Hari is in the east, Allah is in the west.
Look within your own heart, for there
you will find both Karim and Rama.
All the men and women of the world
are his living form
Vain, too, are the distinction of caste.[35]

If we survey the scriptures of various religions we will find that the fundamental values of all the religions are the same. There presentation may be different in style and illustration. Hinduism lays special stress on courtesy and kindness and respect for all life and tolerance to all men. The religion of Islam lays special emphasis on the brotherhood of man. The Mohammedan faith has bound all members in a close bond of brotherhood and they are ready to help each other at all times. The Buddhist religion has taught us to respect and love God's creatures and to hold fast to the doctrine of non-violence (*ahimsa*). The Christian religion has taught us that God is a loving Father and that he loves us individually and cares for each one of us. The fatherhood of God implies the brother-hood of man. Each one of us has a religion. We are born into a family which follows some religion or other.[36] Dr. Radhakrishnan says, "Every religion has its pope and crusades, idolatry and heresy-hunting. The cards and the game are the same, only the names are different. Men are attached for denying. Religious piety seems to destroy all moral sanity and sensitive humanism."[37] That is why religious pluralism has now become the order of the day and cross-cultural communication[38] has been realised as prominent theme to establish social harmony and world peace at large by putting collective efforts for combating racial prejudices and religious dogmas.

Krishnamurti believes that, "there is only one truth the freedom from all hungering and thirsting. All else is mere illusion, infinite in its varieties, its glories. The saint, the sinner, the slave, the victor, the man of virtue and the so-called spiritual man, all are equal in their illusion, all rooted in their longing. Immense space and time may separate them from each other, but the saint who has gone beyond the sinner has merely moved from an inferior illusion to a superior. "Perfect freedom will not be achieved by means of systematic limitation. Virginity of mind will not discovered in a context of predetermined beliefs and dogmas."[39]

Universality of Religious Ethics

At the end of Mahabharata, a great epic of India gist of the religious ethics is described in the following manner:

"O King! Listen to the quintet essence of religion and having heard put it into the practice of your life. Do not do unto others which is not liked or prized by you."[40]

While referring to "The way of the Superior Man" Confucious has given us a lofty and aristocratic moral code. He says: *"What you do not wish others to do unto you, do not unto them"*. This saying very much resembles with the saving of the Mahabharata, quoted above. After about five century, Jesus Christ also. Subsequently, many philosophers including Socrates, Aristotle etc. and the scholar poets like Kalidasa, Goethe etc. Confucious identified morality with intelligence, and preached not humility and gentleness, but the full development of personality.

Whether it is meditation, prayer, or any other spiritual work of this type all have the same contents and theme though they may differ in form and the manners of performance. Richard W. Chilson has rightly observed: "The spiritual insights from our religious traditions can be presented apart from their religious dress. So there is no need for you to affirm that there is a God or that Jesus is the Messiah in order to embark upon this experiment, just as you need not believe Gautam is the Buddha in order to begin Buddhist meditation."[41] Proverbially, it is said that prayer is a conversation between God and Man. It can also be said as the process that allows us to open up more and more fully to the whole of reality. Then Western and Eastern – both the spiritual traditions provide a way of experience this reality. Let's examine the following prayer of the little man of Assissi:

> Lord, make me a channel of thy peace
> that where there is hatred, I may bring love;
> that where there is wrong, I may bring the spirit of forgiveness
> that where there is discord, I may bring harmony;
> that where there is error, I may bring faith;
> that where there is despair; I may bring hope
> that where there are shadows; I may bring light
> that where there is sadness, I may bring joy.
> Lord, grant that I may seek rather
> to comfort than to be comforted;
> to understand than to be understood
> to love than to be loved.
> For it is by forgetting self that one finds;
> it is by forgiving that one is forgiven
> it is dying that one awakens to eternal life.[42]

This prayer is used by the people of all faiths in 132 countries of the world striving for social harmony, peace and prosperity. Fundamental values like truth non-violence, peace, love, good conduct etc. are also common to all the faiths of the world.

The eternal values like truth, non-violence, peace, love etc. had been well woven and interwoven in the ancient literature of the East including the ancient books of China and great epics like Ramayana and Mahabharata. Therefore, it will not only be unfair but unhistorical also to say that all ideas of non-violence as the gift of Buddha or Christ. The eternal human mind, out of which spring all Buddhistic or Christian notions of moral life, was always conscious of the importance of such eternal values. The *Ramayana* speaks of the earliest birth of these ideas in the dawn of civilisation.

Prayer

One of the prominent components of the religion is the prayer which is found in all the religions of the world right from their inception. It is found in the Vedas as well as in the Ancient books of China, in Buddhism, Jainism, Confucianism etc., Hymns or Richas of the Vedas are but Prayers only to various nature-Gods like Indra, Varuna, Agni, Usha etc. "It is said that we can notice a transition from naturalistic and anthropomorphic ploytheism through transcendent monotheism to immanent monism in the pre-Upanishadic philosophy. The personified forces of nature first changed into real gods and these later on, became mere forms of one personal and transcendental God, the "Custodian of Cosmic and Moral Order', who himself, later on, passed into Brahman or Atman which is both immanent and transcendent. The Mantra portion has been called the religion of nature, of the poets; the Brahmana retualism', the religion of low, of the priests; the Upanishadic portion, the religion of spirit, of the philosophers."[43] According to Greek thought "Philosophy is the interplay of science and religion. Gone were the anthropomorphic and largely immoral Gods, but religion refuses to be thrown out of human life. Throw it through the doors and it comes again through the windows. Socrates was guided by a voice (daimon) and was subject to ecstacy or trance akin to what Shri Ramkrishna experienced frequently. Then both Plato and Plotinus speak of meditation which man can rise to great heights in his spiritual attainments. But the religion of mysticism coupled with idealism of Plato and advaitic kind of philosophy in Plotinus. However, Aristotle kept largely to science, and, Aristotelianism remained the most important philosophy for sustaining science both in the world of Arabs and Europe."[44]

Chinese Religion

There is no Chinese religion as such. There are many religions being practised in China among the people of China. According to Will Durant, "There is no Chinese Buddhism and Chinese Mohammedanism; there is, among the people, fetichistic religion of spirits and images, and totemism of sacred animals... There is, among all but the young Nationalists, a stringent ancestor-worship, through which the dead rule the living in almost every act of life.

There is the religion of Laotse, the Tao or Way, almost absorbed now by Buddhism, but still producting saints to self-denial and meditation. And finally there is Confucianism, the religion of the educated classes in China for hundreds of years."[45]

Confucianism: A Religion or Philosophy

Confucianism is better described as a philosophy rather than a religion. He did not teach theology nor taught about any personified God or Goddess. For Confucious religion was a way of life in true sense of the term. He never entertained the questions pertaining to death, other world, rebirth etc. He used no super-natural terms to highlight his philosophical tenets. When a pupil asked him what were man's duties to spirits, Confucious answered: "Before we are able to do our duty the living, how can we do it by the spirits of the dead?"[46] And when the pupil, persisting, asked about death, the Master said: "Before we know what life is, how can we know what death is? To give one's self earnestly to the duties due to men, and while earnestly respecting spiritual beings to keep away from them, what may be called wisdom."[47]

Religious Ethics of Lao-tse

Here we would like to produce below the gist of religious ethics of Lao-tse on the basis of the book titled as "Wisdom of Chinese."[48]

"Requite injury with kindness. To the good I will be good; to the evil also I would be good, in order to make them good. With the faithful I would keep faith; with the unfaithful I would also keep faith, in order that they may become faithful. He who has no faith in others will find no faith in them, keep behind, and you shall be put in front, he that bends shall be made straight. He who is great makes humility his base. He who, conscious of being strong, is content to be weak, - he shall be paragon of mankind. To know, but to be as one not knowing is the height of wisdom. The sage knows what is in him but makes no display; he respects himself, but seeks no honour for himself. All things in nature work silently; they come into being and possess nothing, they fulfil their function and make no claim.

All thinks alike do their work, and then we see them subside. When they have reached their bloom each returns to its origin. Returning to their origin means rest, or fulfilment of destiny. This reversion is an eternal law. To know that law is wisdom. Do nothing by self-well, but rather conform to the infinite Will, and everything will be done for you."

Selflessness, cleanliness and emotional calm are the preliminaries to arriving at full Self-knowledge, but they must be climaxed by deep meditation. "Bide in silence, and the radiance of the spirit shall come in and make its home." For this to happen, all outward impressions must be stilled and the senses withdrawn to a completely interior point of focus. Postures paralleling the Indian *asanas* are recommended and the breath must be similarly controlled. It must be done with all softness and delicacy. The result will be a condition of alert waiting known as "sitting with a blank mind". This type of empty or black mind is prerequisite for meditation. In Japan, Zen Buddhism highlights this type of meditation, which is very close and similar to Indian *"Yogic sadhana"*. This concept is not confined to the East only. St. John of the Cross offers an identical promise:

"Without labour you shall subject to the peoples, and things shall be subject to you." According to Tao such a person rules without even being known to rule:

"The sage relies on actionless activity...
Put himself in the background, but is always to the fore.
Remains outside; but is always there
Is it not just because he does not strive for any personal end
That all his personal ends are fulfilled."[49]

Thus, we see that religious experience is more than a subjective state of consciousness. It points to a trans-subjective spiritual principle wherein value coincide with Reality. But religion should not be taken as mere faith in a super-sensible Reality as the seat and source of all values. It is also the emotional reaction to that ultimate Reality. Such reactions or actions should be channelized for making one's life happy and harmonious.

Common Salient Features

In spite of many diversifications of opinion in terms of origin, rites, rituals, beliefs, ways of worship and various other external points all the religions have certain features in common. According to Dr. Radhakrishnan:

"Every religion has its popes and crusades, idolatry and heresy-hunting. The cards and the games are the same, only the names are different. Men are attached for affirming what men are attached for denying. Religious piety seems to destroy all moral sanity and sensitive humanism. It is out to destroy other religions, not for the sake of social betterment or world peace but because such an act is acceptable to one's own jealous God."[50]

Religions may also differ in meaning and scope, their involvement in spiritual or material strivings of a man; but all of them agree:

(i) That religion is ultimately concerned with something that is beyond man and the world, i.e. with the supernatural Reality, whether it is conceived as a personal God or impersonal Absolute or Nirvana etc.[51]

(ii) That it shows human beings the way to establish communion or unity with that Reality and to attain the supreme goal of his or her life.

(iii) That the truth or mystery of religion or dharma cannot be attained or discovered by human mind or reason; it is known through the word or revelation received by the seers, prophets etc. from the Divine Being himself or through some supernatural source.

(iv) That the good of the individual and the society lies in obeying and following the commandments or injunctions that are laid down in the scriptures which embody revelation.

(v) That religion embodies the moral, the spiritual and all other higher and noble values of life which should be cultivated by the people, individually as well as collectively.

According to some organised religions, the state should be governed in accordance with the laws laid down in the scriptures or in the books that derived their authority from the scriptures. It is this view which leads to the alignment or identification of a particular religion with state and raises the demand for religious constitutions in some countries even today. The Islamic world bears a clear witness to it.

Characteristics of a Spiritual Man

The first sign that you are becoming religious is that you are becoming cheerful. When a man is gloomy, that may be dyspepsia, but it is not religion....Misery is caused by sin, and by no other cause....If you have a clouded face, do not go out that day, shut yourself up in your room. What right have you to carry this disease out into the world?[51]

The real spiritual man is broad everywhere. His love forces him to be so. Those to whom religion is a trade are forced to become narrow and mischievous by their introduction into religion of the competitive, fighting, and selfish methods of the world.[52]

Why do we see wickedness?....We see the world as we are. Suppose there is a baby in a room with bag of gold on the table and thief comes and steals the gold. Would the baby know it was stolen? That which we have inside, we see outside. The baby has no thief inside and sees on thief outside. So with all knowledge, do not talk of the wickedness of the world and all its sins. Weep that you are bound to see wickedness yet. Weep that you are bound to see sin everywhere, and if you want to help the world do not condemn it. Do not weaken it more. For what is sin and what is misery, and what are all these, but the results of weakness? The world is made weaker and weaker everyday by such teachings. Men are taught from childhood that they are weak and sinners. Teach them that they are all glorious children of immortality, even those who are the weakest in manifestation. Let positive, strong, helpful thoughts enter into their brains from very childhood. Lay yourselves open to these thoughts, and not to weakening and paralysing ones. Say to your own minds, "I am He, I am He." Let it ring day and night in your minds like a song, and at the point of death declare, "I am He." That is the Truth; the infinite strength of the world is yours.....Let us be brave. Know the truth and practise the Truth. The goal may be distant but awake, arise, and stop not till the goal is reached.[53]

Do you not know the history of the world where the power of the prophets lay? Where was it? In the intellect? Did any of them write a fine book on philosophy, on the most intricate rationalisations of logic? Not one of them. They only spoke a few words. Feel like Christ and you will be Christ; feel like Buddha and you will be a Buddha. It is feeling that is the life, the strength, the vitality, without which no amount of intellectual activity can reach God.[54]

There are two sorts of courage. One is the courage of facing the cannon. And thē other is the courage of spiritual conviction. An emperor who invaded India was told by his teacher to go and see some of the sages there. After a long search for one, he found a very old man sitting on a block of stone. The emperor talked with him a little and became very much impressed by his wisdom. He asked the sage to go to his country with him. "No", said the sage, "I am quite satisfied with my forest here." Said the Emperor, "I will give you money, position, wealth. I am the Emperor of the world. 'No', replied the man, I don't care for those things.' The Emperor replied 'If you do not go, I will kill you. The man smiled serenely and said, 'That is the most foolish thing you ever said, Emperor. You cannot kill me. Me the sun cannot dry, fire cannot burn, sword cannot kill, for I am the birthless, the deathless, the ever-living omnipresent spirit.' This is spiritual boldness, while the other is the courage of a lion or a tiger. In the Mutiny of 1857 there was a Swami, a very great soul, whom a Mohammedan mutineer stabbed severely. The Hindu mutineers caught and brought the man to the Swami, offering to kill him. But the Swami looked up calmly and said, 'My brother, thou art He, thou, art He' and expired. This is another instance.[55]

Here we should not forget that scientific foundation of Religious truths are necessary if we are to avoid the extravagancies of merely emotional Religion. The emotional man who is unrestrained by intellectual considerations, is often, in danger is being inclined to fall into absurdities. A great attention to scientific demands will emphasise the necessity of our thought and will save religion from depending merely upon the authority, and thereby, becoming 'Dogmatic'. Science is more theoretical whereas religion is always practical. Theory and practice both are natural operations of human mind and as such both should take care of so that human life on the planet earth may become harmonious and happy.

Any religion's effectiveness depends mainly upon three things as far as its social concern is taken into account – its influence over people's lives; its capacity to achieve certain specified goals; and consideration of desirability those goals in terms of some other, external criteria. History tells that, at times, religion exerted a powerful role in social affairs of a man or a group of people. According to Wilson, "Religion's business is to keep men travelling hopefully, rather than to organise their arrival. In the transformation of experience, religion confers meanings, regulates emotions and communicates values. For this reason, its language is always ambiguous, denoting but simultaneously evoking and evaluating. Whereas science excludes the emotive and evaluating in order to operate more effectively at the cognitive level.... Because life is full of decisions men need more than cognitive knowledge: they need interpretation, and interpretations entail emotional response and a sense of values. It is at these levels that the profundity of religious doctrine is discovered, and it is for this reason that religion participate in a wider spectrum of experience that do other systems of knowledge."[56] Therefore, we should ensure religion's influence on social mores is wholesome without being forcibly imposed. A.N. Whitehead has rightly said:

"Thus an attack upon systematic thought is treason to civilisation. Yet the great minds who laid the foundations of our modern mentality – John Look, for example – has reason for their dissatisfaction with the traditional dogmatic theology, though that partially misconceived the grounds upon which they should base their attitude. Their true enemy was the doctrine of dogmatic finality...."[57]

Priesthood

Priesthood is the important dimensions of the religion in practice. In oriental as well as occidental traditions, we find that priesthood has been responsible for many malpractices, which went a long way in bringing a bad name for the religion concerned. The heterodox sects like Jainism and Buddhism emerged in India mainly because of the corrupt priesthood. Of course, there were host of other socio-economic factors also responsible for the fall of Hinduism in ancient India.

Baha'u'llah, the founder the Bahai faith has rightly observed: "The day for professional priesthood in past. In former times it was necessary for a group of people to specialise in administering the religious affairs of the community, and the sincere efforts of many selfless and devoted monks and priest who dedicated their lives the helping the uneducated masses and acquainting them with their religious obligations are not to be forgotten or belittled. The requirements of this age, however, differ from those of past ages. Today, every individual should receive a sound moral and academic education, be encouraged to took into religious teaching with an unbiased mind, and accept full responsibility for his own beliefs and action."[58]

In Bahai faith, therefore, there is no professional priesthood. Every member, man or woman, is called upon to contribute his or her share in conducting the affairs of the community. Such duties as the performance of the Bahai's, marriage ceremony and the carrying out of official burial rites are discharged under the auspices of Spiritual Assemblies.

In this very vein condemning the scrupulous role of the elergy Swami Vivekananda said: "First bread and then religion. Material civilisation, nay, even luxury, is necessary to create work for the poor. Bread! Bread! I do not believe in a God who cannot give me bread here, giving me eternal bliss in heaven! Pooh! India is to be raised, the poor are to be fed, education is to spread, and the evil of priestcraft is to be removed.....Root-up priestcraft from the old religion, and you get the best religion in the world." Though he had all praise for Hinduism; but he was very critical of the dogmas and alubious role of priests. That is why he suggested to remove the evils of priesthood. Besides Vivekananda there had been many social reformers who showed a great concern over the evil of priestcraft and tried their best to modify and cleanse it. According to Dr. Karan Singh:

> "This (effort of Brahmo Samaj) was the first deliberate attempt in modern India to reform Hinduism and to cleanse its of undesirable encrustation that had developed around it over the

centuries."[59] Dr. B.R. Ambedkar who was also a great critic of evils of priestcraft, who wanted to prescribe certain qualifications and prerequisite for the priests. He was a great antagonist of Hinduism. On 25th December, 1927, 'Manu Smriti' was burnt at Mahad under his leadership. Mr. Dhananjay Keer, the biographer of Dr. Ambedkar, says that this was the indicative of the quantum of annoyance and antagonism he had towards Hinduism. This very phenomenon was equally true of Christianity also. Will Durant has rightly said, "Christ had brought the Kingdom of God nearer to earth; but he has been misunderstood, and in place of God's Kingdom, the Kingdom of priest has been established among us."[60]

The phenomenon mentioned above has been described in simpler words by Rasheedduddin Khan. He said: "It is sad to see philosophers 'throttling' the simple doctrines of the prophets and their 'incarnations' in abstruse jargon for intellectual exploitation of the masses. The tradesmen of religion are turning it into a commercial transaction between God and Man with themselves acting as middlemen and power-hungry individuals are playing on religious sentiments in order to occupy blood drenched throne."[61] Let's now realise that entire world, may be Eastern or Western, is moving towards multi-religious character, where all the religions have fair and frank role to play provided they do not become detrimental to the other one. Fast growing awareness of cross-cultural communication is changing or rather has changed it into a 'global village' and nationalism has been reduced to its tribal character.

The perception and experience of Chinese is not very different from the above feeling. As far popular Taoism, one way to approach the basic power of the universe is through magic. From this approach to the power of Tao comes popular Taoism, the Taoism of the masses. Huston Smith feels that "To pass from the lofty heights of the *Tao Te Ching* to the priestcraft of popular Taoism is like passing from a crystal mountain spring to the thick, fetid waters of a stagnant canal. Mysticism becomes mystification and religion is perverted into necromancy and sorcery. There have been long epochs in

China's history when Taoism in its popular form could be characterised in little more than a funeral socket."[62] May it be religion of the East or West one thing is very common that whenever people tried to institutionalise the religion or legalise the simple summons of the prophets, evils crept into the religion in a natural but vigorous way.

Futurology of Religion

In Social Sciences, the concepts are changing very fast. That is why every discipline is in search of its exact future and as such 'futurology' is taking shape as a systematic discipline in itself. Alike many other branches of knowledge the scholars have predicted the 'futurology' of religion also, i.e. synthesis of Science and Religion. International seminars are being held on this very theme. Recently on 8-9th January, 1997, one of such conferences was held at Calcutta. Such synthesis alone can make our religion practices free of dogmas and superstitions and enable the religion to face the challenges of new world-order. Wilson has rightly remarked: "The new world-order, I believe, will be dominated by essentially rational and technical arrangements. That order will lack substantive values, and it will operate in accordance with procedural, that is to say, instrumental values. The emergent social system will not function in response to any set of specifical religious conceptions of human or social purpose. Religious organisations will surely continue, and some of their representatives may well be publicly conspicuous, but it is different to envisage the social system accepting the primacy of spiritual values or being significantly influenced by religious concerns. The strength of the emerging rational and technical social order will lie in its transcendence of national, cultural and religious differences, and in the objectivity of the criteria that will be established for a wide range of international, social and political activities.[63]

We would like to conclude this chapter by the following:

"From Dharma comes success
From Dharma comes happiness
Dharma brings everything
Dharma is the world's essence."[64]

—Ramayana

With Exalted feeling of devotion, Sufi Saint wrote—

I am no Christian, No Jew, No Muslim
Nor of the East, nor of the West
Nor of the land, nor of the sea
Nor of India, China or Bulgaria
Nor of the world or the next or heaven or hell
My place placeless, my trace traceless
Neither body nor mind—all is the life of my beloved.

REFERENCES

1. For details please refer to the author's book titled as "*An Introduction to the Equality of Religions*" wherein Eastern as well as Western thoughts on religion have been elaborated.
2. यतो भ्युदयनिः श्रेयसुसिद्धि स धर्मः ।

— Maharishi Kanad

3. नमो धर्माय महते धर्मो धारयते प्रजाः ।
यत् स्याद् धारणसायुक्तं स धर्म इत्युदाहतः।।

— The Mahabharata

4. वेदः स्मृतिः सदाचारः स्वस्य च प्रियमात्मनः।
एतच्चतुर्विधं प्राहुः सक्षाद्धर्मस्य लक्षणम्।।

— Manu Smriti II.12

धृतिः क्षमा दमो स्तेयं शौचमिन्द्रियनिग्रहः।
धीर्विणा सत्यमक्रोधो दशकं धर्मलक्षणम्।।

— *Ibid.* VI.92

5. आहारनिद्राभयमैथुनं च समानमेतत् पशुभिर्नराणाम्।
धर्मो हि तेज्ञामधिको विशेषो धर्मेण हीनाः पशुभिः समानाः।।

— Niti Shatak

6. परहित सरिस धर्म नहिं भाई।
परपीड़ा सम नहीं अधमाई।।

—Ramcharit Manas

Compare-
अष्टादशपुराणेषु व्यासस्य वचनद्वयम्।
परोपकारः पुण्याय पापाय परपीड्नम्।।

— Maharishi Vyas

7. *Tiruvalluvar*, compiled by S. Maharajan, p.69.
8. *Ibid.*
9. *Subramaniam Bharti*, compiled by Prema Nandkumar, p.120.
10. R.N. Tagore, *Sadhana*, p.33.
11. *Galib*, compiled by M. Mujib, p.50.
12. *What Religion Is*—in the words of Swami Vivekananda (Ed. by John Yale, who later on becomes Swami Vidyatmanand), p.6.

13. *Ibid.*, p.1.
14. Dr. S. Radhakrishnan, *Religion & Society*, p.68.
15. Dr. S. Radhakrishnan, *An Idealistic View of Life*, pp.33-34.
16. Charles T. Gorham, *Ethics of the Great Religions of the World*, pp.84-85.
17. *Religion and World History – A selection from the works of Christopher Dawson*, Edited by James Oliver and Christian Scott, p.35.
18. For details please see - 'Religion and Truth as Experienced by Mahatma Gandhi' in the Author's book titled as '*Equality of Religions*', pp.127-32.
19. Raymond Dawson, *Confucious*, p.37.
20. Dr. S. Radhakrishnan, *Hindu View of Life*, p.13.
21. कर्मण्येवाधिकारस्ते मा फलेषु कदाचन।
   मा कर्ममलहेतुर्भ: मा ते संगो स्त्वकर्मणि।।

   — Bhagvadgita
22. चातुर्वर्ण्यम् मया सृष्टं गुणकर्मविभागश:।

   — Bhagvadgita
23. लोकानां तु विवृद्धयर्थ मुखबाहूरुपादत:।
   ब्राह्मणं क्षत्रियं वैश्यं शूद्रं च निखर्तयत्।।

   — Manu I.31
24. चत्वारो वर्णा ब्राह्मणक्षत्रियवैश्यशूद्रा
   तेषां पूर्व: पूर्वो जन्मत: श्रेयान् ।।५।।

   —Apastamba Dharmasutra 1-1
25. त्रयो वर्णा ब्राह्मणस्य वशे वर्त्तेरन्।
   तेषां ब्राह्मणो धर्मान् प्रब्रूयात्।
   तं राजा चानुशिष्यात्।

   — Vashistha Smriti 1.40-41
26. *Valmiki Ramayana*, Condensed and Transcreated by P. Lal, p.276.
27. *Ibid.*, pp.276-77.
28. *Ibid.*, p.279.
29. D.D. Kosambi, *An Introduction to the Study of Indian History*, p.169.
30. *Swamy Vivekananda on India and her problems*, p.19.
31. Dr. S. Radhakrishnan, *An Idealistic View of Life*, p.79.
32. सुनहु सखा कह कृपानिधाना, जेहि जय होइ सो स्यंदन आना।
   सौरज धीरज तेहि रथ चाका, सत्य सीलदृढ़ ध्वजा पताका।
   बलविवेक दम परहित घोरे, छपा कृपा समता रजु जोरे।
   ईस भजनु सारथी सुजाना, विरति चर्म संतोष कृपाना।
   दान परसु बुधि सक्ति प्रचंडा, वर विग्यान कठिन कोदण्डा।
   अमल अचल मन त्रोन समाना, सम जम नियम सिलीमुख नाना।
   कवच अभेद विप्र गुरू पूजा, एहि सम विजय उपाय न दूजा।
   सखा धर्मस्य इस रथ जाकें, जीतन कहं न कतहुं रिपु ताकें।

   — Ramacharit Manas
33. *Confucious, The Analects* (Lun Yu), Penguin Books, (XVII)-6.
34. Mahabharata of Vyas, Transcreated by P. Lal, p. 321.
   अहिंसा परमो धर्मस्तथहिंसा परं तप:।
   अहिंसा परमं सत्यं यतो धर्म: प्रवर्तते।। — Anushasan Parvan 115/23

अहिंसा लक्षणो धर्म इति धर्मविदां विदुः।
यदहिंसात्मकं कर्म तत् कुर्यादात्मवान् नरः।।

—*Ibid.*, 116/12

अहिंसा परमो यज्ञस्तथाहिंसा मरं फलम्।।
अहिंसा परमं मित्रंमहिंसा परमं सुखम्।।

— *Ibid.*, 116/29

35. Quoted from *Medieval Indian Culture*, A.L. Shrivastava, p.47.
36. For details, please see the Chapter "Religious Pluralism and Human Values" in the author's book titled as '*Equality of Religions*'.
37. Dr. S. Radhakrishnan, *An Idealistic View of Life*, pp.33-34.
38. On this theme the author has contributed an independent volume titled as 'Crosscultural Communication–A Global Perspective'.
39. Luis, S.R. Vas, *Mind of J. Krishnamurti*, p.281.
40. श्रुणुष्व धर्मसर्वस्व श्रुत्वा चैवावधर्यताम्।
 आत्मनः प्रतिकूलानि परेषां न समाचरेत्।।
41. Richard W. Chilson, *I can Pray, You can Pray*, p.3.
42. Quoted in "Enlightened Citizenship", p.325.
43. C.D. Sharma, *A Critical Survey of Indian Philosophy*, p.15.
44. Y. Masih, *A Critical Survey of Western Philosophy*, p.3.
45. Will Durant, *Pleasures of Philosophy*, p.352.
46. Brown B., *The Wisdom of the Chinese*, p.31.
47. Quoted in *Pleasure of Philosophy*, p.353.
48. Brown, B., *The Wisdom of Chinese*, pp.85-120.
49. Quoted in *Religions of Man*, p.188.
50. Dr. S. Radhakrishnan, *An Idealistic View of Life*, pp.33-34.
51. *Complete Works of Swami Vivekananda*, Vol. I, pp.164-65.
52. *Ibid.*, Vol. V., p.60.
53. *Ibid.*, Vol. II, p.87.
54. *Ibid.*, Vol. II, p.307.
55. *Ibid.*, Vol. II, pp.84-85.
56. Bryan Wilson and Daisaku Ikeda, *Human Values in Changing World*, pp.331-32.
57. A.N. Whitehead, *Adventure of Ideas*, p.191.
58. Gloria Faizi, *The Bahai Faith*, pp.95-97.
59. Dr. Karan Singh, *Essays on Hinduism*, p.27.
60. Will Durant, *Story of Civilisation*, p.80.
61. Rasheeduddin Khan (Ed.), *Composite Culture of India and National Integration*, p.14.
62. Huston Smith, *Religions of Man*, p.186.
63. *Human Values in a Changing World*, p.187.
64. धर्मादर्शः प्रभवति धर्मात् प्रभवते सुखम्।
 धर्मेण लभते सर्वं धर्मसारमिदं जगत्।।

— Aranya Kand

7

KNOWLEDGE
Material Versus Spiritual

"The premise which is common in the last analysis to all philosophies and soteriologies in Asia is that knowledge whether it be that of books or mystical gnosis is the only absolute way leading to supreme bliss in this world as well as in the next world. A careful examination would reveal the fact that 'knowledge' does not mean knowing the things of this world, nature, social life, or laws regulating both nature and man. Rather, it is the philosophical knowledge of the 'meaning' of life and world. It is naturally understood that such a knowledge cannot be replaced by Western empirical learning, and that it should never be sought by empirical means, if we are to do justice to the purpose to that learning."

— Max Weber[1]

He, whose mind is unattached everywhere, who has subdued his self and whose thirst for enjoyment has completely disappeared, reaches through sannyasa (the path of knowledge), the highest perfection of actionlessness, i.e. freedom from the bondage of karma through God-Realization."

— Mahabharata[2]

"Release from the circle of life and death is possible through knowledge. Knowledge is nothing but to have proper perception of spiritual phenomena."

— Mahabharata[3]

"The one, whose evil deeds are not washed away, does not attain (such) knowledge. After having attained such knowledge he attains the bliss supreme."[4]

Knowledge is to Know Both

According to Confucious knowledge is both. "It is to know both—what one knows and what one does not know."[5] In answer to Fan Hsu's question the Master said, "To love one's fellow-men is Manhood-at-its best. To know them is to have knowledge."

Since this was not yet clear to him, the Master continued, "If you will appoint upright persons to the places now help by the crooked, you will be making the crooked straight."

Then Fan Hsu retired and reported the conversation to Pu Shang, "what does he mean?" inquired Fan Hsu.

"Rich indeed are those words of his! When Shun ruled the world, making his selection from the whole group, he elevated Kao Yao to high position, and those who were not Men-at-their-best were set aside. When Tang the victorious, founder of the Yin dynasty, ruled the world, he too, choosing from the whole group, elevated I Yin to high position and those who were not Men-at-their-best were set aside."[6]

The state of realizing our relationship with all, of entering into everything through union with God was considered in India to be ultimate end and fulfilment of humanity. Ravindranath Tagore points out: "The sense of the superiority of man in the scale of creation has not been absent from her mind. But she has had her own idea as to that in which his superiority really consists. It is not in the power of possession but in the power of union. Therefore, India chose her places of pilgrimage wherever there was in nature some special grandeur of beauty, so that his mind could come of its world of narrow necessities and realize its place in the infinite."[7]

Supremacy of Spiritual Knowledge : Indian Context

Dr. Bhagvatsharan Upaddhyay observes that with the advent of Upanishadic cult the rivalry for supremacy in the arena of knowledge between the priest class and warrior class had started. The Kshatriyas were prepared to encroach upon the privileges the Brahmanas enjoyed by from the Vedic times. As against ritualism they advocated rationalism and started patronizing profusely - exponents of Ātma-vidyā. Consequently the Brahmanas also propounded various branches of philosophy. The span of this struggle was quite lengthy stretching down to the 2nd century B.C. and resulted ultimately in the political rise of the priest class. On the one side there were priests like Vashistha, Parshurām, Kātyāyan, Turkāvsheya, Rākshasa, Patanjali and Pushya Mitra Shunga, etc., on the other were scholar kings who include Vishwamitra, Devapi, Janmejaya, Ashwapati Kaikeya, Prawahan Jaibli, Ajatshatru Kasheya, Janak Videh, Parshwa Mahavir, Buddha, Vrihadrath, etc.[8] In the *Mahābhārata* we come across many glimpses of this rivalry, such as between Vashistha and Vishwamitra, etc. An example of such a rivalry has been elaborated in the *Rāmāyana* also.

The details of the struggle that took place between Vashishtha and Vishvamitra over the possession of the divine cow Savala shows that the wealth (specially in cattle) of the asrama excited the king's cupidity; he claimed it on the ground that all treasures belong to the king; on opposition he offered various fabulous substitutes as a price, viz. heaps of silver, 14,000 gold-bedecked elephants, 800 golden four-horsed chariots, 1,000 noble horses, any amount of gold and gems; on continued resistance Vishvamitra took away the "asrama" cattle by force, taking advantage of his privileges as a guest[9] but he was subsequently attacked by mercenary Saka, Yavana, Pahlava and other barbarians employed by the Vasistha asrama, and was forced to flee from his kingdom. Vishvamitra re-issued from his forest refuge and ravaged the Vashistha monastery, which was burnt and devastated and whence disciples fled by the hundred and thousand. So that for a time it was like a wilderness, but "Vashistha" rallied the monks and stemmed the Kausika aggression successfully in person; frustrated, king Veshvamitra vowed to become a hierarch himself. This whole episode is nothing but the struggle between the head of a powerful monastery and the king of the land, in which the latter is obliged to bow before heretic influence and prestige, but out of which he emerges successful in a sense, by himself becoming the head of a rival monastic order and institution.

After defeat by Vashistha and his monks, king Vishvamitra, along with his queen, went to the South and engaged in Brahman training where four sons were born to them. After sometime he was recognized in asrama circles as a Kshatriyan teacher (Rajarsi).

Warrior Class and Education

There aware numerous references in the Upanishads where the Kshatriyas are represented as the wisest teachers of spiritual knowledge. But it is needless to multiply examples here. In the Mahabharata their accounts are available in several episodes like Sulbhaakhyan, etc. In the history of Hindu religion and philosophy this warrior class enjoyed a very covetous place. The Upanishads mark a new era in the history of human knowledge. This knowledge "did not belong to any Brahmin before, it belonged in all the worlds to the Kshatriya class (warrior class) alone."

From the internal evidences of the Mahabharata, it is obvious that there were mainly two trends of thought in the society - path of knowledge and path of ritualism. The former leads to salvation whereas the latter leads to heaven and involves several rituals described in the Vedas and allied scriptures. The path of knowledge advocated monism and expressly opposed ritualism. The advocates and exponents of this trend were various famous kings such as Videh Janak, Kaikay Ashvapati, Panchal, etc. They used to arrange and patronize various seminars and assemblies of scholars in which elaborate debates *(shastrartha)* were held in order to affirm and synthesize various currents of thinking about Moksha (salvation) and to open new vistas for further deliberation since "वादे वादे जायते तन्त्वबोध:". True knowledge is obtained through discussion and debate has been our age-old contention. In the Mahabharata it is said that in the place of Videh Janak about a hundered scholars (sages and other masters of various branches of learning) used to stay everyday.[10]

Scholar Kings

There was a good rapport between the priests *(purohits)* and these scholar kings. To the history of Indian philosophy these scholar-kings have contributed substantially, an account of which is recorded in various Upanishads, particularly the Chhandogya Upanishad. In fact the age of the epic was predominantly the age of sacrifices, when prolonged and expensive sacrifices were performed by the kings. Some of the sacrifices continued even for twelve years, which an ordinary king could not afford. But for the Dwapar age, sacrifice has been mentioned as the noble one.[11]

In the Epic age the rulers were almost from the warrior class. Besides the mastery in using arms and various martial arts they used to have indepth study of the Vedas and other scriptures.

In the *Rāmāyana* (1.80.27 ff.), the list of subjects the king is expected to study includes Dhanurveda, Veda, Nitisastra and the art *(siksha)* of elephants and cars, besides the arts of painting *(Alekhya)*, writing *(Lekhya)*, jumping *(langhana)*, and swimming *(plavana)*. In another passage we have mention of writing and numbers *(Lekhyasamkhya)*, of fine arts (Gandharvavidya), logic *(Nyaya)*, polity *(Nitisastra)*, etc.

There are several similar lists in the Mahabharata. Reference has already been made to two such lists (XIII, 104, 125;I, H), where we have mentioned *Sabdasastram* and the sixty-four Kalas together with *Yuktisastram* (i.e. Grammar, fine arts and etiquette). Another list enumerates the following (ii, 11, 25); *Ashtanga-ayurveda* (medicine with its eight branches), Rigveda, Samaveda, Yajurveda, Atharvaveda, Sarvashastrani, Itihasas, Upavedas, Vedangas, Vani of seven kinds, Samas, Shrutisastras (teatises of hymns), various kinds of Gatha literature, Bhashyas *(bhashyani tarkayuktani)*, Nataka, Kāvyas, Kathakhyayikas (Karikah). Hopkins holds the view that probably this list is earlier than the previous one, but both show that "the line of education was away from the Veda and that what time the princes was given to culture, not to religion.".

Hopkins further holds that "as the old royal personal fighting days ended that is, as the princes were more and more expected to be figure heads in war; and drove into battle to watch it from an elephant's back rather than it in a war-car, their older bow-and-sword training was given up; and the time so gained was spent in more effeminate, certainly not more truly intellectual occupations. Perhaps the late Virata, with the cowardly little crown-prince, shows us the step between."

Requisite Qualities of Kings

According to the Mahabharata[12] the king must be learned, receptive, highly witted, of high calibre. The subjects of studies meant for the kings as mentioned above can easily be visualized in Duryodhana's description of various kings who came to participate in the Rajsuya Sacrifice performed by Yudhishthira, though it exaggerated but one can find the truth in the following lines —

आयस्ति ये वै राजानः सत्यसन्धा महाव्रताः ।
पर्याप्तविद्या वक्तारो वेदावभृथाप्लुताः ।।
धृतिमन्तो ह्रीनिषेधा धर्मात्मानो यशास्विनः ।[13]

From the above, it is clear that the kings were not only fond of various branches of learning but were also experts in selected branches of learning. Venkumar king Prithu had profound scholarship in *Vedavedang*, Ved of the bow and Dandniti (statecraft).[14] Yudhisthira was expert in Vedas, moral religious matters.[15] Bhishma was well-versed in several lores including Itihas, puran, spiritual science, Vedas, statecraft, etc.

In Adi Parvan (1.22ff.) the Pandu princes are described as having studied all the Vedas and the various shastras or treatises on duty, etc. Bhishma was a great scholar of his time. He brought up Dhritrashtra, Pandu and Vidur like his own sons. They are described as being purified by the ceremonies of their order, disciplined by study and the vows and practices of studentship and emerging into manhood skilled in studies, Veda-vedangas, archery, polity and various martial arts. Pandu excelled in archery and Dhritrashtra in physical strength.

Though many kings were well-versed in Veda-vedangas they never indulged in priesthood,which was the privilege of the Brahmins exclusively. As it has been specified by the law-givers like Manu, teaching performing sacrifices for others and receiving gifts are special to Brahmins. Similarly "defence or protection of his people" was special to Kshatriyas (the warrior class). According to R.K. Mookerji, "It is also to be noted that such study as was enjoined for a kshatriya might make him sufficiently proficient in the Veda to be able to teach, and teach a Brahmin student who should not go without education for a failure of a Brahmin teacher. Thus, normally, the Kshatriya was only to study and the Brahmin to study as also to teach and perform sacrifices for others. It is thus evident that the study as a qualification of teaching and direction of religious practices will be different in scope and method from that which is followed by occupations not directly depending on or connected with it."[16]

Knowledge and Thought

In Greek thinking "knowledge is perception" was held by the atomist and the sophist. Protagoras and Gorgias are important for holding this theory. In the same way Socrates, Plato and Aristotle are the chief critics of the theory that knowledge is perception. For Socrates and Plato, knowledge means what is universal and valid, that is, consistant and free contradicion. But knowledge cannot be perception according to the definition of knowledge. Perception is momentary and relative to different person, because the perception is what it appears to the perceiving subject, and for him alone. As such each man is the measure of what appears to him true at the moment of its occurrence. In the western philosophy this is knows as the doctrine of *homo measura*, which may appear to be false to others. Indirectly here there is the liar's paradox which looms large in the philosophy of Russel.

Perception and thought both of these are subjective, but there is a slight difference. "According to Democritus, knowledge is due to the motion of atoms. Perception and thought both are due to colision of atoms. In perception the atomic motion is coarse and rough. In thought motion is fine and gentle. *Hence perception and thought do not differ in kind, but only in degree.*[17]

Regarding subjectiveness of the knowledge transcendental which is occupied not so much with objects as with our *a priori* concepts of objects, and with our modes of correlating our experience into knowledge. There are two grades or stages in this process of working up the raw material of sinsation into finished product of thought. The first stage is the coordination of sensations by applying to them the forms of perception—space and time; the second stage is the coordination of the perceptions so developed by applying to them. The forms of conception—the categories of thought.[18]

Presenting an overview of pure reason (which is to mean knowledge) of Immanuel Kant. Will Wurant says:

"At the outset, then Kant flings down a challenge to Locke and the English school. Knowledge is not all derived from the senses, Hume thought he had shown that there is no soul, and no science, that our minds are but our ideas in processon and association, and our certainties but probabilities in perpetual danger of violation. These false conclusions, says Kant, are the result of false premises. You assume that all knowledge comes from "separate and distinct" sensations, naturally these cannot give you necessity, or invariable sequences of which you may be for ever certain. And naturally you must not expect to see your soul, even with the eyes of internal sense….."Further Kant says: "My question is, what we can hope to achieve with reason, when all the material and assistance of experience are taken away.[19]

In fact Kant maintains that there cannot be absolutism with knowledge truth and science. Therefore, there is always scope of logic and reasoning. Knowledge coupled with reasoning happens to be more stronger and effective, may it be the arena of Religion or philosophy, polity or history. This is what he expresses in the preface of *"Critique of Pure Reason"*. It is the rationality which makes a man to think: Christ has brought the kingdom of God nearer to earth; but he has been misunderstood; and in place of God's kingdom, the kingdom of the priest has been established among us.[20] "But excess of Reasoning has also its demerits, as it makes a man more sceptical and incredulous. Swami Vivekananda says: "The practical side of Vedantic morality is necessary as much today as it ever was more necessary, perhaps, than it ever was, for all this privilege claiming has become tremendously intensified with the extension of knowledge. The idea of God and the Devil has a good deal of poetry in it. The difference between God and the Devil is in nothing except in unselfishness and selfishness. The Devil knows as much as God, is as powerful as God; only he has no holiness; that makes him a Devil. Apply the same idea to the modern world; excess of knowledge and power, without holiness, makes human beings devils.[21] Thus we can say that reason should have a positive attitude, holy and pious intention, otherwise it may be detrimental not only for an individual; but, at times, for entire group.

According to the rationalists, the essence of religion lies in our reason or thought. Man's belief in God without reasons would simply be purely subjective. It is reason which guarantees the objectivity and universality of religion. According to Hegel, religion is the divine spirit's knowledge of itself through the meditation of finite spirit. It involves the ultimate unity of the finite and the infinite. Hegel's view has been criticized as his definition of religion is too much intellectual. He emphasises the intellectual aspect or the logical character of God or Absolute and disregarded the conative and volitional aspect. Religion, however, it is not the knowledge of God only but it is an immediate communion with him. Religion without feeling of devotion and religious practices would be a mere abstraction. Religious feelings cannot be separated from its intellectual content. E. Eroll Harris is right to say that, "Religion, in short, is the name for one's total conscious attitude towards life, as it is formed and enlightened by rational awareness and knowledge. Science, in narrower sense, is an integral and indispensable factor in this and in the wider sense, which includes philosophy, it is identical with it. Whichever name one uses and in whatever sense, practical and theoretical aspects are mutually implicated though they may be distinguished, they are never separable".[22] Thus we can say that there is no substantial difference among religion, science and philosophy as far as their aim and objective are concerned since all the three aims at the betterment of human life and peaceful and harmonious society at large.

Knowledge and Faith

If religious consciousness is analysed in term of psychological states we come accross with three elements, i.e. thinking, feeling and willing. In the Eastern Philosophy these elements are inter-related. But the Western thinker like Schliermacher and others hold that feeling is the essence of religion and it cannot consist in knowledge because it is found that many illiterates are also religious minded. The perception of knowledge is quite narrow and one-sided because only literacy is taken as knowledge which is not so. In fact no religion can survive without intellect and activity. But we cannot deny the fact that illiterates can easily be victimised by so called gurus and they suffer from dogmas and superstitions.

Thus we see that faith appears to occupy a kind of middle position in human life; it is neither purely practical nor purely theoretical, but something of both. Commenting on the relationship between knowledge and faith Prof. S.K. Ghosh has rightly observed: "The latter (knowledge) is prompted by an intellectual or an emotional interest, or by both but which does not rest on systematic insight. Faith, on the other hand, is an act of spiritual and self-conscious person who affirms the religious values, and God the supreme value, it be essential to his own soul and to the meaning of the world. It is movement of the conscious and free self which expresses the needs and states the postulates of the spiritual life. Faith so conceived is neither partial nor wavering but speaks of full assurances and an abiding ideal. To deny faith is to deny the spiritual and idealistic view of human life and destiny. Faith is too deeply rooted in human nature and too closely linked with the forward outlook of human life."[23] He further adds: "knowledge and faith are like movements which develop within the wider whole of life and are the outcome of personal and purposive activity of man. Having this much in common, they are otherwise different in their outlook and way of working. Knowledge proceeds by discovering relations between the parts of existence. The process of knowing is a process of eliciting the connection of things and relating them to one another The ideal of knowledge is rationality, or insight into connections of elements within a systematic whole. The work of rationalising ends with unrationalised elements, the individual is not exhausted by the sum of its relations and the process of assigning causes and condition concludes with a confession of ignorance. Hence, the idea of completeness and system, which inspires knowledge is not itself realised by knowledge but is held by faith."[24]

Here it needs mention that above analysis of Mr. Ghosh is based on materialistic knowledge and the spiritual one. Spiritual knowledge has different identity which is based on totally different type of experience. It is said that "the knowledge that Shri Vasudev is dwelling in the heart of every living creature is the eternal and abiding principle of Sanatana Dharma (eternal religion)."[25]

Knowledge, as explained in the beginning, can be classified into two categories knowledge about the world, and knowledge about the supernatural phenomena, which has been termed as Apara (worldly) and para (divine or otherworldly) respectively in the Hindu scriptures. In both the spheres of knowledge teacher has an important role to play. But in the sphere of supernatural knowledge greater importance is attached to gum. It is so because what we call the supernatural or God or supreme consciousness, the self or the Brahman does not belong to the sensory world. The Self cannot be experienced through the five senses - touch, taste, hearing, smell and visualisation. The supreme consciousness is to be realised at a level which is not gross, not even the level of Extra Sensory Perception (ESP); but a subtler level beyond mind and intellect. That is why in this sphere Guru is not only significant but also indispensable.

Here is a piece of advice of a great sage Vyas. Describing the character of knowledge he says:

"Observance of simplicity in words and deeds only leads to attainment of supreme self (Brahma), whereas crookedness meets its own death. This is the essence of knowledge. Rest is futile exercise of mind and speech."[26]

We would like to conclude this chapter with the following illustration of the great Master, Confucious:

"Their knowledge being complete, their thoughts were sincere, their thoughts being sincere, their hearts were then rectified. Their hearts being rectified, their persons were cultivated. Their persons being cultivated, their families were regulated. Their families being regulated, their states were rightly governed, the whole kingdom was made tranquil and happy."[27]

REFERENCES

1. Max Weber, *Aufsatze zur religionsogiologie*, II, pp. 364-65.
2. असक्तबुद्धिः सर्वत्र जितात्मा विगतस्पृहः ।
नैष्कर्म्यसिद्धिं परमां संन्यासेनाधिगच्छति ॥
— Mahabharata, Bhishma Parvan 40.49
3. तत्र संसारचक्रस्य मोक्षो ज्ञानेन दृश्यते ।
अध्यात्मतत्वविज्ञानं ज्ञानमित्यभिधीयते ॥
— *Ibid.*, Anushashan Parvan, Ch. 145
4. न चाप्यक्षीणपापस्य ज्ञानं भवति देहिनः ।
ज्ञानोपलब्धिर्भवति कृतकृत्यो यदा भवेत् ॥
— *Ibid.*, Anushashan Parvan Ch.96
5. *Sayings of Confucious*, II.17.
6. *Ibid.*, XII.22.
7. Ravindranath Tagore, *Sadhana*, p.8.
8. *Bhartiya Samaj ka Aitihasik Anusheelan*, pp.107-108.
9. In Mahabharata (Anushashan Parvan) there are a few episodes depicting extraordinary privileges allowed to the guests.
10. तस्य स्म शतमाचार्या वसन्ति सततं गृहे ।
दर्शयन्तः पृथग्धर्मान्नाना पाषण्डवादिनः ॥
— Mahabharata XII.224.27
11. ततः परं कृतयुगे त्रेतायां ज्ञानमुत्तमम् ।
द्वापरे यज्ञमाहुर्दानिमेव कलौ युगे ॥
— Mababharata XII.224.27
12. Mahabharata, XII.118.10–18.
13. Mahabharata II.49. 1-2.
14. *Ibid.*, XII.59.105-106.
15. *Ibid.*, XII.16.5, 19.1.
16. *Ancient Indian Education*, 3rd Edition, p.337.
17. Quoted in '*A critical History of Western Philosophy*' by Y. Masib, p.182
18. Will Durant, *Story*, pp.267-68.
19. Quoted from *Story*, pp. 265-66.
20. Quoted from *Story*, p.280.
21. *What Religion Is*, p.47.
22. E. Eroll Hariss, *Revelation through Science and Philosophy*, (London, 1958), p.28.
23. S.K. Ghosh, *Philosophy of Religion*, p.80.
24. *Ibid.*, p.81.
25. भगवान् वासुदेवो हि सर्वभूतेष्ववस्थितः ।
एतज्ज्ञानं हि सर्वस्य मूलं धर्मस्य शाश्वतम् ॥ — Mahabharata
26. सर्वं जिह्मं मृत्युपदमार्जवम् ब्रह्मणः पदम् ।
एतावान् ज्ञानविषयः किं प्रलापः करिष्यति ॥
— Mahabharata XV.11.4
27. *Living Thoughts of Confucious*, p.41.

8

WORK CULTURE AND CONFUCIANISM

"Great Man abstains from what he does not know. If the designations are not accurate, language will not be clear. If language is not clear, duties will not be carried out. If duties are not carried out, rites and music will not flourish, then punishment will not be specific. If punishments are not specific, then the people will do nothing without getting into trouble. Hence when Great Man has given something a name it may with all certainty be expressed in language, when he expresses it, it may with certainty be set in operation. In regard to his language Great Man is never careless in any respect."

— Confucious

Cultural Postulates

As every culture needs a sort of philosophical base, in the same way work culture is also based on some philosophy. Besides the value tenets which are explained below our work-culture has some philosophical bases also. Religion and Philosophy are interdependent. Both stand in relation to man only. That is why they are able to provide guidance for an ideal work culture. Law of Karma is one of them. Dr. S. Radhakrishnan says : "The Law of Karma is not to be confused with either a hedonistic or a juridical theory of rewards and punishments. The reward of virtue for virtue is not a life of pleasure nor is the punishment for sin and pain. Pleasure and pain may govern the animal nature of man but not his human. Love which is a joy in itself suffers; hatred too often means perverse kind of satisfaction. Good and evil are not to be confused with material well-being and physical suffering."[1]

For any good work-culture harmonious ethical and personnel management is necessary which may result into a smooth human relationship between two persons or among the group. Confucius has laid a great stress on virtues of the administrator as well as the administered ones. "On this account, the ruler will first take pains about his own virtues. Possessing virtue will give him the people. Possessing people will give him territory. Possessing the territory will give him its wealth. Possessing the wealth, he will have resources for expenditure."[2] He adds: Virtue is the root; wealth is result."[3] Virtuous acts or deeds will, sooner or later, automatically fetch the fortunes. One need not worry about that. This is what Bhagvadgita says: "Only duty is thy concern, not the fruit".[4] Lord Krishna exhorted Arjuna to perform his duties dwelling in Yoga relinquishing attachment.[5] Maharshi Raman, a great mystic of our time also believed in the theory of karmite laws. He says: "All the actions that the body is to perform are already decided upon at the time it comes into existence, the only freedom you have is whether or not to identify yourself with the body."[6] If one acts a play the whole part is written out before hand and one acts as faithfully whether one is Caesar who is stabbed or Brutus who stabs, being unaffected by it because one knows one is not that person. In the same way he who realizes his identity with the deathless self acts his part on human stage without fear and anxiety, hope or regret, not being touched by the part played.

There is a co-relation between the work and time. Proverbially it is said that time and tide wait for none. No good work-culture can be inculcated without good management of time. Comparing the time with a bright coloured bird Lei Shuyan has rightly said in his poem "Time" that good worker should always value the time, welcome the opportunity lest it is too late. He says:

> That bird that has flown casually
> From the palm of our hand

Is flying farther and farther away
It took its flight at the very moment
When we were hesitating what to do.
When we suddenly realize
That the bright colourful bird
Is the opportunity we can never retrieve
The only thing to do is to shout and chase after it.
The bird used to sing and dance for us
To show tender generosity or to cry warningly to us
But now it has jumped from our palm onto our shoulder.
With agony and anxiety we keep chasing
After the only bird that belongs to ourselves
When it abandons us and flies off
We are deprieved of everything and have nothing left
Oh, that beautiful bird named time.[7]

Human Values and Work Culture

Philosophically speaking values are those standards or a code for moral behaviour conditioned by one's cultural tenets and guarded by conscience, according to which human being is supposed to conduct himself and shape his life-patterns by integrating his beliefs, ideas and attitudes to realize cherished ideals and aims of life. The good of many or all should be taken as sole criterion for values. Psychologically in the context of instructional objectives valuing falls under Affective Domain. Affective domain has five major categories—receiving (attending), responding, valuing, organisation and characterization by value or value complex. The third category valuing includes the individual's commitment to a certain goal, idea or belief. The fourth category builds up a value-system that includes his behaviour. The last category in this texonomy is "Characterization by value or value complex". At this stage of development, the individual acts assiduously and consistently in accordance with the values he has internalised.[8]

In fact, value lacks universal defination. According to Rokeach, Values are beliefs about how one ought or ought not to behave, or about some state of existence worth or not worth attaining. Values are abstract ideals, positive or negative, that represent a person's belief about ideal modes of conduct and ideal terminal goals.[9] A value is a standard we use to influence the values, attitudes and actions of others; it is like yardstick we use to guide the actions, attitudes, comparisons, evaluations, and justifications of ourselves and other.[10]

Cultural tenets are main fountain-heads for various moral, ethical, social and cultural values of the group or the society. That is why the value system of one society or country differs from the other. They are guarded and governed by one's own faith and religion. Practically speaking religion is of two types—Religion eternal and Religion operational or Yuga-dharma. The former stands unchanged irrespective of time and place and so are the eternal values like truth, love, peace, non-violence etc. Whereas the operational values take shape or design as per the time and place. They are subject to change and as such we may call them changeable values.

Human being is not merely the product of a biological process but it has mind and spirit also as its integral constituents. Therefore, the tendencies of the human being also can be perceived at three level—spiritual, mental and physical. Here we will try to streamline the nature and character of human values at these three levels. At each level we will observe certain positive and negative values. Human being has been considering the positive values as adoptable and similarly negative ones as unadoptable. We can explain these three sets of values through the following classifications:

Spiritual Level

Positive (adoptable values)	Negative (unadoptable values)
Faith	Suspicion
Hope	Dispair
Love	Hatred
Truth	Untruth
Constrain	Pretentiousness
Endurance	Anger
Cooperation	Non-cooperartion
Patriotism	Traitorism
Charity	Self-interest

Reverence	Derision
Theism	Atheism

Among the positive spiritual values faith and reverence these two can be called arch values. Famous saint Tuisidas has compared these two values with Lord Shiva and Godess Parvati "Vande Parvati - Parmeshwarau Shraddha - Vishwas – Roopinau". That is why he craves for devotion only to the feet of Rama as the supreme bliss. He says in Ramcharitmanasa (Ayodhakand) – "I aspire neither for dharma, nor for enjoyment, nor for the liberation; but only for devotion to the feet of Rama life after life. No other boon do I crave."

Similarly in Gita the importance of total surrender (*Samarpana*) has been extolled and the way of faith (devotion) has been described as the best one. The man who constantly adores and worships the Supreme Lord is beloved of Him. Such a man never comes to grief. The Isha Upanishad has decried "those who flaunt their empty knowledge : Those into blinding darkness. But those who delight in theoretical knowledge are even more misled".[11]

When religion is conceived and practised in the right perspective it is bound to bring about a peaceful revolution for making people happier. Dr. Radhakrishnan has rightly observed, "There are certain inmost sanctities of human life which ought to be preserved. The aim of life is not merely to create an earthy Utopia, but to attain a higher and intenser form of consciousness. The pictures of Shiva, Buddha and hundreds of other saints illustrates the truth grasped by Plato, and Aristotle also, that the supreme end of man is contemplation, the freedom and peace of understanding."[12]

According to Confucious, "The first ingredient of humaneness is to have an attitude of reverence in human relationship, as if one were taking part in a religious ceremony, or at least to behave with ceremoniousness and sense of propriety required when receiving an honoured guest. The second ingredient is to show consideration for the feelings of others by not doing to them what you would not like them to do to you, a sentiment which has been compared unfavourably with the golden rule of the Gospels : "Do unto others as you would want that others should do unto you."[13]

Mental Level

Positive (adoptable values)	Negative (Unadoptable values)
Ambition	Aimlessness
Resolution	Unsteadiness
Simplicity	Complexity
Friendship	Enmity
Wisdom	Doltishness
Optimism	Pessimism
Self-confidence	Self-deception

For worldly progress of human beings ambition is one of the motivative factors. It leads a person to resolve to achieve the goal. Simplicity, friendship and wisdom are the tools or ways for the journey. Optimism and self-confidence are main source of strength in a person. Many men recognise the predominance of destiny, fortune or luck, while others believe in individual efforts. In Indian culture four aims (*Purusharthas*) have been mentioned—Piety, worldly prosperity, gratification of senses and liberation. Of these first three are mere *purusharthas*, whereas liberation (*Moksha*) is the supreme object of human pursuit. Individual effort is the dominant factor in the pursuit of piety and liberation. One who relegates these two to the sphere of destiny remains deprived of their benefit.

Regarding the principle of friendship Confucious has candidly advised : "Friendship should be maintained without any presumption on the ground of one's superior age, or station, or the circumstances of his relatives. Friendship with a man is friendship with his virtue, and does not admit of assumptions of superiority."[14]

Physical Level

Positive (adoptable values)	Negative (Unadoptable values)
Non-violence	Violence
Expertness	Clumsiness
Carefulness	Carelessness
Clarity	Confusion
Pleasure	Agony
Zeal	Idleness
Strength	Lassitude

Our vision and verve can play better if we have clarity of visualizing and for handling the thing or the work in hand. If satisfaction is there one will derive the pleasure out of it. This type of pleasure may generate zeal and strength in man and he will be able to work with regour and vigour. By working with full zeal he will reach his destination. But for this sincere efforts are very essential. "Sincerity is that whereby self-completion is effected and its way is that by which man must direct himself. Sincerity is the end and beginning of things; without sincerity one does not accomplish the self-completion of himself. With this quality he completes other mean and things also."[15]

In spite of the desirability of individual's freedom, one has to conform his deeds and action as per the norms of the concerned organisation. An efficient organisation should also appreciate and encourage these innovative practices of the functionaries allowing them a sort of desired autonomy in the selected areas so that overall interest of the organisation is safe-guarded. Prof. A.N. Whitehead has rightly said "For the great professional organizations, so long as they are efficient, should be able to demonstrate the dangers of extravagant notions. In this way, where sudden action is not in question, reason has obtained an entrenchment which should be impregnable. Indeed, individual freedom, standing apart from organisation, has now its indispensable role. For all organizations are liable to decay, and licence for outside criticism is the best safeguard for the professions."

If each individual strive hard to shape and concretise healthy work-culture the society will definitely reach the penackles of glory. For development of such noble work-culture in each of the dealings of the individual some positive and constructive value-orientation is a must. In this context Confucious talk about *Cultivation of persons*. It depends upon the rectifying of mind. He says : "If a man be under the influence of passion, he will be incorrect in his conduct. He will be the same, if he is under the influence of terror, or under the influence of fond regard, or under that of sorrow and distress.

When the mind is not present, we look and do not see; we hear and do not understand; we eat and do not know the taste of what we eat.

"This is what is meant by saying that the cultivation of the person depends on the rectifying of the mind."[16]

Similar tips have been given for the ruler or the administrator to regulate his own conduct as he stands as the guiding star for the people. When the ruler treats compassionately the young and helpless, the people also follow his footprints. Following these hints of Confucious he can regulate his own conduct :

"What a man dislikes in his superiors, let him not display in the treatment of his inferiors; what he dislikes in inferiors, let him not display in the service of his superiors; what he hates in those who are before him, let him not therewith precede those who are behind him; what he hates in those who are behind him, let him not therewith follow those who are before him; what he hates to receive on the right, let him not bestow on the left; what he hates to receive on the left, let him not bestow on the right: this is what is called "The principle with which, as with a measuring- square, to regulate one's conduct."[17]

Cultural Priorities

The then Prime Minister of Japan, Mr. Masayoshi Ohira, in January, 1979, initiated several Study Groups in Japan with certain interesting terms of reference. They were, "The Garden City State Concept Study Group", "The Age of Culture Study Groug", "The Study Group on Economic Performance in the Cultural Age", "The Historical Evolution of Science and Technology Study Group", etc. The reports of these groups are published by the "Foundation for Advanced Information and Research, Japan". The reports recognise that rapid industrialisation had produced what were referred to as the "advanced nations diseases", in the societal structure. One of such is the "growth of individualisation". They create neurotic individualistic possessive tendencies, characteristic of an acquisitive society. These tendencies, the reports predicated, produce a conflict with the growing consensus for evolving a cultural society and fostering of interdependence. The Report[18] on the Historical Evolution of Science and Technology says :

"In the highly industrialized society isolated and alienated individuals have created the main cause of 'illness' of civilized countries which has reduced significantly the vitality of the society. It may be interpreted as an expansion of the living space of mankind being limited by the barrier of "finiteness of the globe". "..... Life, for instance, cannot be understood simply as an aggregate of elements but the concept of self-organisation is the most important key to understand various life phenomena. It has been remarked in recent years that cells in a living body transforms energy from one form to another directly and very efficiently, by the co-operation of the whole and individual elements. This is a subject to be studied in the context of 'holonic path' concept."

Economic Management

Speaking of the "Economic Management in the Age of Cultural Priorities" the Report says :

"In order to secure existence with honour and vitality in the coming 2lst century, what harmony should be realized between people, culture and economic principle and how should economic management be undertaken? The following five basic philosophies may be sought after in economic management in the age of cultural priorities :

(1) Respect for humanity
(2) Respect for Independence
(3) Respect for Creativity
(4) Respect for Regionality
(5) Respect for Internationality."

Referring to what the values are, the Report says :

"In any age and in any society, if a question is made to the people living therein, 'Are you happy?', not a few of them would answer, 'Yes'. There exist some fundamental life values, including the feeling of happiness and worthiness of life, which will not change, even if time elapses and the environment changes. They are something relating to the essence of people's desires. However, the latter assumes various forms in the current of times, diversifies the contents of 'life values' and thus appears as the change. It is, therefore, important in the study of 'life values' to grasp the essence of people's desires which does not vary with the lapse of time and then study the change of life values in the current of time."

Referring to *Modernisation* in the West, the Report says:

"The 'modern age' was ushered in with the industrial and civil revolutions in Europe. In science, this took the form of 'atomism'; in politics, economics, and society, it gave birth to 'individualism'. The Latin word 'individual' and the Greek word 'atom' are identical in meaning."

Referring to the "*Affluent Society at a Turning Point*", the Report says :

"Faced with a deteriorating natural and living environment, scientific and technological stagnation, resource and energy restrictions, and the worsening trade-off between energy restrictions, and the worsening trade-off between demand control and welfare policies, the economic vitality of the developed countries has failed. In addition, they are plagued by the "developed nations' disease", symptoms of which are deep-rooted-inflation, slowing economic growth, growing unemployment, loss of vitality in the private sector, the decline of business activity (loss of incentives to invest), government bankruptcy and huge fiscal deficits, balance of payments deficits, etc."

Second is a cultural and social viewpoint. The affluent society has altered the desires, behavioural patterns and social structures of its people.

These changes include the formation of a new middle class, the fragmentation of values, and the appearance of a social pathological 'phenomenon', the so-called "advanced nations' syndrome", in rich societies.

Modernity and Modernization

The influence of centuries of modernization and industrialization on society has been the appearance of the British 'disease', or more generally, the "developed nations' disease" or the 'Civilization disease'. This malaise affects not only the economies of the countries involved, but its symptoms penetrate the political and social spheres as well. As a result, the advanced industrial societies are faced not only with declining economic vitality, but also with a variety of manifestations of anomie, such as decreasing political unity, terrorism, crime, juvenile delinquency, suicide, anxiety and depression, alcoholism, drug addiction, the loss of the will to work, and sexual confusion."

Does the ancient Indian tradition have any answers to these growing myths of modernity? "No other country on our planet earth", said a well-known artiste, "has nourished and integrated human aspirations and spiritual wisdom in an amazing continuity for more than four thousand years, than this continent called India. From the beginning of time, perhaps even further back than imagination can take us, there is evidence of a sophisticated culture with both a social and political order."

The artiste said: "The guru-shishya parampara emphasised the importance of learning and hermitages were their places of dwelling. Our civilization was born from nature, the greatest thoughts were nurtured amongst sylvan surroundings. Students came from far and wide away and were integrated into a highly intellectual approach to living."

Gurudev Rabindranath Tagore said of India :

"I love India, not because I cultivate the idolatry of geography, not because I have had the chance to be born in her soil, but because she has saved through tumultuous ages the living words that have issued from the illuminated consciousness of her greater sons : Brahma is Truth, and the unity of all beings is in Brahma."

Without the development of the inner culture of man all our worldly possessions become the means of his own destruction, science and technology, if recognised as ethic-neutral, will surely destroy our great civilisation. Without a perception of the morality of the means and ends intellect becomes a self-stultifying instrument. The scornful impatience of the egoist wrecks his mission.

The ideals of the ancient Indian culture are not only *Atmoddhara* but also *Jagath hithaya*. Without respect for ethical principles, an acquisitive society cannot ensure happiness of its members. Indeed as Aldous Huxley points out :

> "The ethical doctrines taught in the Tao Te Ching, by Gautama Buddha and his followers on the Lesser and above all the Greater Vehicle, in the Sermon on the Mount and by the best of the Christian saints, are not dissimilar. Among human beings who have reached a certain level of civilisation and of personal freedom from passion and social prejudice there exists a real consensus gentium in regard to ethical first principles."

Indeed, happiness is the result of *Iṇdriya jaya*. If the leaders of the polity do not possess this attainment, the consequence will be that the political organisation will be corroded from within. Political power will then be perceived as an instrument of plunder and those exercising such power seek to perpetuate their own power irrespective of the morality of the means.

If we go through the various media reports on socio-economic affairs of East Asia in general and Indian subcontinent in particular during the current decade we will see that the words like *Value-based politics*, *morality of the means*, *social service* etc. have lost their dictionary meaning and have been relegated to the background of history. Political leaders are loosing fast their credibility and political powers perceived as an instrument of plunder. But we cannot change this scenerio overnight by any magic or super-natural power. Daisakuikeda has rightly said :

"Nonetheless, it is often difficult to keep even organizations formed on lofty principles operating on a high level of morality and spirituality since the act of organizing automatically involves authority, which in turn generates desire for advantages and fame. In spite of the need to ensure that only the noblest and the wisest achieve them. Places of great authority are frequently secured by persons whose sole motivation is the desire for power or glory."[19]

Though this statement is from the religious context, but it is equally true in politics. Moreover, in both the areas their means and modes are the same, *modus operandi* is the same, tools and techniques are also more or less the same. Point of difference is a group of sufferers only. In the religious organization its detrimental effect is on the spiritual level of the general membership; whereas when the political leaders get corrupted its overall impact is on the various spheres of the society.

According to Confucious, Government is a matter of setting moral example. By quoting three Analects of Confucius Raymond Dawson has tried to trace the foundations of work-culture particularly in the Government Machinary as envisaged by the Ancient Master in the following manner:

Chi K'ang-tzu asked about inducing the people to be respectful and loyal so that they might be encouraged to support him. The Master said : 'if you approach them with dignity, they will respect you. If you are dutiful towards your parents and kind to your children, then they will be loyal. If you promote the good and instruct the incompetent, then they will be encouraged.' (A 2.20)

Someone said to Confucius : 'Why do you not take part in government?' The Master said : 'What does the Book of History say about filial piety? "Only by dutiful towards your parents and friendly towards your brothers, and you will be contributing to government." These virtues also constitute taking part in government.' (A 2.21)

Chi K'ang-tzu asked Confucius about government. Confucius replied saying : 'To govern means to rectify. If you were to lead the people by means of rectification, who would dare not to be rectified?' (A 12.17)

The first of these three quotations shows how the moral

example of the ruler is expected to be reciprocated by the people. Government was largely a matter of operating in the wider context of the state with virtues which were really more appropriate within the narrower context of the family. The ruler must practise filial piety and then his subjects will practise the parallel virtue of loyalty towards him. He must instruct and encourage his subjects as a father instructs and encourages his children. The saying also mentions promotion on merit, a common theme in the late Chou period when there was general hostility towards the old system of hereditary office.

The second quotation gives consolation to those who have no political power by saying that the practice of social virtues within the family must itself make a real contribution to government, since it is contributing to the social harmony which is the purpose of government. So this is the Confucian version of the people's participation in government: they respond to examples sent down from above and contribute to the order of the state by securing harmony within the family, one of the microcosmic units of which the macrocasm of the state is composed. As we saw earlier, this Confucian message was used by imperial governments for the purpose of political control. If clans had their own moral codes and were largely capable of policing themselves, the task of the government in trying to secure civil order was made much easier. From the state's point of view it was convenient if the people contributed to stability and harmony by contentedly practising the constant norms of human behaviour within their families. The precepts of Confucius about government often seem appropriate only to a small and cosy community, and it is remarkable that they should have provided the ideology of an enormous bureaucratic state. This could only happen because of the age-old dogma that the state was the family writ large, and the belief that the family virtues were a structural part of the cosmic order.

Finally, the reply to Chi K'ang-tzu depends on the fact that the words for 'to govern' and 'to rectify' were etymologically related to each other. The task of government was to rectify society and so restore it to ancient virtues. The same word is used in the expression *cheng ming*, 'the rectification of names'. This emphasis on rectification remained a keynote of Chinese political thought, so that political reform has generally been seen as rectification rather than innovation. It has generally been regarded as an attempt to get back to ancient wisdoms and ancient ways, and to understand the teaching of the ancients more clearly and restore society to the norms that they laid down.

What Must a Man be Like Before he Can Take Part in Government?

Confucious was asked the above question by Tzu-chang. The Master said, "If he exhalts the five excellent practices and eschews the five wicked practices he can take part in government."[20]

Five Excellent Practices

1. The gentleman is generous without its costing him anything.
2. He works with others hard without their complaining.
3. He has desires without being greedy.
4. He is causal without being arrogant.
5. He is awe-inspiring without appearing fierce.

According to Confucious *four wicked practices* are as following :

1. To impose the death penalty without first attempting to reform is to be cruel.
2. To expect results without first giving warning to be tyrannical.
3. To insist on a time-limit when tardy in issuing orders is to cause injury.
4. When something has to be given to others anyway, to be miserly in the actual giving is to be officious.

Confucious further adds :

"If a man benefits the common people by taking advantage of the things around them what they find beneficial, is this not being generous without its costing him anything? If a man, in working others hard, chooses burdens they can support, who will complain? If, desiring benevolence, a man obtains it, where is the greed? The gentleman never dare neglect his manners whether he be dealing with the many or the few, the young or the old. Is this not being causal without being arrogant? This gentleman, with his robe and cap adjusted properly and dignified in his gaze, has a presence which inspires people who see him with awe. Is this not being awe-inspiring without appearing fierce."[21]

REFERENCES

1. *An Idealist View of Life*, p. 218.
2. *Confucious*, ed. by Alfred Doeblin, p.47.
3. *Ibid.*
4. *Bhagvadgita* II. 47.
5. *Ibid.*II. 48.
6. *Raman Maharshi*, Ed. by Arthur Osborne, p.35.
7. *Chinese Literature*, Ed. by Tang Jialong, p. 150.
8. For details the author's following books are worth referring - *Value Education: Theory and Practice* (1986), *A Search for Human Values* (1992).
9. Rokeach, *Beliefs, Attitudes and Values*, p. 124.
10. *Ibid.*, p. 160.
11. *The Isha Upanishad*, Shloka-9.
12. *Religion and Society*, p.68.
13. Raymond Dawson, *Confucious*, pp. 40-41.
14. *The Living Thoughts of Confucious*, p. 119.
15. Alfred Doeblin, *Living Thoughts of Confucious*, p. 59.
16. Alfred Doeblin (Edn.), *Ibid.*, p. 44.
17. *Ibid.*, p. 46.
18. Report published by "Foundation for Advanced Information and Research Japan" in 1979.
19. Daisakuikeda and Bryan Wilson, *Human Values in a Changing World*, p. 100.
20. *Confucious* by Raymond Dawson, pp. 67-68.
21. *Confucious : The Analects*, pp. 159-60.

9

ZEN-CULT
Fusion of Complexity and Simplicity

"The simplicity, however, does not always mean the obliteration of all complexity. In some cases, especially under the influence of Zen-cult, the Japanese endeavoured to infuse unlimited complexity into this simplicity.

This tendency emerged especially in such arts as architecture, drawing, and poetry. For example, the void of empty spaces or of silent pauses is often not devoid, in fact of important meaning. Even in the etiquette and conversation of everyday life, silence can be very positive expression at times. The ideal fusion of the complex and the simple was realised by the Chinese people, who loved complicated thinking and whose spiritual life was greatly influenced by Zen-cult, when introduced into Japan, however, this too, was altered by greater simplification."

— Hajime Nakamura[1]

Historically speaking Zen is the Japanese counterpart of the Chinese word 'Ch'an' which is obviously derived from the Sanskrit word 'dhyan' (meditation) which leads to insight. Here it needs mention that as a corollary from its non-theistic basis Buddhism which dispenses with prayer. In view of the degree to which in many other religions, prayer has been abused and debarred by being employed for procuring divine bliss in variou : forms. Instead of prayer Buddha laid emphasis on various types of meditation. Of which the following four are very significant:

1. Meditation on the impurity of body.
2. On the evils which arise from sensation.
3. On the impermanence of ideas.
4. On the conditions of existence.

Zen-Buddhism is more and more ethical in its character and also easier and simpler to grasp for common people. That is why it became very popular in the Far-East countries like China, Japan etc.

Huston Smith writes: "We choose Zen for these reasons. First many students of religions believe it is the purest form of spirituality in the Far-East today. Second, it gives us an opportunity to look at religion as it has appeared among the Japanese. Third, it is the one religion of the Far-East which as it is breaking upon the West in descriptions and translations that have become available only in our generation is causing philosophers (Heideggar), psychotherapists (Erich Fromm and Hubbert Benoit), Writers (Aldous Huxley), and Artists (Die Zen Gruppe in Germany) to take notice."[2]

Like other Mahayanist or any other sect Zen Buddhists claim to trace is perspective back to Gautama himself. Buddhist sermons were incorporated in Pali Canons, which were easily understood by the masses. The followers of Buddha, of course, received the sermons from their master, a higher angle of vision. The classic instance of this is found his Buddha's Flower Sermon. Standing on a mountain with his disciples around him. On this occasion Buddha did not resort to words, rather he simply held aloft a golden lotus. No one understood the meaning of the eloquent gesture except Maha Kashyap whose quiet smile indicated that he had gotten the point. Therefore, Buddha designated him as his successor. The insight that prompted the smile was transmitted to India through twenty-eight Patriarchs and carried to China in 520 A.D. Bodhidharma. From China it entered into Japan in the 20th century, which contains the secret of Zen.

Highlighting the simplicity and practicability of Jen (Zen) Hajime Nakamura says:

"In other words, our life should be guided by through knowledge of previous examples rather than by meditation. Therefore, Confucianist moral theory insists that the concrete contents of Jen, as "The Way" or practical model for morality, should be taught by other persons as knowledge. However, they did not explain how the moral model given by knowledge is related to Jen (Zen) could be affected by knowledge. Also the *Analects* of Confucious, gave no explanation of why "*Jen*" was the very core of morality itself, nor did they give any explanation of "*Yi*" or "*Ti*" which are concrete and practical matters. Again, they did not explain definitely where the basis for morality should be placed, so that in China, "to learn" meant simply "to search for ancient ways"; consequently, "things" or "meaning" is, in fact, nothing but "things which were taught."[3]

Many history books on Buddhism were composed, especially by Zen Buddhists, on the basis of the genealogy of the transmission of doctrines from master to disciples. The Indians, with their deep respect for universal law or doctrines do not mention the transmission from master to disciples as seriously and minutely as the Chinese do. As a result of this high esteem for the master, the Chinese Zen sects in some instances attach more importance to their founders than to Shakyamuni or the Tathagata. That is why Zen Master Ikkyu calls him (Buddha) "as the mischievous creature", though of course, with deep sense of respect and love.

Alike many items of art, literature, sculpture etc. Japan imported Buddhism also through China. Because complicated words and symbols are not used by the Japanese in their thinking. The philosophical theories of Indian and Chinese Buddhism were too profound, abstruse, and complicated to penetrate into the life of the common people of Japan. Consequently, they had to be made simplified. That is why Zen Master Ikkyu said:

Shakyamuni,
That mischeivous creature
Having appeared in the world,
Misled, alas,
How many people!

Shakyamuni is the Japanese name of Gautam Buddha. Ikkyu is a follower of Gautam Buddha having lot of love and respect for Lord Buddha. The above words about Buddha appear to be joking; but it is not so; since he had tremendous sense of respect and love for Buddha. In this context Rajneesh has aptly observed:

> "If some Christian says such a thing about Jesus 'mischievous' Creature"—all Christians will be very much offended. That person will be immediately excommunicated from the Church; he will be condemned as a sinner. You can't call Jesus a mischievous person, because you have never loved him so deeply. You are afraid, love is not afraid. You have not really respected Jesus. You are afraid if you say such things, your respect will be destroyed. But Ikkyu knows the respect is so deep that it can't be destroyed by anything. He can burn Buddha on a cold night - no fear arises. No Christian can do that, no Hindu can do that, no Jain can do that. That simply shows there is some fear; you are afraid it may be disrespectful. But the fear arises if you have some disrespect somewhere."[4]

In one of his discourses Rajneesh says:

> "Zen has no secrets it is said. Zen is all openness. Zen is not a fist: it is an open hand. It is no esoteric ideology. It is down-to-earth, very earthly, very simple. If you miss, that simply shows that you have a very complex mind. If you miss, that simply means that you have been looking for complex ideologies, and Zen simply drags you back to reality, to the breakfast, to the mountain laurels. To this bird calling. To this Buddha calling."[5]

Zen Buddhism equally cares for basic physical needs also a monk approaches a master saying. I have just come to this monastery. "Would you kindly give me some instruction?" The master answers, "Have you eaten your breakfast yet?" "I have", is the reply. "Then go wash your bowls". It is said that this conversation accomplished its purpose. The enquirer was brought to the understanding of Zen.

An ancient master, when he was asked the meaning of Zen, lifted one of his fingers. That was his entire answer. Another kicked a ball. Still another slapped the enquirer in the face. A novice who makes a respectful allusion to the Buddha is ordered to rinse his mouth out and never utter that dirty word again. Someone claiming to understand Buddhism in its purity writes the following stanza:

The body is the Bodhi-Tree
The mind is like the mirror bright,
Take heed to keep it always clean
And lest no dust collect upon it.

He is at once corrected by a very different quatrain which becomes accepted as the true Zen position:

Bodhi (True wisdom) is not a tree
The mind is not mirror shinning
As there is nothing from the first
Why talk of wiping off the dust?[6]

Zen sect was founded in Japan about 1187 by Eisai, a monk who had been in China in 1167 for study. Eisai held that knowledge can be transmitted without words. It may be reached only by contemplation. The essential thing is to the find the Buddha is one's own heart. In order to find it, one must grasp the "fact of utter and entire void". In theory its motto was : "*Oh to be nothing! nothing!*". Because when one tries to be something the process of 'becoming' goes on, and unless we stop *'becoming'*, one's *'being'* is not revealed. *'Being'* reveals only after the 'becoming' ceases. Zen is, of course, a mystical sect. In about 1223 two other teachers, after a visit to China introduced into the Zen teaching the elements of scholarship and research. These together with comtemplation were the way to the goal. According to George A. Barton[7] "This mystical sect became very popular with the *Sarnurai*, or Japanese warriors."

The characteristics of the one with emptiness of mind have rightly been described by Ikkyu, the Zen master in the following stanzas:

A rest on the way back
From the leaky Road
To the Never-leaking Road;
If it rains, let it rain;
If it blows, let it lows.

My self of long ago
In nature non-existent;
Nowhere to go when dead
Nothing at all.

When asked, he answered
No question, no answer
The master Daruma
Must have had
Nothing in his mind.

Our mind
without end,
without beginning.
Though it is born, though it dies
The essence of emptiness!

Ikkyu has explained the doctrine of nothingness (Shunyata) of Buddhism through various simple illustrations. His attitude was very pragmatic. He says: "Do not bother about the goal because how can you know about it? You have never been there! It is in the future. But you can go into the source; you come from there, you can go deeper and deeper into your being and touch the very source. It is there! Nothing is ever lost. Seeking that, you will know the goal too. He asks:

Should you seek
The way of the Buddha
All might long,
Searching, you will enter
Into your own mind.

In this connection, the observation of Rajneesh is interesting. He says:

Nothing good, nothing bad, nothing to gain, nothing to lose. Take it easy.[8]

With this as a reference, further visualising the difference between Epicurian bedonism and a Zen Buddhism he says: "The Zen Buddhist knows, it the Epicurian hedonist does not know it. That's the difference—otherwise there is none—Between the enlightened person and the unenlightened person there is no difference at all, not even a single inch's difference. The enlightened person *knows* it, the unenlightened person does not know about it— that's all. The unenlightened person believes in the distance, in the difference, hence he creates it. The enlightened person has come to know there is no difference. The belief has disappeared."[9]

Search without any idea—that is Buddha's message. Look, just clean your eyes and look. Don't look for something in particular, just look, a pure look into things, into the suchness of things. The eyes have to be clean and pure, otherwise they can project; even a small particle of dust and it will show on the screen of nothingness. Just a little liking disliking, a little choice, and you will create reality.[10]

Zen sometimes attacks human concepts quite violently. This it technique has often the appearance of spiritual shock tactics. Paradoxes are used because it is difficult to express pure experience in the form of ordinary, formal logic. How paradoxical these dialogues can be is illustrated in the following. The Zen master Nan-Ch'uan was asked "What is the Tao?" He replied, "Everyday life is the Tao". "How" pursue the enquirer, "does one get into harmony with it?" "If you try to get into harmony with it, you will get away from it".

A rather explict Zen saying runs as follows:

Like into space it knows no boundaries:
Yet it is right here with us, ever retaining its serenity and fullness;
It is only when you seek it that you loose it.
You cannot take hold of it, nor can you get rid of it;
While you can do neither, it goes on its own way;
You remain silent and it speaks;
You speak and it is silent
The great gate of Charity is wide open
With no obstructions whatever before it.[11]

For Zen masters the best way to express deepest experiences is by the use of paradoxes which transcend the opposites. For example, these are typical paradoxes to be used for meditation: "Where there is nothing, there is all". "To die the great death is to gain the great life". "Drop into the deep chasm and live again after your death". "We have been separated for a long time and have never been part. We met each other throughout the day, and do not meet a moment." Paradoxes like these bring objective thought to a deadlock and from there it is possible to uncover the vital way of turning around.

In the Eastern tradition dating from Upanishads, the inverted tree and two birds are well-known. In *Taittiriyopnishad* there is passage which says, "the sky rests in the earth and the earth rests in the sky." It was carried further by *Vajrayan* Buddhists and various saints of the medieval period. These paradoxes can be understood by the help of symbology of various metaphysical, Yogic and tantric terms. In one of his couplets (*doha*) Kabir says:

Sixty-four lamps lightened in fourteen moons
What moon is there in the house where Going is not.

Here sixty-four stands for arts and fourteen stands for Vidyas (lores). Such paradoxical *padas* of Kabir are called *Ulat-Bansiyan* or *Ulat-Batiyan* (inverted bamboos or inverted talks), for example

Such wonderment did the guru tell
  I remained stunned
The mouse fought the elephant
  one rarely sees
The mouse entered into a hole
  serpent afraid ran
Contrarily, mouse devoured the serpent
  it was a great wonder
The ants uprooted the mountain
  and brought in open
The cock fought the human
  the fish ran after water.

The cow was milking the calf
the calf was giving milk
Such wonderment happened
the deer killed the tiger
The hunter hid himself in the thickest
the rabbit shot arrows
Kabir says make him a guru

Dr. Hazari Lal Dwivedi discusses these poems in a chapter entitled 'Yogic Allegories and *Ulat-Bansiyan*', and quotes from *Kabir Granthavali* (p. 141) another passage, and gives a chart of the three different interpretations by Vishvanath, Vichardas and the traditionalists of 23 such symbolic terms in this *pada*:

(Sants Jagat neend na kyai.....)
O Saints don't sleep while awake
Death does not eat, epochs don't cover
the body is not eroded by old age
Contrary-wise the Ganges absorbs the ocean
and darkness eclipses the sun
The sick man kills nine constellations
the reflection in water gives light
Without feet one runs in ten directions
without eyes sees the world
The rabbit devours the lion,
such wonder who can solve?
The inverted pitcher does not sink in water
the straight one is filled with it
The reason why men are different
with guru's grace they get through
Inside the cave one sees the whole world
outside nothing is seen.
The arrow upturned and killed the hunter
only the brave can follow
The singer when requested cannot sing
the dumb sings always
The juggler's game is seeing the onlookers
A-nhad cause is increased

The statement inspects itself
all this is an inexpressible tale
The earth enters into the sky
this is the word of a man
Without glasses nectar oozes
the river keeps away the water stored
Kabir says he alone is immortal
who drinks *Ram-Sudharasa*.[13]

In paradoxical Zen literature "*Koans*" and "*Mondos*" are of considerable significance. According to the Rinzai sect "*koans*" are engimatic or Paradoxical, non-logical questions, whereas Professor Paul Wienpahl believes the Zen *koan* is logical, if one properly understands it. *Koan* is based on *Mondo*. *Mondos* are brief dialogues between masters and disciples. For example,

Monk: How do we escape the heat when summer comes and the cold when winter is here?

Zen Master Thung-shan: Why don't you go where there is no summer, no winter? Where is such a place? When the cold season comes, one is thoroughly chilled; when the hot summer is here, one swelters.

Sometimes the *koan* seem to contradict each other.
For example,

Monk: What is Buddha?
Master Bo-so: This mind is Buddha.

But no another occasion Bo-so said: "This mind is not Buddha". According to Professor Charles Morris "This is an example of the language of paradox and contradiction. Both of these assertions are no less than ferryboats which lead one to enlightenment."[14] The way of resorting to *koans* can be compared to religions of Tantric Sahajyanis in medieval India, who taught by riddles and engimatic expressions, partly to guard the secrets of their thoughts, partly to avoid abstractions by concrete imagery. Sarahpa was the prominent figures among such Tantric Sahajyanis.

Contribution

Hajime Nakamura observed:

"The unique contribution of Zen to higher religion is its method of reaching and presenting truth. Many different methods of instruction have been used by Zen masters but, whatever the method of instruction, Zen intuition cannot be attained arbitrarily. The true law of the Buddha according to the Zen school must be transmitted from mind to mind and from personality to personality. The Zen motto "A special transmission outside the classified teachings" means that system of teachings based upon the Sutras are not relied upon, and that the true law is transmitted by other means. Therefore, to attain the goal of Zen one must begin by receiving guidance from true master of Zen who has synthesised understanding and action. Under the guidance of the master, the transmission from mind to mind takes place."[15]

Dogen's teaching for the practice of meditation was: "Abandon your body and soul into the abundance of light sent from above and give no thought to them. Do not seek for enlightenment nor reject illusion; do not try to avoid distraction nor attach yourself to them nor dwell on them. Just sit with perfect composure. If you do not prolong distractions voluntarily, how should they occur by themselves? Only sit like the great void, or fire, breathing naturally, do not concern yourself with anything whatever, just keep sitting... if you take no need of them and leave them alone, every distraction will be turned into the divine light of wisdom (*Prajna*)."[16]

The most glorious contribution of Zen lies in its making the age-old tradition of the meditation of the East in the most gentle but graceful way. If the process of meditation is a filled-with joy experience it is like a moon-lit night of the soul, otherwise "a dark night of the soul"[17] as John of the Cross call it.

REFERENCES

1. Hajime Nakamura, *Ways of Thinking of Eastern People*, pp. 564-65.
2. Huston Smith, *Religions of Man*, p. 133.

3. Hajime Nakamura, *Ways of Thinking of Eastern People.*
4. Rajneesh, *Take it Easy.*
5. *Ibid.*, p. 359.
6. Quoted from *Religion of Man*, p. 134.
7. George A. Barton, *The Religions of the World*, p. 236.
8. *Take it Easy*, p. 76.
9. *Ibid.*
10. *Ibid.*, pp. 246-47.
11. Hsuan-Chiao, Cheng-Tao ke 34 in D.T. Suzuki, *Manual of Zen Buddhism* (London, Rider, 1950), p. 115 quoted in Hazime Nakamura, *A Comparative History of Ideas*, p. 406.
12. *Kabir Granthavali*, p. 141.
13. *Ibid.*,
14. Quoted in Hazima Nakamura's *A Comparative History of Ideas*, p. 406.
15. *Ibid.*, p. 405.
16. *Ibid.*, pp. 408-09.
17. Richard W. Chilson, *I Can Pray, You Can Pray*, p. 15.

10

MESSAGE OF VEDAS

Vedas are the most magnificent and the oldest literature of the world. Historians call them the earliest records of Indian History. It is true because Vedas refer to pre-Vedic period, during which the ancient forefathers of Indian peoples had explored the secrets of cosmos and enhanced unique results which are still cherished by the Indians even after centuries. Some historians have felt that the forefathers of Vedic sages must have lived around 10,000 B.C. or even earlier, whereas some fix the date of Vedas on the basis of some astronomical clues recorded in the Vedas and hold that Vedas were composed approximately around 4,500 B.C. Some historians coservatively maintain the Vedas were composed around 2000 B.C.

The antiquity of the Vedas has been a subject of discussion and dispute. According to the ancient Indian tradition it is impossible to determine the period of the composition of Vedas as they are considered to be divine (*Apauruseya)* by some scholars of Vedas. However, some historians have tried to fix-up the antiquity of Vedas. Shri Avinash Chandra Das holds that Vedas could have been composed any time between 250th and 750th century B.C. According to Lokamanya Tilak, the estimated period would be any time between 45th and 50th century B.C. This coincides with the view of Professor Haug, Professor Ludwig and Professor Jacobi. Professor Whitney places this period any time between 12th and 15th century B.C., while Professor Weber places it between 12th and 15th century B.C., Professor Max Muller believes that the Veda was composed during the 13th century B.C.

Source of Knowledge

According to *Brihadāranyak Upanishad* all the four Vedas — Rigveda, Yajurveda, Samaveda and Atharvaveda— are the breath of the Supreme Lord.[1] In many internal evidences we observe the divine character of the Vedas. Veda itself declares that it is the poem of God.[2]

Recitation of Vedic Mantras was encouraged in the society. A person going through the Vedas by his recitation was sure to make his mark as an erudite scholar. Various theistic schools of India have been deriving direct or indirect inspiration from Vedas. Most of the schools held the Vedas as the most reliable source of knowledge. They are enumerated among Praman ('means of knowledge') a seperate division Shabda or Agam ('a testimony of the Vedas'). They thus placed their faith in and devotion to Vedas. According to them these Vedas were an infallible authority on physical and metaphysical matters. An aphorism of the Nyaya Sutra remarks: "The Veda is reliable like the spell and the medical science, because of reliability of their authors".[3]

The *Richas* (hymns) of the Vedas are, in fact, prayers to the gods of Aryans, such as Indra, Agni, Vishnu, Pushan, Mitra, Varuna, Us'a, As'vinau, Dyava-Prthivi, Rudra, Brahmanaspati, Tvas'tr, Vis'warup, Vrs'akapi and others. In these prayers Aryan composers described the exploits of their forefathers as favours confessed on them by Gods. At place the word 'Veer'[4] (brave) also stands for Arya while praying to the above gods. They, in fact, described the achievements of their active and brave forefathers who faught with their enemies capture their cows, houses, grain and all the valuable belongings, burnt and destroyed their fortified towns and massacred them in large numbers.

According to P.R. Deshmukh, "This technique is followed throughout the Richas compiled in the Rigveda. It was lost sight of, as the historical background of Rigveda was not very clear before the Indus excavation. It was not imagined that the fortified towns of enemies of the Aryans described in Rigveda were real and could exist in so ancient a time. The descriptions were supposed to be imaginary, allegorical or at any rate to a very large extent exaggerated. They were taken to be unreal and were never a matter of serious attention for the scholars who tried to interpret the Rigveda. Those who interpreted the puras in the Rigveda as fortified towns also were not very definite about their nature. But after the Indus excavation the entire aspect is changed. What has been described in the Richa could be seen and inferred from the evidence of the excavation."[5]

Teachings

As far as the teachings of Vedas are concerned they are universal and secular in character and acceptable by the people of all lands, faiths and cultures. After Indus excavations some of the doubts regarding their antiquity and historicity have become clear. Scholars believe that Veda stands for giving right knowledge of every branch of learning. To a sociologist it was first among all law-books. To a philosopher it was the origin point of all the schools of philosophy. To a scientist it was guiding-star for all contemporary and succeeding researches. To a poet it was the glorious poetic work replete with eternal human values. In the tenth Mandal of Rigveda Yama (Lord of death) has been described as the messenger of the Almighty. In the Veda he has nothing to do with judging or punishing the departed (as in later mythology), but he has two terrific dogs, with four eyes, which guard the way to his abode. Here are a few thoughts about him (Yama) :

To Yama, mighty king be gifts and homage paid.
He was the first of men that died, the first to brave
Deaths rapid rushing stream. The first to point the road
To heaven, and welcome others to that bright abode.
No power can rob us of the home thus won by thee.
O King, we come; the born must die must tread the path.
That thou hast trod - the path by which each race of men,
In long succession, and our fathers to have passed.
Soul of the dead ! Depart; fear not to take the road -
The ancient road - by which the happy fathers,
Who dwell in bliss with him. Fear not to pass the guards -
The four-eyed brindled dogs - that watch for the departed.
Return unto thy home, O Soul ! The sin and shame

Leave thou behind on earth; assume a shining form -
Thy ancient shape-refined and from all taint set free.[6]

In the later part of the nineteenth century many noted western Indologists presented various important commentries on the Vedas. No doubt, their contribution to Vedic studies is notable; but at the same time lot of confusion was also created due to their own theological prepossessions. Illustrating one example on this count Shri A.C. Bose says:

"The most important of the Vedic deities, Indra symbolises this heroic ideal. Now, to the typical Christian, all the fire and fury associated with heroism is the mark of a barbarous state of existence. Some orientalists have, however, gone to the extent of recognising Varuna, described as the king of universe (other Dieties also are so described) whose noose gets hold of every sinner and whose emissaries roam over the earth, as the ethical Diety, even as the ultimate Reality. But the true Christian with his notion of "the highest ethics" could not find himself well disposed towards the Hero-God, Indra, to whom many of the grandest Vedic hymns are addressed."[7]

This tendency of the western Indologists and some of their Indian disciples led them to enhance, at time, value judgement about rich cultural heritage of India. One of the factors responsible for this tendency was nationalism, which at times made them less objective and more subjective. That is why we find that the verdict of some Indologists and historians (James, Mill, Elliot, Dowson, Maine, Stephen, Wheeler etc.) of aggressive nature, which resulted into bitter attack on Indian culture and way of life.[8] On this phenomena of Indological studies B. Sheik Ali has aptly remarked:

"On the one hand it opened the vast vistas of India's hoary past with its limitless variety and profundity of thought almost in every sector of human life, which by itself was sufficient to intoxicate. The Indian mind with national pride and fervour, and on the other it dragged them into an argumentative and challenging mood in order to give a fitting reply to the problemics of European writers. Unfortunately, the salutary effect of the new found treasure of knowledge was to a great extent neutralised by a frame of mind that judged the past through coloured glasses."[9]

In such circumstances Indian scholars also entered into deep and penetrating investigation and after ransacking the Vedic Literature put forth the objective and balanced conclusions. One such is that of Dr. Radhakumud Mukherji. He says, "The first point of distinction is that the Veda and especially the primordial work known as the Rigveda represents not merely the dawn of culture, but also its zenith. Indian thought is seen at its highest in the Rigveda.... On the one hand it is the first book of India and also of mankind. At the same time it shows the highest point of human wisdom. We see in it the whole process of evolution from its beginning to its completion."[10]

Here we are producing some such *pearls of wisdom* from the Vedas as a message of the East to the people interested in value oriented literature.

Action-Oriented Life

कृतं मे दक्षिणे हस्ते जयो मे सव्यं आहितः ।
गोजिद् भयासमश्वजिद् धनञ्जयो हिरण्यजित् ।।

— अथर्व 7.50.8

यो जागर तमृचः कामयन्ते,
यो जागर तमु सामानि यन्ति ।
यो जागर तमयं सोम आह,
तवाहमस्मि सख्ये न्योकाः ।।

— ऋक् 5.44.14

May your action be filled by hope and enthusiasm.
May your right hand do duty and the left earn victory and success of your efforts.
May your entire entity be endowed with good rewards
Earn a lot, give a lot
May you collect with hundred hands and give as much as thousand hands give.

The Bright Dawn

उदीर्ध्वं जीवो असुर्न आगाद्,
अपप्रागात्तम आज्योतिरेति ।

आरैकपन्था यातवे सूर्याय,
आगन्म यत प्रतिरन्त आयुः ॥

— ऋक् 1.113.16

Awake, O man, the birght dawn is ushering in a new day
The slumber and the darkness of the night are over
The rosy fingers of the dawn have opened the golden gates of the Sun, and cleared the path of progress
May the dawn lead us from triumph to triumph in the long journey of life.

The Rocky River

अश्मवती रीयते सं रभध्वं
वीरयध्वं प्रतरता सखायः ।
अत्रा जहीत ये असन् दुरेवा
अनर्मावानुत्तरेनाभि वाजान् ॥

— अथर्व. 12.2.26

Swim the rocky river of life with courage
Look the hard rocky flux of the life zooms past before you, with the speed of Vaitarni.
With other in mutual comradeship you should cross it bravely, courageously
Leave behind you those inimical to you
Join those comrades who have with a healthy mind and body crossed this river
This, is the only way to obtain affluence in material and spiritual world.

The Divine Fire

तस्य व्रातस्य । एकं तदेषाममृतत्त्वमित्याहुतिरेव ॥

— अथर्व. 15.17.10

Live and work as an act of offering to achieve complete satisfaction of having lived successful life
Remember you are the child of immortality and that all life is

but an offering
Never forget that the nectar-honey of the flower of mercy,
is for those who sacrifice.
Let the sacred flame of divine fire shine bright in your souls.

Contentment

महो अर्णः सरस्वती
प्र चेतयति केतुना ।
धियो विश्वा वि राजति ।।

— ऋक् 1.3.12

Do not covet anyone's wealth
All that lives or moves on earth transient or permanent,
exists in the glory of God
Enjoy what He bestows on you, set not your heart on what
is possessed by others.
This whole universe is an atom in the whole

Our Aspirations

ओइम् । समानी व आकूतिः समाना हृदयानि वः ।
समानमस्तु वो मना यथा वः सु सहासति ।।

— ऋक् 10.191.4

May our aspirations be perfectly harmonious
May absolute accord reign in our minds
May we divide our wealth equally among ourselves, and
reduce disparity
So that we may be welded into strong fellowship and unity.

For the Glory of Your Country

जनं बिभ्रती बहुधा विवाचसं
नानाधमणि पृथिवी यथौकसम् ।
सहस्रं धारा द्रविणं मे दुहां
धुव्रेव धेनुरनपस्फुरन्ती ।।

— अथर्व 12-1-45

Work for the glory of your country and countrymen speaking different dialects
Give due respect to the faith and aspiration of the people
Countless are the resources of your mother
Earth, from whom flow the rivers of wealth in hundreds of streams
Worship your motherland as your worship God
From time eternal, the mother Earth is giving life to her children – you owe debt to her.

For Truth and Justice

समहमेषां राष्ट्रं स्यामि समोजो वीर्यं बलम् ।
वृश्चामि शत्रूणां बाहुनानेन हविषाऽहम् ।।

— अथर्व. 12.1

Let us take a vow to save the honour of our nation
Our wealth, strength and intellect, all shall be dedicated to her
Our marching feet and our striking arms shall drag into the dust the insolent pride of our enemy
The victory shall be ours
We fight for truth and justice and sacrifice all in the sacred cause.

Mutual Love

मा भ्राता भ्रातरं द्विक्षन्मा स्वसारमुत स्वसा ।
सम्यञ्चः सव्रता भूत्वा वाचं वदत भद्रया । — अथर्व 3.30,3

अनुव्रतः पितुः पुत्रो मात्रा भवतु संमनाः ।
जाया पत्ये मधुमतीं वाचं वदतु शान्तिवाम् ।।

— अथर्व 3.20.2

Stability of the family depends on mutual love
May there be no disagreement between brother and brother.
Between son and father
The son must obey and have thoughts similar to his parents, and behave accordingly.

All the relatives must keep good feelings mutually
May they converse with calm sweet words.

Stained Wealth

न ता नशन्ति न दभाति तस्करो,
नासामामित्रो व्यथिरा दधर्षति ।
देवांश्च याभिर्यजते ददाति च
ज्योगित्ताभिः सचते गोपतिः सह ॥

— ऋक 6.28.3

Attempt not to obtain wealth through unjust and condemned ways
Such wealth shall not enhance your happiness
Never will that wealth be useful which is obtained from violence or oppression.
Even the gifting of such sinful wealth will not be holy and these who accept such wealth also disillusioned or find it useless.

The War Within

यदा त्वष्टा व्यतृणत्पिता त्वष्टुर्य उत्तरः ।
गृहं कृत्वा मर्त्यं देवाः पुरुषमाविशन् ।
पाप्मानो नाम देवताः ॥

— अथर्व 11.8.18-9

स्तेयं दुष्कृतं वृजिनं, सत्यं यज्ञो यशो बृहत् ।
बलं च क्षत्रमोजश्च, शरीरमनु प्राविशन् ॥

— अथर्व 11.8.20

भूतिश्च वा अभूतिश्च क्षुधश्च सर्वास्तृणाश्च शरीरमनु प्राविशम्

— अथर्व 11.8.21

तस्माद्वै विद्वान् पुरुषामिदं ब्रह्मेटि मन्यते ।
सर्वा ह्थस्मिन् देवता गावो गोष्ठ इवास्ते ॥

— अथर्व 11.8.31-2

Continue fighting against sins till the end
Virtues and sins are eternally bound together in human body
When the divine architect planned and fashioned the human

form, all the evils and virtues entered the mortal frame and made it their home
Theft, wickedness, thirst, hunger, live there
with truth, wisdom, content, nobility and faith
Joy and grief, jealousy and nobility, amazing
darkness and glorious brightness, are all
woven in a cloth of one human soul, thus it
becomes complete by opposite qualities
And thus it is that the soul walled within
mortal body is called Brahma.

Speak No Evil, See No Evil

भद्रं कर्णेभिः शृणुयाम देवा
भद्रं पश्येमाक्षिभिर्यजत्राः ।
स्थिरैरङ्गैस्तुष्टुवांसस्तनूभि -
व्यशेम देवहितं यदायुः ।। — ऋक् 1.89.8

Resolve to hear only noble words and speak good words
For a calm and a happy life resolve that only
noble words shall you utter
Only a good sight our eyes would reveal
And by the grave of Lord you shall keep a
strong and healthy body
This firm resolution will make you strong to
serve and suffer for the common good of humanity.

Reason Is Higher

मूर्धानमस्य संसीव्याथर्वा हृदयं च यत् ।
मस्तिष्कादूर्ध्वः प्रैरयत् पवमानोधि शीर्षतः ।। — अथर्व 10.2.26

Give prominence to intellect over emotions
God has housed your emotions heart and
your logical mind in one body
Do not be swayed away by emotions, not be
carried away by mere logic

Obtain inspiration from heart, but guidance
from brain and go forward with steady steps
The place of reason is higher than the place of heart : !
Try to develop your intellect on the same
principles which your enlightened and inspired seers
adopted.

Truth Is Simple and Easy

सुविज्ञानं चिकितुषे जनाय सच्चासच्च वचसी पस्पृधाते ।
तयोर्यत्सत्यं यतरदृजीयस्तदित्सोमो वति हन्त्यासत् ॥

—ऋक् 7.104.12

Speak the truth, it is easy and simple
To silence the questioning of man about truth
and falsehood, both have been explained by scriptures
Amongst these the lasting truth has been
Propounded in a simple and lucid style
Falsehood is devious : it could well be the cause of destruction
Truth is simple and easy
Follow the truth.

The Spiritual Bliss

इति वा इति मे मनो गामश्वं सुनयामिति ।
कुवित्सोमस्यापामिति ॥ ऋक् 10.119.1
प्र वाता इव दोधत उन्मा पीता असंयत ।
कुवित्सोमस्यापामिति ॥ ऋक् 10.119.2
उन्मा पीता असंयत रथमश्वा इवाशवः ।
कुवित्सोमस्यापामिति ॥ ऋक् 10.119.3
अहं तष्टेव बन्धुरं पर्चयामि हृदा मतिम् ।
कुवित्सोमस्यापामिति ॥ ऋक् 10.119.5
नहि मे अक्षिपच्चनाच्छान्त्सुः पञ्च कृष्टयः ।
कुवित्सोमस्यापामिति ॥ ऋक् 10.119.6

Resolve not to hanker after material lust
Resolve to remain free from being jailed in the cage of
temporal body

Embark on spiritual journey. Give up all
possessions, and all acute desires
endeavour to be pious and wise mould your
thoughts under divine guidance
As a carpenter bends down and straighten his
wood, you mould the wishes make your soul unclean
try to be pure, serene and selfless in your service
Cease to doubt and have firm faith on your deliverance
A divine trance will be on you. You will be detached
All your mortal visions will have faded, your fears vanished
like breaking bubbles. Your riddles solved and conflicts
melted into divine unity.

Adhere to Your Duties

उत त्वः पश्यन न ददर्श वाचमृत त्वः श्रृण्वन्न शृणोत्येनाम् ।
उतो त्वस्मै तन्वं वि सस्रे जायेव पत्य उशती सुवासाः ।।

—ऋक् 10.71.4

अक्षण्वन्तः कर्णवन्तः सखायो मनोजवेष्वसमा बभूवुः ।
आदघ्नास उपकक्षास उ त्वे, हृदा इवस्नात्वा उत्वे ददृश्रे ।।

—ऋक् 10.71.7

Adhere to your Dharma - your beneficial
duties - and follow the path ordained by God;
for not alike are the grasping power of all men,
not the penetration of all intellects alike
Some have eyes but bereft of the eyes of
knowledge, they are unable to see
Some have ears, but devoid of the true hearing power, are
unable to hear
All are born with different capabilities, they try
To transcend their own entities. But these who
Follow the road ordained by the Lord, surely
Obtain real intellect and courage.
They have never to confront the face of defeat
But there exist these fortunate devotees of
Lord before whom the divine voice sheds its
mystery and reveals its true form.

The Wheel of the Laws

न देवानामति व्रतं शतात्मा च न जीवति ।
तथा युजा वि वावृते ॥

—ऋक् 10.33.9

The laws of the Supreme are inviolable
That any one, however might his soul be, will
be crushed under the wheel of laws, if he defies
them through ego and ignorance
Lead your life in conformity with these divine laws
Only then your soul will receive the blessings
of immortality, from your divine protector.

Keep Awake

मा त्वा मूरा अविष्यवो,
मोपहस्वान आ दभन् ।
माकीं ब्रह्मद्विषो वनः ॥

— ऋक् 8.45.23

O man, keep awake! Let not fools lure you or the cunning beguile you
Those God-denying hypocrites can never be true benefactors
They will try to belittle your dignity exploit your generosity
Do not be waylaid by them
Do not fall into their trap.

The Temple of God

यो अग्निं तन्वो दमे,
देवं मर्तः सपर्यति ।
तस्मा इद्दीदयद वसु ॥

— ऋक् 8.44.15

Human body is the temple of God
One who kindles the light of awareness within gets true light
By concentrating mind to look inside, the inner vision is

illuminated
The joys of life are not for those who keep their mind unclean and extrovert
The mysteries of life are revealed to one who keep his mind vigilant all the times of life
Keeps the sacred flame of your inner shrine constantly bright and glowing.

The Human Body

अष्टचक्रा नवद्वारा, देवानां पूरयोध्या ।
तस्यां हिरण्मयः कोशः स्वर्गो ज्योतिषावृतः ॥
तस्मिन् हिरण्मये कोशे, त्यरे त्रिप्रतिष्ठिते ।
तस्मिन् यद् यक्षमात्मवन्त तद् ब्राह्मविदो विदुः ।

— अथर्व 10.2.31-321

Human body is symbol of universal existence
Within human body, there exists an invincible fortress city of the gods, with eight wheels and nine doors
That is the shrine of immortal soul, illuminated with divine lights
The soul seals within itself the Lord of the whole universe, it is He whose mystery is revealed to the enlightened.

Quest Within Your Soul

परीत्य भूतानि परीत्य लोकान्
परीत्य सर्वाः त्रदिशो दिशश्च ।
उपस्थाय प्रथमजातस्य
आत्मनात्मानमभि सं विवेश ॥

— यजुः 32.11

Find the eternal object of your quest within your soul
Enough have you wandered during the long period of quest !
Dark and weary must have been the ages of
Your searching ignorance and groping helplessness

At last when you turned your gaze inward,
suddenly you realised the bright light of faith
and lasting truth was shining around you
With rapturous joy, you found soul of the
universe – the eternal object of your quest
the searching mind at last finds the object of his
search within his own heart
His inner vision is illuminated by purity of his mind.

Rejoice With Nature

वसन्त इन्नु रन्त्यो ग्रीष्म इन्नु रन्त्यः ।
वर्षाण्यनु शरदो हेमन्तः शिशिर इन्नु रन्त्यः ।।

— साम पूर्वार्चिक 6.3.13.2

Rejoice in all the moods of nature, experience
the unseen divine glory manifested in various forms
The spring is a season of flowers and scented
breezes which gladden our hearts
The summer has a beauty of its own
The rain with its dark clouds and dazzling
flashes, bathes the entire earth with its raining splendours
The autumn and winter too possess their own
Charm and beauty.

Of Faith in Him

ऋचो अक्षरे परमे व्योमन्
यस्मिन् देवा अधि विश्वे निषेदुः ।
यस्तन्न वेद कि मृचा करिष्यति
य इत्तद्विदुस्त इमे समासते ।

— ऋक 1.164.39

Remember ! of no use is the chanting of psalms
or singing verses, if it reveals not the Supreme
being under whose command all natural forces are working
For the man who has no faith in God, the
Veda has no use for him

Those alone attain true happiness who know
The Supreme being, who have firm faith in Him.

Leave the Rest to God

स नः पप्रिः पारयाति स्वस्ति नावा पुरुहूतः ।
इन्द्रो विश्वा अति द्विषः ।।

— ऋक् 8.16.11

Perform your duty and leave the rest to God,
have deep faith in God's justice
The world is torn by strifes, enmities and rivalries
In this dark whirlpool of turbulent streams of life.
Only the all-powerful God may carry us
across the ocean of troubles
Only he can captain our vessel and bring it to the shore of divine fulfilment
The waves of the stormy sea will become calm at his nod
Therefore dedicate all your thoughts and
desires to God with full faith
Only He can bless you to conquer your
Troubles through his divine mercy.

REFERENCES

1. अस्य महतो भूतस्य निश्वसितम् एतद्
यद् ऋग्वेद यजुर्वेद सामवेदो अथर्वांगिरसः । — Brihadranyakopnishad
2. पश्य देवस्य काव्यं न ममार न जीर्यति। —Atharva Veda 10.8.32
3. मान्त्रायुर्वेदच्च तत्प्रामाण्यमाप्ताप्रामाण्यात् । — Nyaya Sutra 2.1.68
4. अस्माकं वीरा उत्तरे भवन्तु । — Rig Veda 10.103.11
(Mall all brave persons be crowned with triumphant progress.)
5. P.R. Deshmukh, Indus Civilization, Hindu Culture & Rigved, p.39.
6. Various hymns of the 10th Mandal of Rigved. Translation by M.M. Williams, Indian wisdom, p.19.
7. A.C. Bose, *The call of the Vedas*, Introduction.
8. For details author's book titled "Contribution of Western Indologists" may be referred to.
9. B. Sheik Ali, *History: Its Theory and Method*, p.249.
10. Radhakumud Mukherji, quoted by A.C. Bose, *In call of the Vedas*, p.16.

11

THE MESSAGE OF BHAGAVADGEETA

The Mahabharata, the great epic is one of the most important sources of history. From the study of this epic many valuable information regarding civilisation and culture of that time is revealed. On one hand it is marvellous epic of growth embodying of the excellence and elegance, on the other it is compendium of many social and cultural customs and corrections.

According to Hopkins, "upon the original story, the Bharata, have been grafted many 'secondary tales' (*Upakhyanas*), and upon these, and apart from these have been inserted whole poems of romantic, ethical, and theological character, having nothing to do with the course of the Epic itself. We must, however, remember that our Epic has been enlarged in two ways: first, by a natural expansion of matter already extant; secondly, by unnatural addition of new material. The twelth book may serve as a type of the latter; the eighth, of the former". Hopkin's conclusion is that "even the modern Epic, the full completed work, is not as a whole unimportant in the elucidation of the customs of India in the Middle Ages, reaching back more than 2,000 years."

Importance

Shrimad Bhagavadgeeta, herafter called *Geeta*, is a part of *Mahabharata*, as we have mentioned elsewhere. It runs from the Chapters 23rd to 40th of the V book, i.e. Udyoga Parvan. It has assumed the position of universal interest, being the representative scripture of Hinduism as the Bible and Quran are that of Christianity and Islam respectively. Its teachings have gained tremendous appreciations not only in India; but throughout the world. There are hundreds of editions of *Geeta*, Geeta Press (Gorakhpur) Library alone comprises about 1300 editions of *Geeta*. It has been published in 32 different languages including eight foreign languages. Keeping in view its grandeur and glory Jayadayal Goyanka has rightly observed, "it contains the highest esoteric doctrines. It is the essence of Vedas; its language is so sweet and simple that man can easily understand it after a little practice; but the thoughts are so deep that none can arrive at their end even after constant study throughout life-time. Everyday they exhibit new facts of truth, therefore, they remain ever fresh and new. When scrutinized with a concentrated mind possessed of faith and reverence every verse of *Geeta* will clearly appear as full of mistery. The manner in which the *Geeta* describes the virtues, glory and secrets of God is hardly found in any other scripture or in other books, the teachings are generally mixed up, more or less, with worldly subjects, but the *Geeta* uttered by the Lord is such an incomparable book that not a single word will be found in it, devoid of some spiritual import."

That is why at the end of *Geeta* Vedvyasa has himself said:

गीता सुगीता कर्त्तव्या किमन्यैः शास्त्रविस्तरैः ।
या स्वयं पद्मनाभस्य मुखपद्माद्विनि सृताः ॥

Antiquity of *Geeta*

He advises us to study the *Geeta* carefully, i.e. after reading the text, its meaning and idea should be gathered and held in the mind.

S.C. Roy, a great scholar, in his "The Bhagvadgeeta and Modern Scholarship" has made a good attempt in reviewing the results of researches on *Geeta* and *Mahabharata* comprehensively and systematically. According to the author *Geeta* is a gospel of love and peace and not of War, as T.M.P. Mahadevan has also interpreted in his "Is Gita a Gospel of War" the teaching of *Geeta* consistently with the doctrine of non-violence. Roy holds that the

Geeta in its original form was an Upanishadic treatise, which was later on interpolated into the great epic like many other didactic episodes; but until and unless these are clear and concrete evidences there is no point in saying that the *Geeta* is an interpolation. Main conclusion of Roy are as below, which deserve our attention:

(i) The text of the *Geeta* has remained substantially unaltered in spite of numberless interpolations that have take place in other portions of the Great Epic; (ii) the *Geeta* naturally linked both by language and by thought with the thoughts of the Upanishads and has always been associated by the Indian tradition more with the Vedanta philosophy than with the Shankhya-Yoga; (iii) Garbe's theory of interpolation in the *Geeta* is entirely without foundation; (iv) the Krishna of the *Geeta* is not the same historical or mythical person who deified in the Vaishnava scriptures like the Harivamsa, the Bhagavata Purana and the Vishnu Purana; nor are the teachings of the *Geeta* the same as those of the Narayaniya section of the Mokshadharma of the Great Epic; (v) the *Geeta* was not written by a sectarian 'poet for a particular sect, but is meant to be and has always been a sacred code of devotion; philosophical insight and moral and religious culture, universally accepted by all seekers after God, irrespective of caste, creed and colour; (vi) a few verses here and there betray a foreign origin and may have been added by sectarian writers and these seem to have found entrance into this popular scripture along with other interpolations; (vii) the *Geeta*, in its original form, was an Upanishadic treatise, independent of the Epic *Mahabharata*, and was later on incorporated into the Epic along with other didactic episodes; (viii) the object of the poet of the *Geeta* was to teach humanity the sublime art of self-control and self-conquest in the midst of trials and temptations of world, and to encourage the human soul in fighting its battles in spiritual life; (ix) Krishna is not the central of the *Mahabharata* in its extant form, nor was he the inspiring deity for the author of the original Bharata. The Epic, as well as the *Geeta* in its original form, was neither Krishnaite nor Vishnuite; (x) the *Geeta* was a much earlier work than the Bhagavata episode in the Mokshadharma, and also much older than the Anugita (2); (ix) the *Geeta* was composed by a Rishi the Upanishadic age, a poet-philosopher who was a Reformer of the religious and social life of the Contemporary Vedic Aryan as well as non-Vedic and non-Aryan people.

Here with going much deep into the authorship and antiquity of *Geeta* we will try to summarise the teachings of *Geeta* and separate sub-headings, which otherwise needs independent volume.

Manliness

Yield not to unmanliness Ill does it become thee. Yield not to dejection. It is unmanly, disgraceful and contrary to the attainment of heaven.[3]

Self-Reliance

A man should uplift himself by his ownself, so let him not weaken this self. For the self is the friend of oneself, and this self is the enemy of oneself. The self (the active part of our nature) is the friend of the self, for him who has conquered himself by this self. But to the unconquered self, this self is inimical (and behaves), like (an external) foe.[4]

Knowledge

Verily there exists nothing in this world purifying like knowledge. Even if thou be the most sinful amongst men, yet by the raft of knowledge alone thou shalt go across all sin. As blazing fire reduces wood into ashes, so does the fire of knowledge reduce all karmas to ashes.[5] I shall tell thee that Supreme knowledge, which is above all other knowledges, having known which the sages have attained the highest perfection.[6]

The Divinity of Man

The unreal never is. The real never is not. Men possessed of the knowledge of the Truthfully know both these. That by which all this is pervaded. That know for certain to be indestructible. None has the power to destroy this Immutable.

As are childhood, youth and old age, in this body, to the embodied soul, so also is the attaining of another body. Calm souls are not deluded threat. Even as a man casts off worm-out clothes, and puts on others which are new, so the embodied casts off worm-out bodies, and enters into others which are new.

The soul is never born, nor does it die. It is not that, not having been it again comes into being. This is unborn, eternal, changeless, ever-itself. It is not killed when the body is killed. This (Self), weapons cut not; This, fire burns not; This water wets not; and This wind dries not. This Self cannot be cut, nor burnt, nor wetted, nor dried, Changless all-pervading, unmoving, immovable, the Self is eternal.[7]

The Insight of Yoga

The wisdom of Self realisation has been declared unto thee. Hearken thou now to the wisdom of Yoga, endued with which thou shalt break through the bonds of Karma. In this, there is no waste of the unfinished attempt, nor is there production of contrary results. Even very little of this Dharma protects one from the great terror. In this, there is but a single one-pointed determination. The purposes of the undecided are innumerable and many branching. Be thou free from the tried of the Gunas, free from (the thought of) getting and keeping, and established in the Self.[8]

Why One Should Work

In the beginning (of creation), the two-fold path of devotion was given by Me to This world:— the path of knowledge of for the meditative, the path of work for the active. By non-performance of work none reaches worklessness; by merely giving up action, no one attains to perfection. Verily none can ever rest for even as instant, without performing action; for all are made to act; helplessly indeed, by the Gunas, born of Prakriti. He, who restraining the organs of action sits revolving in the mind thoughts regarding objects of senses, he of deluded understanding, is called a hypocrite. But, the controlling the senses by the mind, unattached, directs his organs of action to the path of work, he excels. Do thou perform obligatory action for action is superior to inaction, and even the bare maintenance of the body would not be possible if thou art inactive. The world is bound by action other than those performed for the sake of *Yajna*; do thou, therefore, perform action for Yajana alone, devoid of attachment.[9]

How One Should Work Duty

The right is to work only —but never to the fruits thereof. Be thou not the producer of the fruits of (thy) actions; neither let thy attachment be towards inaction. Being steadfast in Yoga perform actions, abandoning attachment, remaining unconcerned as regards success and failure. This evenness of mind (in regard to success and failure) is known as Yoga. Work (with desire) is verily far inferior to that performed with the mind undisturbed by thoughts of results. Seek refuge in this evenness of mind. Wretched are they who act for results. Endued with this evenness of mind, one frees onself in this life. Devote thyself, therefore, to this Yoga. Yoga is the very dexterity of work. The wise, possessed of this evenness of mind, abandoning the fruits of their actions, freed for ever from the fetters of birth, go to that state which is beyond all evil.[10]

The Yoga of Work

He who perfoms his bounden duty without learning to the fruit of action—he is a renouncer of action as well as of steadfast mind; not he who is without fire, nor he who is without action. Know that to be devotion to action, which is called renunciation. For none becomes a devotee to action without forsaking *Sankalpa*. For the man of meditation wishing to attain purification of heart leading to concentration, work is said to be the way for him; when he has attained such (concentration), inaction is said to be the way. Verily, when there is no attachment, either to sense-objects or to actions, having renounced all *Sankalpas*, then is one said to have attained concentration.[11]

Therefore, do thou always perform actions which are obligatory, without attachment:— by performing action without attachment, one attains to the highest. Verily by action, alone, Janaka and others attained perfection:— also, simply with the view for the guidance of men, thou shouldst perform action.[12]

Therefore, at all times, constantly remember Me, and fight. With mind and intellect absorbed in Me,[13] thou shalt doubtless come to Me. Renouncing all actions to Me, with mind centred on the self, getting rid of hope and selfishness, fight— free from (mental) fever.[14]

The Wise also Work to Set an Example

But the man who is devoted to the Self, and is satisfied with the Self, and content in the Self alone, he has no obligatory duty. He has no object in this world (to gain) by doing (an action) nor (does he incur any loss) by non-performance of action, —nor has he (need of) depending on any being for any object. As do the unwise, attached to work, act, so should the wise act, (but) without attachment, desirous of the guidance of the world. One should not unsettle the understanding of the ignorant, attached to action; the wise (himșelf) steadily acting, should engage (the ignorant) in all work. Whatsoever the superior person does, that is followed by other. What he demonstrates by action, that, people follow.[15]

The Source of Evil and Its Cure

But by what impelled does man commit sin, though, against his wished, constrained as it were, by force? It is desire—it is anger, born of the Rajoguna: of great craving, and of great sin: know this as the foe here (in this world). As fire is enveloped by smoke, as a mirror by dust, as an embryo by the secundine, so is knowledge covered by desire. Knowledge is covered by this, the constant fee of the wise, the unappeasable fire of desire. The senses, the mind and the intellect are said to be its abode: through there, it deludes the embroided by veiling his wisdom.

Therefore, controlling the senses at the outset, kill it, the sinful, the destroyer of knowledge and realisation. The senses are said to be superior (to the body); the mind is superior to the senses; the intellect is superior to the mind; and that which is superior to the intellect is He (the Atman). Thus, knowing Him who is superior to the intellect, and restraining the self by the Self, destroy that enemy the unseizable fee, desire.[16]

The Yoga of Knowledge

Humility, unpretentiousness, non-injury, forbearance, uprighteness, service to the teacher, purity, steadiness, self-control, the renunciation of sense-objects, and also absence of egoism; reflection on the evils of birth, death, old age, sickness and pain, non-attachment, non-identification of self with son, wife, home and the rest, and constant even-mindedness in the occurrence of the desirable and the undesirable, unswerving devotion to Me by the Yoga of non-separation, resort to sequestered places, distaste for the society of men, constant application to spiritual knowledg, understanding of the end of true knowledge; this is declared to be knowledge, and what is opposed to it is ignorance.[17]

Freed from attachment, fear and anger, absorbed in Me, taking refuge in Me, purified by the fire of knowledge, many have attained My Being. He who sees inaction in action, and action in inaction, he is intelligent among men, he is a Yogi and deer of all action. Whose undertakings are all devoid of plan and desire for results, and whose actions are burnt by the fire of knowledge, him, the sages call wise. Devoid of attachment, liberated, with mind centred in knowledge, performing work for Yajna alone, his whole Karma dissolves away. Knowledge-sacrifice is superior to sacrifice (performed) with (material) objects. All action attains its consummation in knowledge.

Know that knowledge, by prostrating thyself, by questions, and by service; the wide, those who have realised the Truth, will instruct thee in that knowledge. Knowing which, thou shalt not, again get deluded like this, and by which thou shalt see the whole of creation in (thy) Self and in Me. In good time, having reached perfection in Yoga, one realises that oneself in one's own heart.[18]

Need for Shraddha

The man with Shraddha, the devoted, the master of one's senses, attains (this) knowledge. Having attained knowledge one goes at once to the Supreme peace. The ignorant, the man without Shraddha, the doubting self, goes to destruction. The doubting self has neither this world, nor the next, nor happiness. With work renounced by Yoga and doubts rent as under by knowledge, actions do not bind him who is poised in the Self. Therefore, cutting with the sword of knowledge this doubt the Self, born of ignorance, residing in thy heart, take refuge in Yoga.[19]

Knowledge is enveloped in ignorance, hence do beings get deluded. But whose ignorance is destroyed by the knowledge of Self—that knowledge of theirs, like the sun, reveals the Supreme (Brahman). These who have their intellect absorbed in That, whose self is That; whose steadfastness is in That, whose consummation is That, their impurities cleansed by knowledge, they attain to non-return (*Moksha*).[20]

Peace Within

Whose happiness is within, whose relaxation is within, whose light is within, that Yogi alone, becoming Brahman, gains absolute freedom. With imperfections exhausted, doubts dispelled, senses controlled, engaged in the good of all beings; the Rishis obtain absolute freedom. Released from lust and anger, the heart controlled, the Self realised, absolute freedom is for such Sanny-sins, both here and hereafter… Knowing Me as the dispenser of Yajnas and asceticisms, as the Great Lord of all worlds, as the friend of all beings, he attains peace.[21]

Vision of Equality

The knowers of the Self look with an equal eye on a Brahmana endowed with learning and humility, a cow, an elephant, a dog, and a pariah. (Relative) existence has been conquered by them, even in this world, whose mind rests in evenness, since Brahman is even and without imperfection; therefore they indeed rest in Brahman. Resting in Brahman, with intellect steady, and without delusion, the knower of Brahman neither rejoiceth on receiving what is pleasant, nor grieveth on receiving what is unpleasant.

With the heart concentrated by Yoga, with the eye of evenness for all things, he beholds the Self in all beings and all beings in the Self. He who sees Me in all things and sees all things in Me, he never becomes separated from Me, nor do I become separated from him. He who, being established in unity, worships Me, who is dwelling in all beings, whatever his mode of life, that Yogi abides in Me. He who judges of pleasure of pain everywhere, by the same standard as he applies to himself, that Yogi is regarded as the highest.

He sees, who sees the Lord Supreme, existing equally in all beings, deathless in the dying.[22]

Equanimity

Notions of heat and cold, of pain and pleasure, are born only of the contact of the senses with their objects. The have a beginning and an end. They are impermanent in their nature. Bear them patiently. That calm man alone who is the same in pain and pleasure whom these cannot disturb, will be able to attain to immortality. Having made pain and pleasure, gain and loss, conquest and defeat, the same, engage thou then in battle. So shalt thou incur no sin.[23]

Whose heart is filled with satisfaction by wisdom and realisation, and is changeless, whose senses are conquered, and to whom a lump of earth, stone, and gold are the same: that Yogi is called steadfast. He attains excellence who looks with equal regard upon well-wishers, friends, foes, neutrals, arbiters, the hateful, the relatives, and upon the righteous and the unrighteous alike.[24]

The Middle Path

(Success in) Yoga is not for him who eats too much or too little—nor for him who sleeps too much or too little. To him who is temperate in eating and recreation, in his effort for work and in sleep and wakefulness, Yoga becomes the destroyer of misery.[25]

The Yoga of Mind Control

The Yogi should constantly practice concentration of the heart, retiring into solitude, alone, with the mind and body subdued, and free from hope and possession. Having in a cleanly spot established his seat, firm, neither too high nor too low, made of a cloth, a skin and *Kusha*-grass, arranged in order; there, seated on that seat, making the mind one-pointed and subduing the action of the imaging faculty and the senses, let him practise Yoga for the purification of the heart. Let him firmly hold his body, head and neck erect and still (with the eye balls fixed, as if) gazing at the tip of his nose, and not looking around. With the heart serene and fearless, firm in the vow of a Brahmachari, with the mind controlled, and ever thinking of Me, let him sit (in Yoga) having Me as his supreme goal. Thus always keeping the mind steadfast, the Yogi of subdued mind attains the peace residing in Me,—the peace which culminates in Nirvana (*Moksha*).

When the completely controlled mind rests serenely in the Self alone, free from longing after all desires, then is one called steadfast (in the Self). 'As a lamp in a spot sheltered from the wind does not flicker',—even such has been the simile used for a Yogi of subdued mind, practising concentration in the self.

When the mind, absolutely restrained by the practice of concentration, attains quietude, and when seeing the Self by the self, one is satisfied in his own Self; when he feels that infinite bliss—which is perceived by the (purified) intellect and which transcends the senses, and established wherein he never departs from his real state; and having obtained which, regards no other acquisition superior to that, and where established, he is not moved even by heavy sorrow;—let that be known as the state, called by the name of Yoga,—a state of severance from the contract of pain. This Yoga should be practised with perseverance undisturbed by depression of heart. Abandoning without reserve all desires born of *Sankalpa*, and completely restraining, by the mind alone, the whole group of senses from their objects in all directions,[26] with the intellect set in patience, with the mind fastened on the Self, let him attain quietude by degrees; let him not think of anything. Through whatever reason the restless unsteady mind wanders away, let him, curbing it from that, being it under the subjugation of the Self alone.

Verily the supreme bliss comes to that Yogi, of perfectly tranquil mind, with passions quieted; Brahman—become, and freed from taint. The Yogi freed from taint (of good and evil), constantly engaging the mind thus, with ease attains the infinite bliss of contact with Brahman.

Without doubt, the mind is restless, and difficult to control; but through practice and renunciation, it may be governed. Yoga is hard to be attained by one of uncontrolled self; but the self-controlled, striving by right means, can obtain it.[27]

Steps to Spiritual Life

Those who, fixing their mind on Me, worship Me, ever steadfast, and endowed with supreme *Shraddha*, they in My opinion are the best versed in Yoga. Fix thy mind on Me only place thy intellect in Me; (then) thou shalt, no doubt, live in Me hereafter. If thou art unable to fix thy mind steadily on Me, then by *Abhyasa*-Yoga do thou seem to reach Me. If also thou art unable to practise *Abhyasa*, be thou intent on doing actions for My sake, thou shalt attain perfection. If thou art unable to do even this, then taking refuge in Me, abandon the fruit of all action, self-controlled. Better indeed is knowledge than (blind) *Abhyasa*; meditation (with knowledge) is more esteemed than (mere) knowledge than meditation the renunciation of the fruit of action; peace immediately follows renunciation.[28]

The True Devotee

He who hates no creature, and is friendly and compassionate towards all, who is free from the feelings of 'I' and 'mine', even-minded in pain and pleasure, forbearing, ever content, steady in meditation, self-controlled, and possessed of firm conviction, with mind and intellect fixed on Me, —he who is thus devoted to Me, is dear to Me. He by whom the world is not agitated and who cannot be agitated by the world, who is freed from joy, envy, fear and anxiety, —he is dear to Me. He who is free from dependence who is pure, prompt, unconcerned, untroubled, renouncing every undertaking; —he who is thus devoted to Me, is dear to Me. He who neither rejoice, nor hates, nor grieves, nor desires, renouncing good and evil, full of devotion, he is dear to Me. He who is the same to friend and foe, and also in honour and dishonour, who is the same in heat and cold, and in pleasure and pain; who is silent, content with anything, homeless, steady-minded, full of devotion; —that man is dear to Me. And they who follow this Immortal Dharma, as described above, endued with *Shraddha*, regarding Me as the Supreme Goal, and devoted; —they are exeedingly dear to Me.[29]

The Divine Promise

Persons whom meditating on Me as non-separate, worship Me in all beings, to them thus every zealously engaged, I carry what they lack and preserve what they already have. I am the same to all beings; to Me there is none hateful or dear. But those who worship Me with devotion, are in Me, and I too am in them. If even a very wicked person worships Me, with devotion to nothing else, he should be regarded as good for he has rightly resolved. Soon does he become righteous, and attain eternal Peace; boldly canst thou proclaim, that My devotee is never destroyed.[30]

Verily, there is destruction for him, neither here nor hereafter: for the doer of good never comes to grief.[31]

The Way of the Godly

Fearlessness, purity of heart, steadfastness in knowledge and Yoga; almsgiving, control of the Senses, Yajna, reading of the Shastras, austerity; uprightness; non-injury, truth, absence of anger, renunciation, tranquility, absence of calumny, compassion to beings, uncovetousness, gentleness, modesty, absence of fickleness, boldness, forgiveness, fortitude, purity, absence of hatred, absence of pride; these belong to one born for a divine state.[32]

The Way of the Demoniac

There are two types of beings in this world, the divine and the

Asurika. The divine have been described at length; hear from Me, of the *Asurika*. Ostentation, arrogance and self-conceit anger as also harshness and ignorance, belong to one who is born for an *Asurika* state. The persons of *Asurika* nature, know not what to do and what to refrain from; neither is purity found in them nor good conduct; nor truth. They say, 'The universe is without truth, without a (moral) basis, without a God, brought about by mutual union; with lust for its cause; what else?' Holding .this view, these ruined souls of small intellect and fierce deeds, rise as the enemies of the world for its destruction. Filled with insatiable desires, full of hypocrisy, pride and arrogance, holding evil ideas through delusion, they, work with impure resolve. Beset with immense cares ending only with death, regarding gratification of lust as the highest, and feeling sure that is all; bound by a hundred ties of desire, given over to lust and wrath, they strive to secure by unjust means hoards of wealth for sensual enjoyment.

'This today has been gained by me; this desire I shall obtain; this is mine, and this wealth also shall be mine in future; 'That enemy has been slain by Me, and others also shall I slay. I am the Lord, I enjoy, I am successful, powerful and happy'. 'I am rich and well-born. Who else is equal to Me? I will sacrifice, I will give, I will rejoice.' Thus deluded by ignorance, bewildered by many a fancy, covered by the meshes of delusion, addicted to the gratification of lust, they fall down into a foul hell. Self-conceited, haughty, filled with the pride and intoxication of wealth, they perform sacrifices in name, out of ostentation, disregarding ordinance. Possessed of egoism, power, insolence, lust and wrath, these malignant people hate Me (the Self within) in their own bodies and those of others.

The divine state is deemed to make for liberation, the *Asurik* for bondage; grieve not, thou art born for a divine state.[33]

The Three Gunas and their Transcendence

Sattva, Rajas, and *Tamas*, — these *Gunas* born of *Prakriti*, bind fast in the body the indestructible embodied one. When, through every sense in this body, the light of intelligence shines, then it should be known that *Sattva* is predominant. Greed, activity, the undertaking of actions, unrest, longing — these arise when *Rajas* is predominant.

Darkness, inertness, miscomprehension, and delusion — these arise when *Tamas* is predominant. He who hates not the appearance of light (the effect of *Sattva*), activity (the effect of *Rajas)*, and delusion (the effect of *Tamas*), (in his own mind), nor longs for them absent, he who, sitting like one unconcerned, is moved not by the *Gunas*, who knowing that the *Gunas* operate, is Self-centred and swerves not; alike in pleasure and pain, Self-abiding, regarding a clod of earth, a stone and gold alike; the same to agreeable and disagreeable; firm, the same in censure and praise, the same in honour and disgrace, the same to friend and foe, relinquishing all undertakings — he is said to have gone beyond the Gunas.[34]

Three Kinds of Penance

Worship of the Devas, the twice-born, the Gurus and the wise, purity, straightforwardness, continence, and non-injury are called the austerity of the body. Speech which causes no vexation, and is true, as also agreeable and beneficial, and regular study of the Vedas, — these are said to form the austerity of speech. Serenity of mind, kindliness, silence, self-control, honesty of motive, — this is called the mental austerity.

This threefold austerity practised by steadfast men, with great *Shraddha*, desiring no fruit, is said to be *Sattvika*. That austerity which is practised with the object of gaining welcome, honour worship, and with ostentation, is said to be *Rajasika*. That austerity which is practised out of a foolish notion, with self-torture of for the purpose of ruining another, is declared to be *Tamasika*.

Three Kinds of Gifts

To give is right, —gift given with this idea, to one who does no service in return, in a fit place and to a worthy person the gift is held to be *Sattvika*. And what is given with a view to receiving in return, or looking for the fruit, or again reluctantly, that gift is held to be *Rajasika*. The gift that is given at the wrong place or time to unworthy persons without regard or with disdain, that is declared to be *Tamasika*.[35]

The Kinds of Knowledge

That by which the one indestructible Substance is seen in all beings, inseparate in the separated, know that knowledge to be *Sattvika*. But the knowledge which sees in all beings various entities of distinct kinds as different from one another, know thou that knowledge as *Rajasika*. Whilst that which is confined to one single effect as if it were the whole, without reason and without foundation in truth; —that is declared to be *Tamasika*.

Three Kinds of Intellect

That which knows the paths of work and renunciation, right and wrong action, fear and fearlessness, bondage and liberation, that intellect is *Sattvika*. That which has a distorted apprehension of *Dharma* and its opposite and also of right action and its possible, that intellect is *Rajasika*. That which enveloped in darkness regards *Adharma* as *Dharma* and views all things in a perverted light, that intellect is *Tamasika*.

Three Kinds of Will

The fortitude by which the function of the mind, the *Prana* and the senses, are regulated, that fortitude, unswerving through *Yoga*, is *Sattvika*. But the fortitude by which one regulates (one's mind) to *Dharma*, desire and wealth, desirous of the fruit of each from attachment, that fortitude, is *Rajasika*. That by which a stupid man does not give up sleep, fear, grief, despondency and also overseeing conceit, that fortitude, is *Tamasika*.

Three Kinds of Happiness

And now hear from Me, of the threefold happiness. That happiness which one learns to enjoy by habit, and by which one comes to the end of pain; that which is like poison at first, but like nectar at the end; that happiness is declared to be *Sattvika*, born of the translucence of intellect due to Self-realisation. That which arises from the contact of object with sense, at first like nectar, but at the end like poison, that happiness is declared to the *Rajasika*. That happiness which begins and results in self-delusion arising from sleep, indolence and miscomprehension, that is declared to be *Tamasika*.[36]

Three Kinds of Renunciation

The renunciation of obligatory action is not proper. Abandonment of the same from delusion is declared to be *Tamasika*. He who from fear of bodily trouble relinquishes action, because it is painful, thus performing a *Rajasika* relinquishment, he obtains not the fruit thereof. When obligatory work is performed, only because it ought to be done leaving attachment and fruit, such relinquishment is regarded as *Sattvika*.

The renunciation of *Kamya* actions, the sages understand as *Sannyasa*; the wise declare the abandonment of the fruits be all works as *Tyaga*: Relinquishment has been declared to be of three kinds. The work of *Yajna*, gift and austerity should not be relinquished, but it should indeed be performed; (for) *Yajna*, gift and asuterity are purifying to the wise. These works should be performed, leaving attachment and the fruits.[37]

True Renunciation

He should be known a constant *Sannyasi*, who neither likes nor dislikes; for, free from the pairs of opposites, he is easily set free from bondage. Children, not the wise, speak of knowledge and performance of action, as distinct. He who truly lives in one, gains the fruits of both. The plane which, is reached by the *Jnanins* is also reached by the *Karmayogins*. Who sees knowledge and performance of action as one, he sees.

Renunciation of action is hard to attain without performance of action; the man of meditation, purified by devotion to action, quickly goes to Brahman. With the mind purified by devotion to performance of action, and the body conquered, and senses subdued, one who relies one's Self, as the Self in all beings, through acting, is not tainted.

He who does actions forsaking attachment, resigning them to Brahman, is not soiled by evil, like unto a lotus-leaf by water. Devotees in the path of work perform action, only with body, mind senses and intellect, forsaking attachment, for the purification of the heart. The well-poised, forsaking the fruit of action, attains peace, born of steadfastness; the unbalanced one, led by desire, is bound by being attached to the fruit (of action).[38]

The relinquisher endued with *Sattva* and a steady understanding and with his doubts dispelled, hates not a disagreeable work nor is attached to an agreeable one. Action cannot be entirely relinquished by an embodied being, but he who relinquished the fruits of action is called a relinquisher. The threefold fruit of action — disagreeable, agreeable and mixed,— accrues to non-relinquishers after death, but never to relinquishers.[39]

The Path to Perfection

Devoted each to his own duty, man attains the highest perfection. How engaged in his own duty, he attains perfection, that hear.

From whom is the evolution of all beings, by whom all this is pervaded, worshipping Him with his own duty, a man attains perfection. Better is one's own *Dharma*, (though) imperfect, than the *Dharma* of another well-performed. He who does the duty ordained by his own nature incurs no evil. One should not relinquish the duty to which one is born, though it is attended with evil; for all undertaking are enveloped by evil, as fire by smoke.

He whose intellect is unattached everywhere, who has subdued his heart, whose desires have fled, he attains by renunciation to the supreme perfection, consisting of freedom from action. Brahman become, tranquil minded be neither grieves nor desires; the same to all beings, he attains to supreme devotion unto Me. Resigning mentally all deeds to Me, having Me as the highest goal, resorting to *Buddhi-Yoga*, do thou ever fix thy mind on Me.

The Lord dwells in the hearts of all beings, causing all beings, by His Maya, to revolve, (as if) mounted on a machine. Take refuge in Him with all they heart, by His grace shalt thou attain supreme peace (and) the eternal abode.[47]

The Perfect Life

When a man completely casts away all the desires of the mind, satisfied in the Self alone by the Self, then is he said to be one of steady wisdom. He whose mind is not shaken by adversity, who does not hanker after happiness, who has become free from affection, fear wrath, is indeed the sage of steady wisdom. He who is everywhere unattached not pleased at receiving good nor vexed at evil, his wisdom is fixed. When also, like the tortoise drawing in its limbs, he can completely withdraw the senses from their objects then his wisdom becomes steady.

Objects fall away from the abstinent man, leaving the longing behind. But his longing also ceases, who sees the Supreme.

The turbulent senses do violently snatch away the mind of even a wise man, striving after perfection. The steadfast, having controlled them all sits focused on Me as the Supreme. His wisdom is steady, whose senses are under control.

Thinking of objects, attachment to them is formed in a man. From attachment longing, and from longing anger grows. From anger comes delusion, and from delusion loss of memory. From loss of memory comes the ruin of discrimination, and from the. ruin of discrimination he perishes.

But the self-controlled man, moving among objects with senses under restraint, and free from attraction and aversion attains to tranquillity. In tranquillity, all sorrow is destroyed. For the intellect of him who is tranquil-minded, is soon established on firmness. No knowledge (of the Self) has the unsteady. Nor has he meditation. To be unmeditative there is no peace. And how can one without peace have happiness? For, the mind which follows in the wake of the wandering senses carries away his discrimination, as a wind (carries away from its course) a boat on the water. Therefore, his knowledge is steady, whose senses are completely restrained from their objects.

That man who lives devoid of longing, abandoning all desires without the sense of 'I' and 'mine', he attains to peace. This is to have one's being in Brahman. None, attaining to this, becomes delude Being established therein, even at the end of life, a man attains to oneness with Brahman.[41]

What is our *Kartavyam Karma*? What is to be done? This very important question having universal appeal and concern. This is the most difficult question; but *Geeta* has answer to it, Dr. Karna Singh calls *Geeta— Sangharsha Shastra* ('A treatise on Struggles'). Lord Krishna has himself realised complexity of duty. He says— *Gahno Karmno Gaith* (Thick and tangled is the way of action). Dr. Karna Singh has rightly observed:

"The theory of correct action should not be purely for selfish purposes, although the self is obviously involved; it should not be a necessary evil, because we have to act. Action must be positive joyous, affirmative action, it must be an offering to the divine. This is the important point. It does not matter what it is we are doing; what is important is the psychological and spiritual input into the action."[42]

In the eighteenth chapter there is an important *shloka* which says that by worshipping through one's action the divinity that pervades the entire cosmos man moves towards perfection—

सर्वकर्माण्यपि सदा कुर्वाणो मद्व्यपाश्रयः ।
मत्प्रसादादवाप्नोति शाश्वतं पदमव्ययम् ।।

If the action is detached, there is an inner freedom and inner dedication. One does not become obsessed. Thus *Geeta* leads us from detached action of Humanism and from sublimed Humanism to Divinism. At the end *Geeta* also tells us about five contributory factors[43] for the accomplishment of all actions. They are—(1) The body; a seat of all activity and organs of action, (2) *karta* (a man), (3) different kinds of organs, (4) divergent activities of various kinds, and (5) destiny.

Thus, we see that Geeta's approach to the problems is quite viable and practical. The technique adopted by Lord Krishna, whose divine personality makes him an ideal teacher, is remarkably sound and reveals a depth of psychological insight like all great teachers, he does not "teach", does not merely repeat the philosophy of his predecessors, he develops it. He combines the known and familiar techniques of his times—the Yoga of knowledge, Yoga of action and Yoga of devotion—into an integral Whole resulting into an "*inward religion, profound and subtle, but simple*". It is true that divinity is attributed to him, which is but natural for all the great teachers attain the divine heights. Therefore, though we speaks the ordinary language of the common man, but it becomes unique and immortal when it is transformed by the personality of the speaker.

Shri Krishna's technique illustrates one of the most established and well recognised ideal of teacher-taught relationship, which is not only cordial and harmonious; but also quite conducive to the teaching-learning process. Shri Krishna's technique also illustrates the soundness of the dialectical principle of teaching. The guru's answers follow the pupil's questions in succession, resulting in the composition of "*an integrated eirenicon*" (a treatise on peace). *Geeta* is an eirenicon in the sense that it is a treatise on metaphysics, ethics and psychology dealing, with the problem of human conduct whose solution is a pressing need for man if he wishes to live without inner discord. In *Geeta* we find together the Vedic cult of sacrifice, Upanishadic concept of transcendent Brahma, Bhagvad creed of compassion, dualism of Sankhya, Monism of Vedanta, meditation of Yoga, reasoning and passion of Buddha etc.

Educational Thought

All selfless teachers desire to inspire and elevate their pupils by making them conscious of their inner selves. Krishna also desires to uplift his pupil, Arjuna by making him conscious of inner self. The term 'education' is derived from the Latin word "*educare*", meaning "to lead out", "to bring up", "to raise" or "to elevate". Krishna does make all our efforts "to elevate" Arjuna who needed his advice and guidance at the time of a great illusion.

Krishna's educational thought process as embodied in his psychological hierarchy is more or less in conformity with A.F. Shand's Theory of Sentiments,[44] which has enriched present day educational thought to a considerable extent. According to this theory "a sentiment is not a single state of feeling but a system of feeling organised with reference to a particular object". Moreover, a sentiment has a considerable degree of stability, and "*generates its own peculiar qualities which tend to recur in analogous sentiments.*" It is just possible to form sentiments of love in respect of such notions as justice, truth, honour etc. Similarly we can form complementary sentiments of hatred for injustice, lying dishonour etc. McDougall, the well-known British Psychologist, sheds valuable light in the context of educational thought on the subject pointing out that "moral sentiments tend to be bipolar". Other psychologists[45] have also enhanced their thoughts on the subject.

It is significant for educators to realise that moral sentiments follow successively the order of "*concrete particular concrete general and abstract*". In the present context Arjuna develops a love for a particular person for Krishna, his teacher. This development leads to the formation of "*the concrete particular sentiment*" in Arjuna's mind Krishna's spiritual strength has a tremendous impact on Arjuna's vacilating mind. Thus we have various kinds of sentiments, some higher, some lower, some positive, some negative etc. But the *master sentiment*,[46] a determinant of the one's character, is noteworthy. The task of a teacher is to see that his little charges form right sort of sentiments, otherwise he will turn as 'kill-joy'- enemy of Learning, who help his pupils to form sentiments of hatred for knowledge and scholarship. Constant watch is essential on such teachers.

When Krishna exhorts Arjuna to control his senses, he is helping him to organise his instincts. These, in their turn, would vitalize his emotions. The latter would organise themselves into a system resulting in the formation of worthy system, a foundation of worthy character. In terms of Shand's Theory of Sentiments, Krishna makes an appealing effort to elevate his pupil's character by helping him to form his pupil's character by helping him to form moral sentiments. Such as love[47] for courage, truth, honour and duty. In fact by making Arjuna conscious of their aspirational value, he convinces him that they are ideals which he should accept.

In terms of modern educational psychology Krishna helps Arjuna to make a "Will decision". As we have said that the central value of *Geeta* is "devotion", it is a scripture of heart and not that of head, of faith not of reasoning of reverence not of logic. No one, ever convinced anybody by logic. To convince a man, you must appeal to his self-interest, his desires, his wills. Will Durant has rightly observed:

"Character lies in the will, and not in the intellect, character too is continuity of purpose and attitudes: and there are will. Popular language is correct when it prefers the heart" to the "head", it knows (because it has not reasoned about it) that a "goodwill" is profounder and more reliable than a clear mind; and when it calls man "shrewed", "knowing" or "cunning" it implies its suspicion and dislike. "*Brilliant qualities of mind win admiration, but never affection*", and "*all religions promise a reward... for excellence of will or heart, but none for excellence of head or understanding.*"[48]

The Message

The message of *Geeta* perceived by K.M. Munshi,[49] a great scholar, is as follows:

"God is and informs and upholds Creations; the Spirit is His expression in man and the Law of the Spirit is supreme.

The aim of a man's efforts is and should be to transform himself, his fellow-beings and the material world so that the Spirit is revealed in life and God becomes manifest.

To understand, to fulfil and to follow the Law of Moral Causation is the first step towards the discovery and revelation of the Spirit in life. In its aspects the non-violence, truth, non-stealing, non-waste and non-possession this law supports the Moral Order in the universe. It is inreluctable; it imposes upon man the need to care for the purity of means as much as for ends. No man may achieve good by wicked means, be a devil in order to emerge as a God.

The divine element in man is the Fundamental Aspiration which yearns for Light, Love, Beauty, Bliss, Joy, Freedom and Calm. Because of this, he is not an atom moved by Physico-Chemical laws; not merely a unit of life, like an amoeba; not a bundle of instinctive reactions, like an animal, not even a thinking machine as he believes himself to be. Because of it, he is a spark of divinity whose destiny leads towards God."

REFERENCES

1. Jaya Dayal Goenka, Preface to *Geeta*, pp. 5-6 (Pocket Edition).
2. In *Mbh.* Arjuna asked Krishna at the end of the war to repeat what he had told him in the beginning. Krishna showed his inability to do so. Of course, he gave a substitute for "*Geeta*", which is called the "Anugeeta", an important portion of *Mbh.* Particularly with philosophic point of view.
3. कुतस्त्वा कश्मलमिदं विषम समुपस्थितम् ।
अनार्यजुष्टमस्वर्ग्यमकीर्तिकरमर्जुन ।।
क्लैव्यं मा स्म गमः पार्थ नैतत्त्वटयुपपद्यते ।
क्षुद्रं हृदयदौर्बल्यं त्यक्त्वोत्तिष्ट परंतप ।।

— *The Bhagavadgeeta,* II.2-3.

4. उद्धरेदात्मनाऽऽत्मानं नात्मानमवसादयेत् ।
आत्मैव हयात्मनो बन्धुरात्मैव रिपुरात्मतः ।।
बन्धुरात्मनस्तस्य येनात्मैवात्मना जितः ।
अनात्मनस्तु शत्रुत्वे वर्तेतात्मैव शत्रुवत् ।।

— VI. 5-6.

5. अपि चेदसि पापेभ्यः पापकृत्तमः ।
सर्व ज्ञानप्लवेनैव वृजिनं संतरिष्यति ।।
यथैधांसि समिध्दोऽग्निर्भस्मसात्कुरूतेऽर्जुन ।
ज्ञानाग्निः सर्वकर्माणि भस्मसात्कुरुते तथा ।।

— IV. 36-37.

6. XIV. 1.
7. नासतो विद्यते भावो नाभावो विद्यते सः ।
उभयोशिप दृष्टोऽन्तस्त्वनयोस्तत्त्वदर्शिभिः ।।
अविनाशि तु तद्विद्धि येन सर्वमिदं ततम् ।।
विनाशभव्ययस्यास्य न, कश्चित्कर्तुमर्हति ।।

— II. 16-17, XII. 20-24

8. एषा तेऽमिहिता साख्ये बुद्धिर्योगे त्विमां श्रुणु ।
बुद्धया युक्तो तथा पार्थ. कर्मबन्धं प्रहास्यति ।।
नेहाभिक्रमनाशोऽस्ति प्रत्यवायो न विद्यते ।
स्वल्पमप्यस्य धर्मस्य त्रायते महतो भयात् ।।
व्यवसायात्मिका बुद्धिरेकेह कुरुनन्दन ।
बहुशाखा ह्यनन्ताश्च बुद्धियोऽव्यवसायिनाम् ।।

— II. 39-41.

9. नियतं कुरु कर्म त्वं ज्याषो ह्यकर्मण ।
शरीरयात्रापि च ते नं प्रसिद्धयेदकर्मणः ।।
यज्ञार्थात्कर्मणोऽन्यत्र लोकोऽयं कर्मबन्धनः ।
तदर्थ कर्म कौन्तेय मुक्तसडगः समाचर ।।

— III. 8-9.

10. Ch. II. 47-61.

11. Ch. VI. 1-4.

12. तस्मादसक्तः सततं कार्यं कर्म समाचर
असक्तो हयाचरन् कर्म परमाप्नोति पुरुषः ।।
कर्मणैव हि संसिद्धिमारिथता जनकादयः ।
लोकसग्रहमेवापि संपश्यन् कर्तुमर्हसि ।।

— III. 19-20.

13. Ch. VIII. 7.
14. Ch. III. 30.
15. Ch. III. 17-26.
16. Ch. III. 36-43.

17. अमानित्वमदम्भित्वमहिंसा क्षान्तिरार्जदम् ।
आचार्योपासनं शौचं स्थैर्यमनिग्रहः।।७।।
अमानित्वमदम्भित्वमहिंसा क्षान्तिराजेवम्।
आचार्योपासनं शौचं स्थैर्यमनिग्रहः।।७।।
इन्द्रियार्थेषु वैराग्यमहंकार एव च।
जन्ममृत्युजराव्याधिदुःखदोषानुदर्शनम।।८।।
असक्तिरनाभिष्वङ्गः पुत्रदारगृहादिषु।
नित्यं च समचित्तत्वमिष्टानिष्टोपपत्तिषु।।६।।
मयि चानन्ययोगेन भक्तिव्यभिचारिणी।
विविक्तदेशसेवित्यभरतिर्जनसंसदि।।१०।। VIII. 7-11

18. Ch. IV. 10, 18, 23, 33-38.

19. श्रद्धावाँल्लभते ज्ञानं तत्परं संयतेन्द्रियः ।
ज्ञानं लव्ध्वा परां शान्तिभचिरेणाधिगच्छति।।३६।।
अज्ञश्चाश्रध्धनश्च संशयात्मा दिनश्यति ।
नायं लोकोस्ति च परो न सुखं संशयात्मन ।।४०।।
योगसंन्यस्तकर्माणं ज्ञानसंछिन्नसंशयम् ।
आत्मवन्तं न कर्माणि निबध्नन्ति धनजयः ।।४१।। IV. 39-41

20. नादते कस्यचित्पापं न चैव सुकृतं विभुः ।
अज्ञानेनावृतं ज्ञानं तेन मुह्यन्ति जन्तवः ।।१५।।
ज्ञानेन तु तदज्ञानं येषां नाशितमात्मनः ।
तेषामदित्यवज्ज्ञानं प्रकाशयति तत्परम् ।।१६।।
तदबुद्धयस्तदात्मानस्तन्निष्ठास्तत्परायणाः ।। ।।
गच्छन्त्पुनरावृत्तिं ज्ञाननिर्धूतकल्माषाः ।।१७।। V. 15-17

21. Ch. V. 21-23

22. विद्याविनयसम्पन्न ब्राह्मणे गति हस्तिनि।
शुनि चैव श्वपाके च पण्डिताः समदर्शिनः।।१८।।
इहैव तैर्जितः सर्गो येषां साम्ये स्थितं मनः।
निर्दोष हि समं ब्रह्म तस्माद् ब्रह्मणि ते स्थितंः।।१६।।
न प्रहृष्येत्प्रियं प्राप्यं नोद्विजेद्धत्राप्य चाप्रियम्।
स्थिरबुद्धिरसम्मूढो ब्राह्माविद् ब्रह्मणि स्थितः।।२०।।

V. 18-20, VI. 29-32, XIII. 27, etc.

23 Ch. II. 14, 15, 38.

24. Ch. VI 8-9.

25. नात्यशनस्तु योगोऽन्ति न चैकान्तमनश्नतः।
न चाति स्वप्नशील्स्य जागृतो नैव चार्जुन।।१६।।
युक्ताहारविहारस्य युक्तचेष्टस्य कर्मसु।
युक्तस्वप्नावबोधस्य योगो भवति दुःखहा।।१७।।

26. Ch. VI. 10-24.

27. शनैः शनैरुपरमेद बुद्धया धृतिगृहीतया। VI. 16-17
आत्मसंस्थं मनः कृत्वा न किंचिदपि चिन्तयेत्।।२५।।
यतो यतो निश्चरति मनश्चञ्चलमस्थिरम्।
ततस्ततो नियम्यैतदात्मन्येव वशं नयेत्।।२६।।
प्रशान्तमनसंह्येनं योगिनं सुखमुत्तमम्।
उपैति शान्तरजसं ब्रह्मभूतमकल्मषम्।।२७।।
युञ्जन्नेवं सदाऽऽत्मानं योगी विगतकल्मषः।
सूखेन ब्रह्मसंस्पर्शमन्यन्तं सुखमश्नुते।।२८।। VI. 25-28
असशयं महाबाहो मनो दुर्निग्रह चलम्।
अभ्यासेन तु कौन्तेय वैराग्येण च गृह्यते।।३५।।
असंयताम्मा योगो दुष्प्राय इति मे मतिः।
वश्यात्मना तु यतता शक्योऽवाप्तुमुपायतः।।३६।। VI. 35-36

28. **मय्यावैश्य मनो ये मा नित्ययुक्ता उपासते।**
श्रद्धया परयोपेतास्ते मे युक्ततमा मताः।।२।।
मय्येव मन आधत्स्व मयि बुद्धिं निवेशय।
निवसिष्यसि मऽयेव अत उर्ध्व न संशयः।।८।।
अथ चित्तं समाधातुं न शक्नोसि मयि स्थिरम्।
अभ्यासयोगेन ततो मामिच्छाप्तुं धनंजय।।९।।
अभ्यासेऽप्यसमर्थोऽसि मत्कर्मपरमो भव।
मदर्थमपि कर्माणि कुर्वन्सिद्धिमवाप्स्यसि।।१०।।

अथैतदप्यशक्तोऽसि कर्तुं मद्योगमाश्रितः।
सर्वकर्मफलत्यागं ततः कुरु यतात्मवान्।।११।।
श्रेयो हि ज्ञानमभ्यासाज्ज्ञानाद्ध्यानं विशिष्यते।
ध्यानात्कर्मफलत्यागस्त्यागाच्छन्तिरनन्तरम्।।१२।। XII. 28-12

29. Ch. XII. 13-20.

30. अनन्याश्चिन्तयन्तो मां ये जनाः पर्युपासते।
तेषां नित्याभियुक्तानां योगक्षेमं वहाम्यहम्।।२०।।
समोऽहं सर्वभूतेषु न मे द्वेष्योऽस्ति न प्रियः।
ये भजन्ति तु मां भक्त्या मयि ते तेषु चाप्यहम।।२६।।
अपि चेत्सुदुराचारो भजते मामनन्यभाक्।
साधुरेव स मन्तव्यः सम्यग्व्यवसितो ङि सः।।३०।।
क्षिप्रं भवति धर्मात्मा शश्वच्छान्तिं निगच्छति।
कौन्तेय प्रतिजानीहि न मे भक्तः प्रणश्यति।।३१।। IX. 20, 29-31

31. Ch. VI. 40.

32. अभयं सत्त्वसंशुद्धिज्ञानयोगव्यवस्थितिः।
दानं दमश्च यज्ञख्य स्वाध्यायस्तप आर्जयम्।।१।।
अहिंसा सत्यमक्रोधस्त्यागः शान्तिरपैशुनम्।
दया भूतेष्वलोलुप्त्वं मार्दवं हीरचापलम्।।२।।
तेजः क्षमा धृतिः शौचमद्रोहो नातिमानिता।
भवन्ति संपदं दैवीमभिजास्य भारत।।३।। XVI. 1-3

33. Ch. XVI. 5-18.

34. Ch. XIV. 5, 11-13, 22-25.

35. Ch. XVII. 2-22.

36. Ch. XVIII. 20-39.

37. काम्यानां कर्मणां न्यासं संन्यासं कवयो विदुः।
सर्वकर्मफलत्यागं प्राहुस्त्यागं विचक्षणाः।।२।।
त्याज्यं दोषवदित्येके कर्म प्राहुर्मनीषिणः।
यज्ञदानतपः कर्म न त्याज्यमिति चापरे।।३।।
निश्चयं श्रुणु मे तत्र त्यागे भरतसत्तम्।
त्यागो हि पुरुषव्याघ्र त्रिविधः संप्रकीर्तितः।।४।।
यज्ञदानतपःकर्म न त्याज्यं कार्यमेव तत्।
यज्ञो दानं तपश्चैव पावनानि मनीषिणाम्।।५।।
एतान्यपि तु कर्माणि सङ्गं त्यक्त्वा फलानि च।
कर्तव्यानीति मे पार्थ निश्चितं मतमुत्तमम्।।६।। XVIII. 2-6

38. Ch. V. 3-12.

39. न द्वेष्टयकुशल कर्म कुशले नानुष्ज्जते।
त्यागी सत्त्वसमाविष्टो मेधावी छिन्नसंशयः।।१०।।
न हि देहभृता शक्य त्यक्तु कर्माण्यशेषतः।
यस्तु कर्मफलत्यागी स त्यागीत्यभिधीयते।।११।।
अनिष्टमिष्टं मिश्र च त्रिविधं कर्मणः फलम्।
भयत्यत्यागिना प्रेत्य न तु संन्यासिनां कथित्।।१२।।

40. Ch. XVIII. 45-49, 61-62.

41. Ch. II. 55-72.

42. Dr. Karna Singh, *Essays on Hinduism*, p. 64.

43. अधिष्ठानं तथा कर्ता करणं च पृथग्विधम्।
विविधाश्च पृथक्चेष्टा दैवं चैवात्र पञ्चमम्।।

44. In his book titles as "Foundations of Character" A.F. Shand calls the disposition of Love, hate respect etc., as sentiments. These "sentiments" are nothing but values. Love, respect, devotion, reverence etc. are positive values whereas hatred, enmity, envy etc. are negative values. We have dealt with this subject in a separate chapter styled as "Education for Values". The "Theory of Sentiments" is also expounded in McDougal's "Social Psychology".

45. Compare – Nunn, T.P. , "*Education : Its Data and First Principles*", p. 164. According to Rose – "Sentiment is not born with us like instincts, it is an acquired organisation of dispositions in the mental structure." McDougal opines that it "involves an individual tendency to experience certain emotions and desires in reaction to some particular object."

46. When various sentiments are being formed, there is one strong sentiment which dominates others. This is the master sentiment under which other sentiments work in harmony and are controlled by it. When there is no possibility of a conflict between sentiment, when the inter-related system works, well, character is vigorously consistent and strong.

47. In this very treatise we have mentioned that the central value of *Geeta* is devotion which consists of two values apparently—Love and reverence. Love implies various allied values in its various forms, as Satya Sai Baba have perceived them—
Love as thought is Truth
Love as action is Right Conduct
Love as feeling in Peace
Love as understanding in Non-violence
(Education in Human Values, compiled by Lorained Burrows,p.70).

48. Will Durrant, *The Story of Philosophy,* pp. 313-14.

49. K.M. Munshi ,*Bhagwad Geeta and Modern Life* (BVB),p. 203.

12

WAYS OF AJIVIKAS

It is universally acknowledged fact that Biology and Genetics can explain some of the many differences that distinguish individuals from each other; but determining why a certain person should have his own unique genetic composition? This is beyond the powers of science to give satisfactory answer. Fate, which seems to be only answer, plays a striking role in non-hereditary aspects of individual and human lives as well.

Who Were Ajivikas

Gosal or Muskary (Mankkhali) Gosal, a contemporary of Gautam Buddha and Mahavir, was a great exponent of determinism. He was born in a cow-pen, where his parents took refuge while on a pilgrimage during a rainy season. Therefore, he was named "cowpen" (*Gosal*). The school established by the sage Monki is called *Ajivika*, a sect which came into existence along with Buddhism and Jainism. As per the Jain tradition Mahavir and Monki lived together for number of years. In Jain and Buddhist literature he is called Mankhalii Gosal. A.L. Basham, in his famous book "*Wonder That India Was*" has mentioned Gosal as Maskari, in fact, *Maskari* was a title. Patanjali, a noted grammarian and an author of 'Mahabhashya' (a commentary on Ashtadhyayee of Panini), has explained the word 'Maskari' like this: "Don't work, don't work, peace is better for us—one who says like this—is called Maskari".[1]

Gosal reportedly asserted : "There is no cause, either ultimate or remote, for the depravity (state of being corrupted) of beings; they become depraved without reason and without cause. There is no cause either proximate or remote, for the rectitude of beings, they became pure without reason and without cause. The attainment of any given condition, of any character, does not depend either on one's own acts, or on the acts of another, or on human effort. There is no such thing or power or energy or human strength or human vigour. All animals, all creatures (with one, two or more senses), all beings (produced from eggs or in a womb), all souls (in plants) are without force and power and energy of their own".[2]

The doctrine of Gosal was a sort of theism, which can rightly be called 'Ultra-theism', seeds of which are found in abundance in Hindu scriptures. Mahābhārata say:

> "when men are ripe for ruin, even a straw
> Has power to crush them, like a thunderbolt".[3]

At many places the doctrine of 'pre-destination' has been critised also. Valmiki says that those are coward and impotent, who depend upon the destiny (fate); noble and brave persons never look forward to the luck or fate for their fortunes.[4] In this connection, in Mahābhārata we find a very balanced and practical view. Vyasa compares the endeavour of the individual and the destiny with the two wheels of the chariot, whose function is not accomplished even if one of these two is missing.[5]

Determinism Vs. Indeterminism

In the Shanti Parvan of Mahābhārata, consoling the Pandavas Vyas says that they are grieving to the point of distraction because—

> "This grief is pointless.
> What is born, die; what's united, divides.
> Destiny rules us all.
> Like bubbles on a stream, things come and go.
> Friends do not bring joy, nor enemies misery;

Wisdom does not bring wealth, nor wealth happiness
Destiny rules us all."[6]

Further in the Mahabharata itself we find a very balanced disposition about the duty and destiny. If the life is a chariot, duty (deeds) and destiny — these two are its wheels. For the movement of the chariot as the functioning of both the wheels is necessary, so is the case of life. Good fortunes can be achieved or misfortunes can be lessened or eliminated by good deeds provided the fate is also favourable to an individual.

Confucious also says : "life and death are governed by fate, and riches and honours depend upon sky. If Great Man is faultlessly respectful, if he is humble within the rites of his fellow men, then in the whole, wide world, all are his brothers. How can a Great Man complain that he has no brothers?"[7]

Bhartrihari, in his *Nitishataka*,[8] has quoted an incident highlighting the prominence of destiny in human life: "One night a mouse cut out a hole into bamboo basket, and thus entering into its; interior, it became the morsel of a hungry serpent that had long been imprisioned there, and consequently deprived of all power and hope of further life; but appeased its hunger by the flesh of the mouse God had sent it, it now came out of its prision by the same path and became a free creature. Here you see that fate and fate alone is the real cause of good and evil to all men." One can experience such incident in real life when we are busy in doing some work or performing the essentials, all of a sudden some most desired or undesired come in between and elevate or relegate our planning. This is a part of a life or game we have to play whether we like it or not. Through another analogy of the feeler and container he says that a pitcher can fetch only the same quantity of water regardless to its being sunk into a well or sea. Similarly one is sure to get the quantity of wealth whether small or great according to one's preordained fortune; and it can never be more or less, no matter one is cast into the midst of a sandy desert, or on the top of the famous golden mountain, the *Meru.*"[9]

What Gosala preached was a doctrine of utter fatalism saying that, "No amount of virtue and assertions could hasten or shorten the natural biological process of rebirths, that goodness did not help towards the final release".[10] The only consolation seemed to be that in the end, each life-monad having passed through the inevitable 84 lacs of aeons would finally find peace. No matter what one did, one could neither change or shorten the end nor the inexorable progress towards it. Even if one became an ascetic, it was only because he was destined for it. Each and every aspect of life and activity was predetermined and just as a ball of string (top) when thrown, would go only as far as string unwound, so too, the fool and the wise would alike, run their course till they finally found.

Law of Karma and Pre-destination

"The law of Karma does not support the doctrine of predestination. There are some who believe that only the pre-destination of certain souls to destruction is consistent with divine sovereignty. God has a perfect right to deal with his creatures even as a potter does with his clay. St. Paul speaks of 'vessels of wrath fitted to distruction'. Life eternal is a gracious gift of God. Such a view of divine sovereignty is unethical. God's love is manifested in and through law."

Notwithstanding his diving deep into the sea, or ascending up the peak of the mountain Meru, the famous golden mountain, or defeating his enemies in battle, or learning with proficiency the different sciences and arts or commerce, husbandry, and service; or crossing like a bird the endless sky, a man with all his efforts is quite unable to effect anything contrary to his fate; for, there is no doing against one's destiny whose course is wholly unavoidable.[10]

For a person swinging between determinism the following piece of advice of Vivekananda is quite pertinent. He says, "we make our destiny. His sun shines for the weak as well as for the strong. His wind blows for saint and sinner alike. He is the lord of all, father of all, merciful and impartial. Do you mean to say that he, the Lord of creation , looks upon the pretty things of our life in the same light as we do? What a degenerate idea of God that would be! He knows what the puppets' play means. Our attempts to lay the blame on him; making him the punisher and the rewarder, are only foolish.

He neither punishes nor rewards any. His infinite mercy is open to everyone, at all times, at all places, under all conditions, unfailing unswerving. Upon *us* depends how we use it. Upon *us* depends how we utilize it. Blame neither God nor anyone in the world. When you find yourselves suffering, blame yourselves, and try to do better."[11]

REFERENCES

1. "मा कृत कर्माणि, मा कृत कर्माणि शान्तिर्वः श्रेयसीत्याहातो मस्करी परिव्राजकः ।"
2. Digha-Nikaya, II, 20-22.
3. Mahabharata, Drone Parvan, 429

   सर्वसाम्यमनायासः सत्यवाक्यं च भारत ।
   निर्वेदश्चाविवित्सा च यस्य स्यात्स सुखीनरः ॥
   एतान्येव पंचवृद्धाः प्रशान्तये ।
   एष स्वर्गश्च धर्मश्च सुखं चानुत्तमं सताम् ।

   — Shanti, 171.2-3

4. क्लीवो वीर्यहीनो यः स दैवमनुवर्तते ।
   वीराः संभावितात्मानो न दैवं पर्युपासते ॥

   — Ramayana, 2.23.16

   cf. (ए) मूढैः प्रकल्पितं दैवं तत्परास्ते क्षयं गताः ।
   प्राज्ञास्तु पौरुषार्थेन पदमुत्तमतां गताः ॥

   (बी) अहले हिम्मत मंजिलेमकसूद तक आ ही गये ।
   बन्दसेतकदीर किस्मत का गिला करते रहे ॥

   — "Chakbasta"

5. ह्येकेन चक्रेन रथस्य गतिर्न विद्यते ।
   न हि पुरुषकारेण विना दैवं हि सिद्ध्यति ॥

   — Mahabharata

   Cf. उद्यमेन हि सिद्ध्यन्ति कार्याणि न मनोरथैः ।
   न हि सुप्तस्य सिंहस्य प्रविशन्ति मुखे मृगाः ॥

   — Panchtantra

6. Mahabharata of Vyas, Transcreated by P. Lal, p. 301.
7. Sayings of Confucious, xii.5.
8. भग्नाशस्य करण्डपीडिततनोर्म्लानेन्द्रियस्य क्षुधा,
   कृत्वाडखुर्विवरं स्वयं निपतितो नक्तं मुखे भोगिनः ।
   तृप्तस्तत्पिशितेन सत्वरमसौ तेनैव यातः पथा,
   लोकाः पश्यत दैवमेव हि नृणां वृद्धौ क्षये कारणम् ॥

   — Nitishataka, 85

9. यद्धात्रा निजभालपट्टलिखितं स्तोकं महद्व धनं,
   तत्प्राप्नोति मरुस्थले पि नितरां ततो नाधिकम ।

तद्धीरो भव वित्तवस्तु कृपणां वृतिं वृथा मा कृथाः,
कूपे पश्य पयोनिधावपि घटो गृहाति तुल्यं जलम् ।।

— Nitishataka, 49

cf. (ए) किस्मत में जो लिखा है, वह आयेगा आपसे
फैलाइए न हाथ, न दामन पसारिए ।।

— 'Aatish'

(बी) निज कर क्रिया "रहीम" कहि सुधि भावी के साथ ।
पांसे अपने हाथ में, दांव न अपने हाथ ।।

— Rahim (Rahiman Vilas)

10. मज्जत्वम्भसि यातु मेरुशिखरं शत्रूंजयत्वाहवे,
वाणिज्यं कृषिसेवनादि सकला विद्याः कलाः शिक्षतु ।
आकाशं विपुलं प्रयातु खगवत्कृत्वा प्रयत्नं परं,
नाभाव्यं भवतीह कर्मवशतो भाव्यस्य नाशः कुतः ।

— Nitishatak, 101

cf. (ए) आकाशमुत्पततु गच्छतु वादिगन्तमम्भोनिधिं विशतु तिष्ठतु वा पथेच्छम् ।
जन्मान्तरार्जितशुभाशुभकृन्तराणां छायेव न त्यजति कर्मफलानुबन्धः ।।

— Shantishatak, Part-III, 21

(बी) एवं प्राग्जन्मसम्बन्धपरायत्तेषु जन्तुषु ।
भाविको वस्तितिक्रामेत्को वा किं कस्य वारयेत् ।

—Kathasaritsagar, Suratmanjari
Lambak, Tarang - 2.170

(सी) पातालमाविशतु यातु सुरेन्द्रलोकमारोहतु क्षितिधराधिपतिं च मेरुम् ।
मन्त्रौषधप्रहरणैश्च करोतु रक्षां यद्भावि तद्भवति नात्र विचारहेतुः ।।

— Suktavali

11. What Religion is, in the words of Swami Vivekananda, Ed. by John Yale, p. 63.

13

MYSTICISM
Eastern Context

It will be a just futile exercise to explain the Eastern Thought without having a peep into the Mysticism, as it had played a definite role in weaving the religious fabric of the East. In quantity as well as in quality the East is far richer and eloquent than the West in mystic expression as well as experience. One of the pertinent and prominent reasons for this had been the willed inclination towards spiritualism and materialism of the East and West respectively.

Mysticism Defined

According to the *Universal Dictionary* of the English language, "a knowledge of ultimate reality and the divine can be gained only by immediate intuition, especially by concentration of the mind on and absorption in the *divine essence* which leads through ecstacy to the revealing." In fact, when the words fail to reach the ultimate, any sort of thought or contemplation too faint away speeding towards the Infinite, how to comprehend the Supreme? Under such phenomena Saints and Mystics make their heart so pure that reality gets reflected undistorted therein. Mysticism transcends sex and nationality, race and religion, colour and creed.

What is an element called mystical? On this Dr. Radhakrishnan says that when anything is not accessible to us in the normal ways—through the ways of reason or intellect we describe it as mystical.

Mysticism is defect of though *only* when it is negative in approach—emphasised only to cover-up explain something. Mysticism, in fact, is a natural and necessary aspect of higher thinking. This can be recognized only when the rational and the scientific ways of understanding realise their limitations and come to perceive the evidence of '*a beyond*' that transcends the rational and scientific ways. According to Radhakrishnan, it is in this sense that there is the presence of a mystical element in religious experience.

Shri Ramkrishna has rightly said: "When one attains Samadhi, then alone comes the knowledge of Brahman, and one attains the vision of God. In that ecstatic realization, all thoughts cease, and one becomes perfectly silent. There in no power speech lift by which to express Brahman. For verily is he beyond power and speech."[1]

This state of mind is really indescribable just like a taste of sweet-meat by a dumb person. Kathopnishad puts it like this: "When the five instruments of knowledge stand still, together with the mind, and the intellect itself does not stir—that, they say, is the highest state. This they consider to be Yoga, this steady control of the senses. The one does become watchful, for Yoga comes and goes."[2]

According to Bhagvadgita such state of mind is true being, unthinkable, indefinable, and yet realizable:

> Utterly quiet
> Made clean of passion
> The Mind of the yogi
> Knows that Brahman
> His bliss is the highest.[3]

In the concept of supermind enhanced by Shri Aurobindo also we find the element of mysticism. We can say that the ascent from mind to supermind is a passage from nature to super nature. Because of this fact it cannot be achieved by a mere effort of our mind or our unaided aspiration. Aurobindo wished that the powers of the Super-conscience must descend into human beings and uplift them and transform their being. According to him spiritual transformation of supermind leads the soul to the apprehension of spiritual unity. He says: "A spiritualised consciousness is achieved and the life falls quiet, the body ceases to need and to clamour, the soul itself merges into the spiritual silence."[4] Here it needs mention that Aurbindo talks of a triple transformation of the supermind : (a) Psychic transformation,(b) Spiritual transformation, and (c) Supramental transformation. The element of mysticism is said to be more implicit and dense in the third type of the transformation.

Global Phenomena

Saints and Mystics are found all over the world. Like in the East there had been a great galaxy of mystics in the West also. To name a few —St. John, St. Paul, Plotinus (205-270 A.D.), St. Augustine (354-430 A.D.), Dionysius, the Areopagite (475-515A.D.), St. Francis of Assissi (1226-1347), St. Therese (Spain), Catherine of Sienna (1347-1380). Germany has also been very famous for her mystics such as Meister Echhart (1260-1329), Tauler (1230-1361), Jacob Boehme (Cobblermystic), Swedenburg (1688-1772, Sweden), H. William Lqw, George Fox, William Blake etc. In the Eastern tradition right from the Vedic age to the modern age of renaissance, from Shankaracharya to Satya Sai of Shirdi there has been a very long tradition of mystics. Most of our ancient sages had "intuitive experience" or *Aparokshanubhuti* as Acharya Shankar has put it. It is the experience beyond words and beyond expression. The great sages like Vyas, Valmiki, Angira, Bhishma, Shukracharya etc. had a sort of vision to assess the things or ideas and foretell the future.[5] The Shaiva saints of South India are known for their overpowering devotion. Saint Kannappa (first or second century A.D.) had such an intense love for Shiva that in the frenzy of his devotion he plucked out one of his eyes. He was about to do the same to the other, he had a vision of the Lord. Tirumular, who belongs to the fifth century, had supernatural powers. He entered the body of a dead shepherd and wrote 3000 verses on religious life. According to him, everyone, who strives for superhuman powers, can obtain them. It is more or less a common belief, which is also confirmed by the Upanishads: "The self-existent pierced the senses outward, and so one looks outward and not within oneself. *Some wiseman, however seeking immortality, and turning his eyes inward, sees inner Self.*"[6] Thus there is no doubt that every Atman contains the seeds of spiritual growth and ultimate realization. The great mystic like Raman Maharshi held that "Everyman is divine and strong in his real nature. What are weak and evil are his habits, his desires and thoughts, but not himself."[7a] Similarly opines Dr. Karan Singh: "However diverse the circumstances, however hostile the environment, Hinduism believes that there is within the human psyche the unquenchable spark of divinity that can, sooner or later, be fanned into the blazing fire of spiritual realization. This concept endows every indivudual with a dignity that immediately places him, in essence, above and beyond social and traditions."[7b]

Monism and Dualism

Our mystic saint poets had not any rigid or confined way. Some believed in the monism, i.e. absolutism of Brahman and adopted *Nirguna* way of devotion, while others believed in the personal theism. But Ramanujachary attempted a harmonious combination of absolutism with personal theism. The attempt is not new. According to Dr. C.D. Sharma: "We find it in the Gita, in the Mahabharata, particularly in the section called Narayaniya, and in the Puranas, notably in the Visnu and the Bhagavata. This tradition was continued by the Alvar saints and their interpreters, the Acharyas to whom Ramanuja was largely indebted. The attempt to combine personal theism with absolutism took three main lines— Vaisnavism, Shaivism and Shaktism accodingly the Personal Divinity was identified with Visnu or Shiva or Shakti. Among the Vaisnavas there are four main sects— Shrisampradaya (*Vishistadvaita*) of Ramanuja, Brahmasampradaya (*Dvaita*) of Madhva, also known as Anandatirtha and Sanakasampradaya (*Davaitadvaita*) of Nimbarka. Chaitanyasampradaya (*Achintybhedabheda*) is treated as a branch of Madhvism.[8]

The credit for propounding special type of Monitheism (*Vishistadvaita*) goes to Ramanuja. He recognizes three things as ultimate and real (*Tattva Traya*). These are matter (*achit*), soul

(*Chit*) and God (*Ishwar*). The first two are absolutely dependent on God. According to Swami Prabhvananda, "To the student of Western Philosophy, Ramanuja's ideas concerning God and the soul bear an astonishing resemblance to ideas on the same subject with which scholastic philsophy concerned itself during the Christian Middle Ages. The personality and the attributes of God, the Heavenly Father, the relation of man to God, the question of free will and divine grace, the submission of the will of a man to a higher will than his, the union of human and divine, the relative positions of reason and love in the divine scheme, the vision of divine love and grace, and the release of the soul from bondage after—it was principally on these topics that the Schoolmen speculated through many hundreds of years, from St. Augustine until the final synthesis of faith and reason in St. Thomas, St. Aquinas, and Ramanuja, living in the tenth century, might well have been the spiritual father of the Christian Dante."[9]

Sufi poet Jala-ud-din Romi (d. 1273) in his one of the Masnavis sings of One True Light:

The lamps are different, but the light is the same:
it comes from beyond If thou keepest looking at the lamp, thou are lost:
for thence arises the appearance of number and plurality Fix thy gaze upon the light, and thous art delivered from the dualism inherent in the finite body.
thou art the Kernel of Existence, the disagreement between Moslem, Zoroastrian and Jew depends on the standpoint.[10]

In the Sufist tradition alike Rumi, the name of al-Hallaj, the great Martyre of Sufism is very notable, who suffered at Baghdad in A.D. 922. His disciple Ibn Fatik relates: "When Husayn Mansur al-Hallaj was brought to be crucified, and saw the cross and nails, he laughed so greatly that tears flowed from his eyes... and when he had finished he uttered a prayer of which I remember only these words.

"O Lord, I beseech thee to make me thankful for the grace that thou hast bestowed upon me in concealing from the eyes of other men what thou hast revealed to me of the splendours of Thy radiant countenance which is without a form, and making it lawful for me to behold the mysteries of Thy inmost conscience which thou hast made unlawful to other men.

And these Thy servants who are gathered to slay me in zeal for thy religon and in desire to win Thy favour, pardon them and have mercy upon them; for verily if Thou hast revealed to them that which thou hast revealed to me, they would not have done what they have done; and if Thou hadst hidden from me that which Thou hast hidden from them, I should not have suffered this tribulation. Glory upto thee in whatsoever Thou in whatsoever thou doest, and glory unto thee in whatsoever Thou willest."[11]

The very conflict between the Religion of the Saint and the Religion of the Prophet came to a crisis in the case of al-Hallaj, whose life and death mark the turning point of the whole Sufi Movement. Christopher Dawson said: " The martyrdom of al-Hallaj is the culmination of the Christian tendencies which were already latent in the earlier Suffi movement. Al- Hallaj founded his ideal of mystical sanctity on the Koranic tradition of Jesus, and this imitation of the Koranic Christ led him on to a literal conformity with the real Christ in His Passion and death."[12]

In the Middle East as well as in India there have been many mystics. To name a few—Iranian Sufis, Habib Hjami (738 A.D.), Ibrahim Adham (875 A.D.), Fazail (803 A.D.); mystics of Islam as Ghzzali (12th century), Sheikh Abdulla Ansari of Herat (1005-1090), Jalal-ud-din Rumi (13th century), Fariduddin-in-Attar (1118 A.D.), Sadi (13th century), Nurid-din-Jami (1414-1492), Faiz (14th century), Abdul Latif of Sindh etc.

There was saint poetess of Basara, who used to go to the house-top and pray as follows: "O my Lord, the stars are shining and the eyes of men are closed, and the kings have shut their doors and every lover is alone with his beloved and here am I alone with thee." Again she would say: "O my Lord whatever share of this world thou dost bestow on me, bestow it on thine enemies, and whatever, share of the next would thou dost give me, give it to Thy friends, Thou art enough for me."

In Islam we find two types of Schools. One is of orthodox

orders which had their individual views on community life and routine of prayers and fasts, and they hardly come out of *zuhd, ibadat, taqua* and *riyadat*— the limits set by their founders. But Shah Abdul Latif of Sindh, like other liberal Muslims (Sufis) attached no sole importance to them. Refuting the significance of orthodox practices of Islam he says:

> Prayers and the sacred fast—
> They too are virtuous things
> But that is another art
> Which brings the beloved face to face[13]

A group of scholars believe that Sufism is the admixture of Neo-Platonism, Zorastrianism, Buddhism, and Indian Monism.[14] Whatever may be the point of its origination but it emerged long ago as the need for the humanity. "The sufis, being in the general framework of the Shart'ah, the correct practices of the quaranic beliefs, followed different individual paths, or *tariqah*, for their spiritual endeavour. With Mansur Hallaj (858-922), metaphysical speculation showed itself prominently in Sufism originally a doctrine of social and philanthropic nature. Mansur Hallaj said, *anal-Haqq* (I am truth) and the orthodox people took his life. Ali b. Uthman al-Hujwiri (b. circa 1000) in his *kashful mahjub* (The Unveiling or the Veiled), the oldest Persian work on Sufism, declared it heretical to say that in the state of *fana* personality merged into or even mixed with the Divine Personality.[15]

Is Guru Dispensable ?

Our scriptures enjoin that Guru is indispensable for achieving knowledge, spiritual or otherwise. We find a grand galaxy of such Gurus (or *Acharyas*) who initiated their disciple on the path of enlightenment. Raman Maharshi maintains that Guru need not necessarily take human form. He himself used to sing hymns to Arunachala. Further he is also reported to have said Mrs. Piggott, an English visitor "Realization is the result of the Guru's Grace more than of teachings, lectures, meditations, etc. These are only secondary but that is the primary and essential cause."[16] Somebody who knew his teaching at second hand suggested that he did not hold it necessary to have a Guru and explained the lack of explicit initiation in that way, but he rejected his suggestion unequivocally. S.S. Cohen has recorded a conversation[17] on this subject with Dilip Kumar Roy, the celebrated musician of Shri Aurobindoashram:

Dilip: Some people report Maharshi to deny the need of a Guru. Other say the reverse. What does Maharshi say ?

Bh.: I have never said that there is no need of a Guru. (Maharshi)

Dilip: Shri Aurobindo often referes to you as having no guru.

Bh.: That depends on what you call Guru. He need not necessarily be in human form—Dattatreya had twenty-four Gurus— the elements, etc. That means any form in the world was his Guru. Guru is absolutely necessary. The Upanishads say that none but a Guru can take a man out of the jungle of mental and sense perceptions. So there must be a Guru

Dilip: I mean a human Guru. The Maharshi did not have one.

Bh.: I might have had at sometime or other. And did not sing hymns to Aurnachala ? What is a Guru ? Guru is god or the Self. First a man prays to God to fulfil his desire but for God himself. So God appears to him in some form or other, human or non-human, to guide him as a Guru in an answer to his prayer.

As a reaction Hinduism raised its head the Arya Samaj and Brahmo Samaj under the leadership of Swami Dayanand Saraswati and Raja Ram Mohan Roy respectively. But these reformers failed to have a comprehensive vision, which only antagonised the vast mass or orthodoxy The main stream of Hindu religion based on eternal springs of Vedant, Buddhism, and the Bhakti movement as expounded by Gaudapada, Shankara, Ramanuj, the Vaishnava saints, and Lord Buddha, began to get dry. It was at this point of time that Shri Ramakrishna came to the scene and fulfilled the Gita's promice[18] by re-establishing the Dharma. About him Mahatma Gandhi says very rightly: "The story of Ramakrishna Paramhamsa's life is a story of religion in practice. His life enables us to see God alone is real and that all else is illusion. *Ramakrishna is a living embodiment of Godliness.*"

Tota Puri, a Vedantik monk, started Ramakrishna on the path of realization of the impersonal Brahman. When the monk expressed his willingness to give him the advaitic doctrine, Ramakrishna said "I will ask permission of the Divine Mother to undergo it." The Divine mother gave him the permission, and Ramakrishna accepted Tota Puri as his guide. Again the experience is best related by Ramakrishna himself:

"The universe was extinguished. Space itself was no more. At first the shadows of ideas floated in the obscure depths of mind. These melted away, leaving a monotonous ticking of the conscience of the ego. Then that too stopped. Nothing remained in existence. The soul was lost in the Self. Dualism was blotted out. Beyond word and beyond thought, I attained Brahman.[19]

Ramakrishna remained in this state continually for three days and three nights, after which his guru brought him back to normal consciousness, much wondering how his disciple had attained this state of *nirvikalpa samadhi* in a day, when he himself had been able to achieve it only after forty years of strenuous practice. It is reported that after Tota Puri's departure, Ramakrishna remained for six months in continuous communion with Brahman. He lost consciousness, and was able to survive only because a monk who was present, realising his condition at the time, forcibly fed him during the few moments he lapsed into consciousness.

Kabir says that those who think lightly of their Guru are Blind, indeed. When God frowns upon you, the Guru is your refuge, but when the Guru frowns, you have no refuge anywhere.[20] Further he says :

If body is a Venomous creeper
    Guru is tank full of nectar
Should you give for Guru your head
    Still the price is for less paid.[21]

He preached a very simple religion based on ethical and moral values. His teaching was based on the authority of his direct realisation of God and thus attacked directly the priestcraft of both Hinduism and Islam.[22] As a result he became an eye-sore for the priests. When Kabir was summoned to the court of Sikandar Lodi he refused to salute the Emperor because for him there was no Emperor except Rama. This arrogance resulted due to unflinching faith in Rama and the allegations lodged by the priests gave a long handle to the emperor to punish him. On different occasions, he got Kabir tied to a stone, thrown into water, also into burning flames, and pushed under the feet of a doped elephent. From each trial Kabir cameout unhurt. Ultimately the Emperor had to submit tc knowledge of the divinity in him.

Alike Kabir, his disciple Raidas (a Cobbler Saint) does not offer any wreath or prayer to God, but he believes in the natural meditation.[23] These saints, such as Paltudas, Dadudas, Charandas, Nanak etc. believed and taught Nirgun Bhakti which included the concept of Shankar's Advaita the oneness of Jiva with the Supreme self. The Yoga practices of Natha Yogis, the religion of love of the Sufis, and Islam's brotherhood of man and the concept of Shankar's Advaita the oneness of Jiva with the Supreme Self. These saints stressed on God's grace as most essential of spiritual illumination. Kabir called it Nirguna, in the sense that He was free from the three Gunas (*sattva – Raja – Tama*) and their derivatives – ego, vanity, attachment, jealousy, anger, senses etc. Kabir says : Rama, Rahim, Keshava, Karim, Allah, Ishwar are the different names of one and the same supreme bliss. Veda, Kuran etc. also confirm this disposition.[24]

Soul and Cosmic Soul

Mysticism moves around the Paramatma and Atma, i.e. Brahman and Jiva and the aim happens to the union of the two, which is possible only through self-realisation. Brahman is related to the cosmos as the soul is related to body. As a man has a soul and a body, and as the soul, though distinct from the body, yet controls and guides it, lives in it. And uses it as an instrument, similarly

Brahman is the soul of the universe, the sources and sustenance of all beings within it, and the ruler over all. This relationship between the soul and cosmic Soul is eternal and for mystic saints it is inseparable, indivisible and imperishable. That's why Raidas says :

"O Lord, you are Sandal, I am water,
Its fragrance is internalized deep in me,
You are the forest, I am indwelling pea-cock,
Look at you as the bird Chakore looks at he moon,
You are lamp, I am its wick fine
Whose flame is burning day and night
You are the thread, I am pearl pure
As borax is mingled with gold pure
O Lord you are the savant, I am servant
O Lord my devotion to thee is so sure
My zeal to repeat name thine intense in gear."[25]

Mysticism of Kabir is mainly based on three aspects his concept of God or Brahman, his concept of soul or Atman, and his concept of Maya or the World as Illusion. Kabir calls Brahma the Primal Principle or the essence. It is beyond time, space, qualities and attributes. It is unaffected by any change. It is absolute and beyond causation – "Neither to the left, nor to the right, nor in front, neither below, nor above, formless."[26] This is what Kathopanishad says about the Brahman – His form is not to be seen, no one beholds him with the eye. He is to be apprehended by the heart, by thought, by mind. Those who know Him thus become immortal."[27] Kabir used many attributes for Brahma which he derived from Buddhist and Nath traditions. He describes his supreme as a Void or Nothingness. But his Shunya is different from the orthodox Buddhist position. It is very near to Shankar's Brahma, which is beyond speech. Kabir describes his god as the experience of sweetness enjoyed by a dumb person. It cannot be communicated, it is inexpressible, indescribable. The mystic trance, to which Kabir refèrs again and again, is some kind of this divine madness. Kenopanishad says – "The eye does not go there, speech does not go, nor the mind. We do not know, we do not understand how wex can instruct one about it. It is other than the known, and also above the unknown. Thus we have heard from the ancients who explained it to us."[28] On this very line Kabir describes his Brahma :

> Beyond Vedas, beyond differences
> beyond sin or virtue
> Beyond knowledge, beyond meditation,
> beyond solid or void
> Beyond dress, beyond alms,
> beyond all snobbery and form,
> Kabir says, beyond the three worlds
> that essence unmatched is.[29]

Mysticism and Literature

As compared to the West the poetry of the East, may it be of ancient, medieval or the modern age, is replete with the mystic expressions. Of these the contribution of the saints of medieval age has been noteworthy. Dawson has rightly observed that "In the West, apart from a view outstanding exceptions, mysticism and literature have followed separate paths, and the man of letters often knows nothing of works which from the religious point of view are spiritual classics. In the East, however, this is not so. *Mysticism* and letters go hand in hand in all the Moslem countries – among the Persians, above all, but also among the Arabs and Turks. The greatest poets have devoted themselves to give literary expressions to spiritual experiences and to fuse poetical and mystical ecstasy in a single flame."[30]

Great Mystical poets of Persia — *Attar, Jalal-ud-din Rumi, Mafiz and Jami* – were good examples of the above statement. We have also some good mystical works of the great Arab mystics such as Ibnul Arabi and Ibnul Farid etc.

For *Tukaram* God is everything. Like many other saints of the medieval age Tukaram describes his lord as par excellence. He says :

> You are more loving than a mother
> You are cooler than the moon

You are more yielding than water
You are a roaring surge of love[31]

In order to lead a spiritual life observance of moral and ethical values is a must. He stands very firm and determined against all miseries and trials. Our saints like Jnandeva, Ekanath, Namdev, Tukaram etc. had to undergo such trials. Due to their firm faith and inflinching belief in God Almighty they could stand by all such trials and came out with flying colours. "Tukaram was also troubled and tested by the people in various other ways. But he was unmoved. He refused the offers of rich presents made by King Shivaji, and when Shivaji, impressed by his renunciation and devotion, desired to become his spiritual disciple, Tukaram advised him to become a disciple of Ramadasa. His inward life, his earnest efforts to realize God, and the sufferings he passed through in order to achieve the Highest – all these represent important phases of a mystic life. In the range of his mystic experience in the lucid and forceful expression of his ideas, in his lofty conception of the purpose of life, and in the vigorous exposition of it to the people at large, he undoubtedly occupies a high place. He rightly describes himself as a coping stone of the edifice of mystic experience, of which Jnandeva was the foundation.[32] He himself describes about his mystic experience saying that he has emptied himself by shading the ego far away and merged himself into the infinite, i.e. Cosmic soul which is eternal non-illusioned and perennially pure for his eternal stay in the formless body cosmic.

"We have built a house in nothingness,
Our eternal stay is in the formless
We have become one with the non-illusion,
We are the recipients of continual unity
Tuka says, now there is no ego left.
I have become one with that which is perennially pure."[33]

Alike saint poets there had been good many saint-poetesses who enriched the mystic literature, namely Aryanayaki Andal, Akka Mahadevi and Goda of the South, Daya Bai, Sahjo Bai of

Maharashtra and Meera Bai of Rajasthan etc. Goda Devi writes about herself: "My healthy bosoms was meant for the lord who carries the discuss and the conch. If there is a talk of human being embracing me as a fox wild licking the offerings in a sacrifice for the immortals above. I shall not continue, O Lord."[34]

Vishnucita took his daughter on a pilgrimage to holy shrines in India. While visiting the temple at Shrirangam, Goda Devi had an ineffable experience of union with the presiding deity, Ranganathan. She merged in the Divine Effulgence. Vishnuchit was inconsolable. The lord assured him that he would wed Goda Devi in Srivillipputtur on Panguni Uthiram day. The wedding of the eternal lord and his spouse takes place year after year in the temple to assure the devotees of the never failing compassionate grace of Goda Devi. Apart from the Srivillipputtur temple to Goda Devi with its year round of festivities, India is dotted with niches to the girl who became a goddess by her unique devotional ministry at the feet of the Divine. She also became a role model for mystically inclined young girls who chose the Divine as their companion on earth. Mira Bai's devotional outpourings and Indira Devi's Krishna songs in our own days are witness to the devotional inspiration generated by Goda Devi.[34]

Dr. Yusuf Hussain says that Sufism was "born in the bosoms of Islam", and that it was not influenced by foreign ideas and practices. He seems to believe that although it flourished in India for several hundred years, yet if remained immune from Indian thought and environment.... As far as the history of this sect in this country is concerned there is no doubt about its having been mixed profoundly by Hindu thought, belief and practices. For example, the very conception of a loving God and the relations between God and soul as one of the beloved and the lover are peculiar to Hinduism and were adopted by the Sufis in India. The Muslim conception of God is that of the Master and relation between god and man in Islam is that between master and servent. Secondly, pacifism and non-violence which were imbibed by the Indian Muslim Sufis are also peculiar to Christianity and to Hinduism, Buddhism and Jainism (the latter three of which had their birth in India). In the third place, some of the ascetic practices, which involved the starving and torturing of the body, such as Chillah-I-mi-kus (the Inverted Chillah, which means the tying of the rope to one's feet and getting one's body lowered into a well and offering prayer in that posture for forty nights) also seem to have been borrowed from the Hindu and Buddhist practices. There were many other details in the ceremonies and practices of the Muslim Sufis particularly of the Chisti order that too were of Indian origin and were certainly due to Hindu environment. The Chistis "adopted many Hindu customs and ceremonials in the intial stages of the development of their *Silsilah* of India. The practice of bowing before the *Shaikh* (head of Khangah), presenting water to visitors, circulating *zanbil* (a bowl made of dried and hollow gourd), shaving the head of new entrants to the mystic circle, audition parties (*sama*) an the Chillah- i- ma'kus had close resemblance to Hindu and Buddhist practices....[35]

Henotheism

Hinotheism, as found in the Eastern Scriptures, in Vedas in particular, is not a simple religious theory, but the symptom of a deep spiritual experience. In henotheism there is no mere toleration, no mere hospitality to another's God, but acceptance of another's God as one's own and as the one divinity. This last is logically puzzling, but it has been part of the mystic experience of great sages and saints at all times. Shri Ramakrishna's religious experience was the contemplation of all Divinity according to the conception of different sects and religions. He used to say –"There is only one God, but endless are his aspects and endless are his names. Call him by any name and worship him in any aspect that pleases you, you are sure to see him.[36]

The seeds of henotheism are found in Indian culture as early as the dawn of civilization. The scholars have traced this trait in Rigveda, the oldest store house of knowledge. This peculiar trait of the Vedic hymns Max Muller has called Henotheism or Kathenotheism. A belief in single gods, each in turn standing out as the highest. And since the gods are thought of as specially ruling in their own spheres, the singers, in their special concerns and desires, call most of all one that god to whom they ascribe the most power in the matter, to whose department if I may say so, their wish belongs. This god alone is present to the mind of the suppliant, with him for the time being is associated everything that can be said of a divine beings – he is the highest, the only God before whom all others disappear, there being in this, however, no offence or depreciation of any other God."[37]

Synthesis

Since the subject of Mysticism is concerned with the soul and God, human divinity, the relation of man to God etc. which is one and the same all over the world and as such there cannot be any line of demarkation between the East and West. Only the context or the examples may differ. It is true that medieval Christianity laid greater emphasis on sin than it to be found anywhere in Hindu Philosophy. That is why in Christianity there is a provision of expiation of sin or sins by confession. In Jain religion also there is a provision of apology during Kshama—Paryushan Parvan. In the teachings of Ramanuja all the other mysteries of Christian theology seem to find their counterpart. In this connection, we may say that the greatest *Christian mystics* attained the height of realization by following Bhakti *yoga* taught by the Indian mystics.

In the realm of mysticism of our time Ravindranath Tagore and Shri Aurobindo—These two are noted as master souls. There is a bond of natural affinity between them. Both of them were seer poets, earned worldwide fame through their famous poetical works Gitanjali and Savitri respectively. If Tagore is the poet of the Dawn, Shri Aurobindo was the poet and prophet of the Eternal Day of the human race. Characterising Tagore's poetry, in reference to a particular poem, Shri Aurobindo once wrote:

"But the poignant sweetness, passion and spiritual depth and mystery of a poem like this, the haunting cadences subtle with a subtlety which is not of technique but of the soul, and the honey laden felicity of the expression, these are the essential." Rabindranath and Aurobindo cannot be initiated because they are things of the spirit and must have the same sweetness and depth of soul before to catch any to these desirable qualities. In the Upanishadic style Tagore also says :

Thou art the sky and thou art the nest as well
O thou beautiful, there in the nest it is thy
Love that encloses the soul with colours and sounds and odours" (*Gitanjali* LXVII)

Bengali poetry is very rich as far as mysticism is concerned. See the symbolic and mystic expression of Chandidas, the father of modern Bengali poetry.

There is a shore poised on a shore,
Upon that a wave
Waves dwell upon Waves
But a few only know or again
It is the lover that knows the sweetness of love
And who is it that pours out this sweetness?
What is that has abandoned all and become The Two
and dwells in the home of Delight?

Shri Aurobindo says, "What is magic to our finite reason is logic of the Infinite. The supramental change", he says, "is a thing decreed and inevitable in the evolution of the earth consciousness, for its upward ascent is not ended and mind is not its last summit. But that the change may arrive, take form and endure there is needed the call from below with a will to recognize and not deny the light when it comes and there is needed the sanction of the supreme from above."[38]

His great monumental epic Savitri based on the famous episode of the Mahabharata called "Satyavan-Savitri episode" is not merely an epic but an exposition of Aurobindo's Sadhana and his mystic thoughts, a mile-stone in the history of mystical poetry. An epic records the exceptional courage of a here. In the whole range world epics, Savitri is unique in this that its here is a woman.

Amid the work of darker powers she is here
To heal the evils and mistakes of space
And change the tragedy of the ignorant world
Into a Divine comedy of joy
And the laughter and rapture of God's bliss.[39]

REFERENCES

1. Kathamrit, Vol. II, pp. 9-10.
2. यदा पंचावतिष्ठन्ते ज्ञानानि मनसा सह ।
   बुद्धिश्च न विचेष्टति तामाहुः परमां गतिम् ॥
   तां योगमिति मन्यन्ते स्थिरामिन्द्रियधारणाम् ।
   अप्रमत्तस्तदा भवति योगो हि प्रभवाप्ययौ ॥

   — Kathopnishad II.3.10-11
3. Gita VI. 27.
4. Sri Aurobindo, *The Life Divine*, p. 802.
5. For details author's book titled as *Pracheen Bhartiya Acarya Parampara* may be referred to.
6. पराञ्चिखानि व्यतृणत्स्वयम्भूः तस्मात्पराङ् पश्यति नान्तरात्मन् । कश्चिद्धीरः प्रत्यगात्मानमैक्षदावृत्तचक्षुरमृतत्वमिच्छन् ॥

7a. *A Search in Secret India*, p.202.

7b. *Essays in Hinduism*, pp. 41-42.

8. Dr. C.D. Sharma, *A Critical Survey of Indian Philosophy*, p. 335.
9. Swami Prabhavanand, *The Spiritual Heritage of India*, p. 315.
10. Nicholson's rendering, quoted from 'Kabir', p. 21.
11. Quoted from *Religion and World Hisotry*, p. 121.
12. *Ibid.*, pp. 123-24.
13. Quoted from Dr. Motilal Jotwani's *Sufis of Sindh*, p. 3.
14. *Encyclopaedia of Islam*, p. 524.
15. Dr. Motilal Jotwani, *Sufis of Sindh*, p. 1.
16. Raman Maharshi (Edited by Arthur Osborne), p. 143.
17. *Ibid.* 143-44.
18. Gita, IV. 7-8.
19. *The Cultural Heritage of India*, Vol. II, pp. 489-90.
20. कबिरा ते नर अन्ध हैं, गुरु को कहते और ।
    हरि रुठे ठौर है, गुरु रुठे नहीं ठौर ॥

    —Kabir Granthavali
21. यह तन विष की बेलरी, गुरु अमृत की खान ।
    सीस दिये जो गुरु मिले, तौ भी सस्ता जान ॥ — *Ibid.*
22. तुर्क मसीत, देहरा, हिन्दू आप आपको धाय ।
    अलख पुरुष घट भीतरै, ताका द्वारा न पाय ॥ — *Ibid.*
23. तोड़ूं न पाती पूजूं न देवा;
    सहज समाधि करुँ हरिसेवा । — Santvani, p. 132

    Compare—

    साधो सहज समाधि भली ।
    गुरुप्रताप जा दिन सो जागी,
    दिन-दिन अधिक जली ।
    जहँ-जहँ डोलौं सो परिकरमा,
    जो कुछ करौं सो सेवा,

जब सोवौं तब करौ दंडवत,
पूजौ और न देवा । — *Ibid.*, p. 134

24. राम, रहीमा, करीम, केसव, अल्लह राम सति सोई ।
बेद कुरान बिसम्भर एकै, और न दूजा कोई ।। — Santvani, p. 24
Compare
कोई राम, कोई अल्लाह सुनावै ।
वै अल्लाह राम का भेद न पावै ।।
— Dadudayal, *Ibid.*, p. 22
'दास मलूक' कहा भरमौ तुम –
राम रहीम कहावत एकै ।
— Malukadas, *Ibid.*

25. प्रभुजी तुम चन्दन हम पानी । जाकी अंग-अंग बास समानी ।
प्रभुजी तुम बन हम मोरा । जैसे चितवत चन्द चकोरा ।
प्रभुजी तुम दीपक हम बाती । जाकी ज्योति बरै दिन राती ।
प्रभुजी तुम मोती हम धागा । जैसे सोनहि मिलत सुहागा ।
प्रभुजी तुम स्वामी हम दासा । ऐसो भक्ति करै रैदासा ।
अब कैसे छूटे नाम रट लागी ।
—Raidas

26. *Kabir Granthavali*, SSD, p. 242.

27. न सन्दृशे तिष्ठति रूपमस्य न चक्षुषा पश्यति कश्चैनम् ।
हृदा मनीषा मनसाभिक्लृप्तो य एतद्विदुरमृतास्ते भवन्ति ।।
— Kathopanishad 2.3.5

28. न तत्र चक्षुर्गच्छ्वति न वागगच्छति नो मनः ।
न विद्मो न विजानीमो यथेतदनुशिष्यात ।।
अन्यदेव तद्विदिनादथो अविदितादधि ।
इति शुश्रुम पूर्वेषां ये नस्तद् व्याचचक्षिरे ।।
— Kathopanishad 1.1.3-4

29. *Kabir Granthavali*, p. 103.

30. Christopher Dawson, *Religion and World History*, p. 120.

31. तू माउलीहुनी मायाळ चन्द्राहुनी शीतल ।
पाणियाहुनी पातळ कल्लोळ प्रेमा च ।।
—Tukaram, edited by Bhalchandra Nemade, p. 63

32. C.H.I., Vol. IV, p. 359.

33. *Tukaram*, edited by Bhachandra Nemade, p. 63.

34. For details please see "Saints and Mystics" published by Ramakrishna Math, Madras.

35. K.A Nizami, *Religion and Politics*, pp. 178-79.

36. Swami Brahmanand, *Ramakrishna Updesh*, p. 132.

37. *The Rigveda*, by Paegi, p. 27.

38. *The Mother*, pp. 83-84.

39. Shri Aurobindo, Savitri III, 2.

14

Dr. SUN YAT-SEN AND CHINESE NATIONALISM

The life and works of Sun Yat-Sen coincided with that period of Chinese history when the country was set to labour a lot to get rid of the existing political and administrative patterns. He took active part in changes, that followed, and championed the cause of revolutionism and republicanism. Although he could not do much for his cause during the turn of the century, he succeeded in overthrowing the Manchus in 1911, and thus achieved his primary goal. But this did not make the country at once a real republic. Yuan Shih-kai and other warlords held the stage for more than a decade, during which period Sun laboured in ambiguity. But he carried on a ceaseless battle against these warlords both materially and ideologically until he reorganised the Kuomintang, the party which he started as his political platform. Yet he ceased to live before his dreams were fulfilled. For more than a quarter of a century he trained the Chinese people with his ideals and policies and after his death he was regarded as the Father of the Chinese nation. Therefore, a study of the development of political ideals and policies under Sun Yat-Sen was not only important, but at the same an interesting one.

Born in a peasant family of a coastal village forty miles away of Canton in 1866 Sun Yat-Sen emigrated to Hawaii to join his elder brother at the age of twelve. He joined a mission school and latter was converted to Protestant Christianity. In the subsequent years he was qualified as a doctor and for a time practised medicine at Macas. He had thus a complete cycle of Western education, and had the idea of overthrowing the Manchus from the beginning. He returned to China in 1894 and soon he founded a republican secret society from a group of compatriots in Hawaii. He contrived to use the country's humiliations in the Treaty of Shimonosheki to organise a *coup d'etat*. But the plot failed; a price was put on his head and he left China in a British vessel not to return again before 1911.

During his exile Sun Yat-Sen travelled extensively in Europe and America, and these travels only deepened his anti-dynastic convictions. He was opposed to the programme of reforms by royal decrees inaugurated by K'ang Yu-wei. Japan at this time became an abode of Chinese students who were attracted by Western knowledge and technique, and many Cantonese merchants settled there. The latter financed Sun's trips abroad while among the former he began to propagate, his anti-dynastic ideologies. By 1905 several secret societies were organised in Tokyo with the representatives from both Central China and the Shanghai area. In that summer Sun Yat-Sen persuaded these secret societies to combine into one grand association, and he thus succeeded in organising the *Tung-meng hui* or the General League, whose political programme was to be expounded in its own newspaper.

This programme of the Tung meng-hui was based on the Sun Yat-Sen established a new military government at Canton in August, 1917. From there he continued to invade the north until he himself was unseated from the Canton Government. Meanwhile China joined the Allies in the First World War at the insistence of T'uan Ch'i-jui, who again was displaced by his Chihli rivals. Sun returned to Canton in 1920 and formed a new military government there. The factional disputes of the warlords in north were intensified in the meantime and China lost in the bargaining at Paris Peace Conference.

The most significant event during the war years was the Russian Revolution and the success of the Bolshevik attracted the Chinese students and intellectuals. The students were inspired to organise the demonstrations on the Fourth of May, 1919 as mark of protest against the failure of the Chinese Government at Varsailles.

Labourers in different places took resort to strikes and the Chinese Communist Party was formed in 1922. Sun Yat-Sen admired Soviet Government and Moscow on its part turned to him to erect a national Government. There were prolonged negotiations between Sun and the Russian advisers, led by Borodin. Communists joined the Kuomintang as individuals, and an alliance between the Communists and the nationalists was thus forged. Sun Yat-Sen proceeded to remodel the Kuomintang, with the Soviet party model in his mind.

The blueprint of the Kuomintang reorganisation was drafted on the Russian model and Sun became its president for life. It was made a policy-making body. In its first Congress held in January 1924, was issued a manifesto to the effect that the Revolution recognised as its enemies the warlords and the imperialist powers associated with them. The Three Principles of the People were published in revised version, Sun added with nationalism the removal of foreign imperialism, and People's rights would thus deprive all counter-revolutionaries of their rights. The principle of People's livelihood was amplified with the addition that landless peasants would be given land, by the State. Their realisation depended upon military victory and for this Whampoa Military Academy was started.

With the reorganisation of the Kuomintang, Sun Yat-Sen resumed his northern expedition. This time he joined the victors of T'uan Ch'i-jui to take advantage of warlord factionalism. But soon he broke with them on the question of the treatment of the imperialists. He refused to join the Ministry of all the Talents, and he died in March 1925.

Thus throughout his career Sun Yat-Sen advocated national integration on republican principles; and it could be achieved by revolutionary upheavals. He taught the Chinese people of the evils of both monarchism and foreign imperialism and devoted his life to demonstrate his ideas. But he died before he could work as the midwife of the nationalist republic. In the words of McAlavy "his doctrine of the Three Principles was to become the Bible of the Nationalists and to ensure that in death his influence far exceeded what it had been during his life. It was a fair estimate of the developments of ideal and policies under Sun Yet-Sen.

The Three Principles of the People

The Three Principles of the People had been the basic ideas of Sun Yat-Sen since they were formulated in 1905. But they were subsequently modified and expressed in the Sun Min Chu I in the context of the post-war developments. Even after his death they remained the basic manifesto of the Chinese Nationalists.

The first of the Three Principles was Min-tsu or People's Nationhood. Originally when it was first conceived in 1905 as a part of the programme of the T'ung-meng-hui, Nationalism connoted only liberation of the Chinese people from the alien Manchu rule. It was plainly anti-Manchuism. It was achieved in 1911, but events since then had demonstrated that the end of Manchu rule did not automatically make the Chinese people a nation. The idea was now confronted with a new bugbear, foreign imperialism, against which the Chinese people needed to cement themselves together into a strong modern state. It was thus widened in scope, and embodied the idea of a unity embracing all groups of people, major and minor. It sounded like a federalism; but Sun Yat-Sen revised it only towards anti-imperialism.

The second was Min-ch'uan, translated as People's Authority or Democracy. Sun proclaimed this principle by attacking the constitutional monarchists as counterparts of 'absolutism'. More positively it would help to establish a republic after the expulsion of the dynasty. Vaguely it would be achieved in three stages; armed revolution, military government, and then after six years a national constitutional government. In 1924 these three stages denoted that the Kuomintang revolution was to be followed by Kuomintang tutelage, during which period the party would handle the affairs until the people irrespective of wealth or class, would be allowed to elect the organs of the State. These organs would include offices to fulfil the traditional Chinese functions of Examination and Censorship, besides a Legislature, an Executive and a Judiciary, of the westem republicanism, the Swiss doctrine of Initiative, referendum, election, recall, Soviet democratic centrism and Chinese ideas of examination and control.

The last of the Three Principles was called Ming Sheng or

People's livelihood. Sun borrowed this doctrine from an American, Henry George and expressed in it a number of theories, which he had come to pass In essence it connected the "equalisation of landownership". Mr. Alervy rightly explained, "It did not envisage the general nationalisation of land in it redistribution, but the restriction of unearned profits by private owners whose land,... had vastly increased by reason of its situation and development of industries and communications through the labour of the community". It was thus a vague doctrine, which failed to solve the problem of peasantry. In 1924, it was implied that its goal was equalisation of land ownership according to value and that the landless peasants would be given land by the State The State would enact labour laws to protect the workers, and large industrial enterprises would be put under public control. With this doctrine Sun Yat-Sen proceeded to fight Capitalism and Marxism at the same time.

These were, in short, the Three Principles of the People enunciated and elaborated by Dr. Sun Yat-Sen. After his death his Sun Min Chu I became the Bible of the Nationalists.

Contribution to Chinese Nationalism: Sun Yat-Sen had promulgated the doctrine of nationalism among the Chinese, when it had been rather a passive factor. Even when he had first propounded it in 1905, he restricted it only to anti-Manchuism. Nationalism in its present details was known to only those Chinese, who had gone abroad to pursue studies. But their number was almost microscopic in relation to the Chinese population.

Chinese nationalism which had been already rooted in its society had a stir immediately after the end of the World War I. Before that the Europeans had brought in their nationalism with their tools and textiles, trinkets and guns. The Western communities, residing in China, had already demonstrated before the Chinese the blessings of industrialism, democracy and nationalism. People in China became aware of the strength of an Asian power in Russia's defeat at the hands of Japan. There had been dissatisfaction among the people but the diplomatic discomfiture of the Chinese delegates at the Paris Peace Conference over Shantung melted the rock. On the Four of May 1919, students demonstrated their resentment in a general strike which resulted in a general boycott of Japanese goods.

Nationalism no longer remained a passive affair; it was publicly demonstrated.

The Russian Revolution of 1917 and the end of Czardom in Russia attracted very much the Chinese Nationalism. Communism entered into China; and the Chinese Communist Party was formed in 1922. The most ardent among the Chinese Nationalists were also attracted by the Bolshevik successes. Dr. Sun Yat-Sen also admired the Bolshevik successes; and began to cultivate good and friendly relations with Soviet Russia. Negotiation began between him and the Soviet advisers headed by Borodin; and Communists were allowed to join the Nationalist Party as individual members. Sun Yat-Sen reorganised the party after the blueprint of the Russian Communist Party.

The objects of Sun-Yat-Sen was a nàtional unification through armed revolution. His experience in the years following 1911, atropined him to change his early conceptions of nationalism. Hence forward, he used it in a broader sense, covering all the Chinese irrespective of Manchus, Chinese, Mongols etc. He also amplified his objectives, namely, democracy and People's livelihood. But to achieve these aims he borrowed a scheme of organisation and a technique of propaganda. He set things for a successful nationalist revolution.

The Revolution of 1911 which ended 267 years' old Manchu rule in China was probably inevitable. The dynasty had lost its moral basis to rule China because of rank corruption, nepotism, incompetence, inefficiency and finally its failure against mounting foreign aggressions. The pulsating national spirit born of Western impact could no longer tolerate the alien and moribund Manchu dynasty and forced it to abdicate: The dynasty was overthrown with a comparative ease largely due to the inherent weakness and the decrepitude of the old order rather than due to the skill of the revolutionists. The peacefulness of political transition from anarchy to Republic was deceptive. China stumbled upon her career as a Republic initiating decades of disorder and turmoil. "The Chinese Republican Revolution 1911-1912, was an attempt to set aside the Confucian monarchy and to replace it with a parliamentary constitutional republic. On paper this Republic appeared to have everything needed for success—constitution, parliamentary procedures, codes of law. But the constitutions were not understood, the parliamentary procedures were not followed, and the law codes were never enforced. What the Republic did not have was much more important than what it possessed. It did not have a people who understood parliamentary institutions, government by law, or the rudiments of democratic responsible citizenship" (Clyde).

The doctrine of nationalism was actually thesised in the Chinese context by Dr. Sun-Yat-Sen. His movements might have been at times adventurous. But it was he, who for the first time felt the need to weed out the foreigners as a basis for positive national growth. He exposed both the positive and negative aspects of Chinese nationalism. Indeed, he was to Chinese nationalism, what Thomas Jefferson was to democracy, and Mazzini was to Italian unification.

15

RELIGIO-SPIRITUAL THOUGHT OF MAHATMA GANDHI

"It is logical that Mahatma Gandhi, weak of body and without material resources, should prove the unconquerable strength of the meek and the humble hidden in the heart of the outraged and destitute humanity of India. India's destiny is bound-up in *Narayana* and not in *Narayani-sena*, in soul force and not muscle. It must uplift human history, transport it from the confused valley of material struggle to the high plateau of spiritual battles, although we may delude ourselves through phrases acquired from the vocabulary of the *West Swaraj*, home rule, not really our goal. Our battle is a spiritual battle, a fight for humanity. We must emancipate man from meshes he has woven around him, free him from the organisations of national selfishness. We must persuade the butterfly that the freedom of sky is better than the shelter of cocoon. In India we have no word for "*nation*". When we loan the word from other peoples it is not suited to us, for we should ally ourselves with *Narayana*, the supreme being, and our victory will be the victory for God's world.... If we can defy the powerful, the rich, the armed by showing the power of immortal spirit, the castle of the giant flesh will crumble into nothingness. And then man will find real swaraj. We, the miserable outcasts of the Orient, we' must conquer freedom for all humanity."

— Rabindranath Tagore[1]

Synthesis

Some critics have pointed out a sort of contradiction in his life style (adopted after 1921) and his thinking. He had adopted all good things from the East as well as West. Krishna Kriplani has rightly said, "It needs to be noted that despite his increasing pride in Indianness the most radical influences on Gandhi's moral and mental outlook were almost all derived from the Western contacts, though these contacts by themselves might not have been characteristically Western. His meticulous regard for hygiene and sanitation, his good habits and dietetic experiments, his insistence on punctuality and his endless curiosity about the why and how of everything could hardly be said to have been inherited from his traditional Hindu background. His moral sensibility and his religious consciousness, too, were at least as much influenced by Jesus, Tolstoy, Ruskin and Thoreau as by Jainism and Gita and the lessons received from his Gujarati jeweller-friend Raychan Bhai. Gandhi's adoption in later life of the loin cloth as dress invested him with an exaggerated Indianness, which was in a way misleading."[4]

Gandhi's Concept of 'Ram Rajya'

As a staunch believer in the theories enumerated in *Ramcharitmanas*, Mahatma Gandhi reposed faith in a benevolent monarchy, which he called 'Ram Rajya'. The basic concept of 'Ram Rajya' was that of a welfare state. But Gandhiji did not elaborate the concept and left in vague just saying that it would fulfil the aspirations and yearnings of deprived disinherited and downtrodden classes of Indian society, it would be superior to any other social system devised by man and known to humanity in historical age, it would excel the democratic system evolved by philosophers and scientists in the West since Magna Charta was forced from King John of England. Thus in the absence of precise connotation of the concept the builders of free India could not derive any concrete guidance. It has given rise to various concepts of the ideal state and created 'a virtual babel'.

Tulsi's Concept of Ram Rajya

Tulsi's concept of Ram Rajya was that of a benevolent monarchy. In Uttarkand of *Ramcharitmanas*, he has given elaborate description of Ram Rajya, salient points of which are as follows:

- Nobody dies in young age; nobody suffers from any pain. Everyone's body is beautiful and afflicted by no sickness. No one is poor or miserable; none is dependent or foolish or without good qualities.
- All are without hypocrisy, devoted to duty and virtue. Both men and women are clever and possess good qualities. All admire virtuous man, scholars and enlightened. All are grateful and no one plays frauds.
- In Ram Rajya all sentient and non-sentient beings are above the consequences of time action and nature.
- In Ram Rajya no one commits sins, so there in no need to use rod to punish; the environments are congenial and favourable; therefore, there is no need to divide and rule the people.
- In forests trees grow and blossom; elephants and lion live together and birds and animals, forgetting enmity, live with love.
- Creepers and trees offer coveted honey, cows give desired milk, the earth grows abundant needs of society.

Goswami Tulsidas was a supporter of autocratic, authoritarian and dictatorial rule in which the ruler transcends humanity which exists merely to make him happy. He instructs the people to docilely bow before his firmness right or wrong. However, certain political values, contained in the above description of Ram Rajya are noteworthy. Justice, health, happiness, brotherhood, doing good to others, concern for countrymen, patriotism—these are central values of Ram Rajya. Tulsi's concept of an ideal citizen was that he should be free not only from ignorance and ill-will but also from disease and want. That means according to him political freedom and equality is incomplete, without economic freedom. He realised from the core of his heart that no duty is higher than doing good to others—

"Parhit saris dharm nahi bhai". Thus we see that total happiness of the people was the sole aim of Ram Rajya. Our seers too have been aspiring to see all persons in society in a healthy, happy and good condition — "Sarve Bhavantu Sukhinah". Merely achieving 'the greatest good of the treatest number' is a western outlook, not ours.

Uniqueness of Polity

The uniqueness of time-honoured Hindu polity has been the delinking of the political power from the economic power and *vice versa* and both of them from the legislative power, that is why our three wings (legislative, executive and judiciary) of the government are having an independent identity and functions. This is said to be an ideal condition, where the deadly combination of any of these two or three (as in communist states) powers getting concentrated in the same hands is eliminated. Thus in our Constitution the judiciary under the direction of the Supreme Court, is independent and free of any influence of the executive and legislature. The fundamental rights of a citizen had been clearly defined and declared inviolable. These rights, among other, include complete freedom of expression and right to form associations; caste distinctions had been annulled throughout in the provisions of the Constitution and untouchability had been abolished and its practice in any form forbidden under articles 15(2) and 16(2).

Secularism and Mahatma Gandhi

On the Indian scenario Gopal Krishan Gokhale, the moderate leader, whom Gandhiji hailed as his 'political mentor' first talked of 'spiritualising politics' but he was not a man of religion, but a secular minded person. But, his commitment to the national cause was praiseworthy. He contended that India's dire need then was of men who could devote all their time and talents to the service of the country. Therefore, he established 'Servants of India Society'. B.R. Nanda observes that "this idea of 'spiritualising politics, of evoking abnegation and self-denial for secular causes, which inspired Gokhale to establish the Servants of India society, also appealed to Gandhi; he applied it to the various ashrams he set up in South Africa and India. But he went further, and extended the application of this idea to the political field. *Satyagraha*, his method of resolving conflicts, drew its dynamics from his deeplyheld religious and philosophical belief, which were not exclusively Hindu. He acknowledged his debt not only to Gita and the Upanishad, but to 'the Sermon of the Mount', and the writings of Tolstoy and Thoreau. One can be atheist or agnostiel, and still practice satyagraha. But it is easier for a man of religion to accept the assumptions on which satyagraha rests. That it is worthwhile fighting, and even dying. For causes which transcend one's personal interests, that the body perishes, but the soul lives, that no oppressor can crush the imperishable spirit of man, that every human being, however, wicked he may appear to be, has a hidden nobility, a 'divine spark' which can be 'ignited'.[5]

In fact Gandhi, in modern times, was the first leader who associated spiritual values like truth and non-violence with practical political affairs very graciously and successfully. For him politics devoid of religion is like a noose for the nation, which may strangle and ultimately destroy it. He himself writes: "... My devotion to truth has drawn me into the field of politics and I can say without the slightest hesitation and yet in all humility that those who say that religion has nothing to do with politics do not know what religion means." For Gandhi religion is identical with morality and truth is the substance of morality. According to Kriplani Gandhi's religion and morality were the same. They were identical terms.

His religious basis of politics did not mean injecting religious bigotry or fanaticism in politics. He did not also mean political exploitation of religion. For example, he supported to Khilafat Movement in 1920-21 on humanitarian ground rather than bargaining considerations. In fact, he was neither a communalist nor a revivalist, he stood for unity of all human beings and was crucified for the sake of fostering unity and brotherhood between the two major communities of India (Hindus and Muslims). The concept of religion he wanted to be the basis of politics is not to be identified with any credal dogmatic theology. He stood for a religious cleaning of the structure of society subsequently resulting in the elimination of gross superstitions and customs that usurped the true spirit of religion. A true religion was to bind man to God and subsequently man to man as he himself says, "I am endeavouring to see God through service of humanity for I know that God is neither in heaven nor down below but in everyone."

Gandhi's spritualisation of politics left two prominent problems for the country. Ravindra Kumar writes, ".... Yet the success of orthodox pluralism, a success confined to the sphere of political mobilisation, left two problems, as a legacy for politics in India after 1947. First, Gandhi's belief that religious cleavages could be healed by using religious loyalties as the basis for nationhood proved to be a miscalculation. With the British Government anxious to exploit every division within society in India, the ideology of orthodox pluralism heightened instead of reducing the gulf between different religious communities. Even in the decades after 1947, therefore, religious and communication solidarities continue to plague politics in India, though it is important to remember that such solidarities often provide a mask for the promotion of class interests. Secondly, the device of drawing the rich and powerful into the national struggle, often through policies which more than protected their interests, ensured that these classes would assume a dominating position in politics after independence. Neither of these consequences, we would emphasise, was Gandhi's seeing. Yet their presence in the structure of contemporary politics in India is a fact which cannot be easily denied."[6]

Thus, we can say that like Plato, Cicero and Kant he gave priority to moral values in social and political life. He believed in the piety of the resources while accomplishing the aim, just contrary to Kautilya and Machiavelli, whose prime concern was the interests of the State rather than piety of the resources. The protagonist of Pakistan ridiculed the phrase 'Ram Rajya' which Gandhi occasionally employed to describe the goal of Indian freedom struggle. This was Gandhi's equivalent for the English term 'utopia'. The great saint Tulsidas used the term 'Ram Rajya' in the context of monarchial form of government. But what Gandhi meant by this 'saintly idiom' was an ideal polity firmly founded on the noble principles of justice, equality and free from exploitation. That is why he broke laws that were unjust. He believed that it was wrong to tax salt which even the poorest people use. Therefore, after having duly informed the then Viceroy he broke such law through 'Dandi March' (Namak Satyagraha). Very violent events like 'Chauri Chaura' (February 1922), Noakhali and others were faced firmly and reconciled by the virtue of his absolute commitment to the eternal values like truth and non-violence.

The moral influence of his personality and his gospel and technique of non-violence cannot be weighed on any material scale, nor its value is confined to any particular creed or country. It is imperishable gift to the entire humanity. Though he was deeply religious in his person; but advocated for a secular state. Louis Fischer[7] noted the strange paradox that Jinnah, who had grown up as a secular nationalist in his younger days, and who apparently had little interest in religion founded a state based on religion, while Gandhi, wholly religious, worked to establish a secular state. Gandhi said, "He did not believe in state religion even though the whole community had one religion. The state interference would probably always be unwelcome. Religion was purely a personal matter...." Therefore, he opposed to state-aid, partly or wholly to religious institutions. He was against the inculcation of denominational and sectarian religious teachings in state institution. Therefore, he did not included religion in the curriculum of 'Basic Education' propounded by him in 1937 at Sewagram (Wardha-Maharashtra); as he was afraid that religions as they are taught and practised today would lead to conflict rather than unity.

He wanted religious education to be the exclusive concern of the religious associations as he regarded it as a matter of personal experience and private judgement. He did not like the organised agencies of the state to meddle with religious considerations of the people. Thus, Gandhi's religious-mindedness did not detract a bit from his concept of secularism, be it politics, education or any other social phenomena. Dr. Verma has rightly observed, "this theory of divided allegiance implying the superiority of the obligation to obey God or the inner conscience is a monumental contribution of Gandhi to political philosophy."[8]

Gandhism: An Aptitude

In his autobiography he made it a point to acknowledge his debt to Tolstoy, Ruskin, Thoreau; but these great Western writers seemed only to have encouraged him along the path he had already chosen for himself. He had deep study of good many Hindu scriptures as well as sacred books of other religions. Apart from the religious and philosophical works such as the Mahabharata, the Bhagvad Gita, the Upanishads, the Bible, the Koran, he studied the writings of Plato, Cailyle, Ruskin, Buckle, Leeky, Geddes, Bernard Shaw, Wells, Kipling, Karl Marx and numerous other writers. He was not sharp intellectually, which he admits in his autobiography. He also said that he is not built for academic writing, action is his domain. He did not have any claim to originality. The eternal values like 'Truth', 'Non-violence' etc. have already been depicted in Vedas and Upanishads as early as the dawn of civilisation. "I represent no new truths", he said, "I do claim to throw a new light on many an old truth". Thus his contribution in the field of religion and philosophy is that he gave new shades of meaning to the age-old values not only at theoretical level, translated also them into action, may it be a political, forum or his own personal life. Before preaching any ideal or principle he himself lived through it. In all humbleness he described himself simply as one "who claims to be a humble searcher of truth knows his limitations, makes mistakes, never hesitates to admit them". The politicians of our time claim to be the followers of Gandhi; but they don't follow the spirit of Gandhism. A big gap between the words and deeds of the politicians is the greatest tragedy of our time.

In fact, '*Gandhism*' is not a system. He never tried to formulate any such system. B.R. Nanda has rightly observed, "Though he expounded his ideas on almost every conceivable subject in thousands of articles and letters over a period of more than fifty years, he never tried to build them into a. system. What is called '*Gandhism*' is, therefore, only a distinctive attitude to society and politics rather than an ideology — a particular ethical standpoint rather than fixed formulate or a definitive system."[9]

Gandhi's Philosophy

Gandhi calls his philosophy the philosophy of satyagraha, a word we may use as such, as it is known throughout the world. This word has been translated and interpreted variously as "passive resistance", "non-violent resistance", "civil disobedience", and so on.

The central ideas of Gandhi's philosophy of action may be reduced to the following principles:

1. God is truth. This truth is not the logical, abstract truth, but the spiritual metaphysical. As truth is the law that supports man and the universe, God is both the law and the law giver.
2. God is love itself. He is not a pure concept, but is affectional, affective, by nature.
3. Truth always prevails over falsity and falsehood in every conflict between the two sides.
4. One should stick to truth. Then one will be supported by truth or being. Falsity leads to non-being, non-existence.
5. As truth, God, and love are one and the same, one should stick to love.
6. One should, therefore, follow the path of non-violence. The opposite of love is violence, the destruction of what opposes us.
7. Man is finite, he is not God; his power, knowledge, and will are limited. He may be mistaken in his own convictions, to which he may stick.
8. In sticking to truth or to what one believes to be truth, one should not destroy another. For man, being finite, may take falsity for truth and may mistake the other to be wrong. Even then one should stick to his truth, until one is convinced that he himself is wrong and the other right. Conflicts thus are inevitable. But no conflict should lead to destruction. Truth will, however, ultimately prevail. If the parties really love each other and are earnest about truth, there will be no acrimony left, whoever be the winner.

9. When truth wins, falsity will be destroyed. If the two parties love each other, the destruction will only be the destruction of false convictions. But no party should try to destroy the other, even when afterwards it is shown to be wrong and not in earnest about truth. God alone has the right to destroy. In his infinite wisdom, he knows what is true and what is false, what is good and what is evil. When he destroys, he destroys in love, not in hatred. As finite beings, we not only cannot be certain of truth, but also cannot destroy in love. Generally in hate only can we destroy. Hate is easy, but love difficult for us. Our duty is to follow only the path of love; we shall then be like God, the law; ground support of our being.

He followed the doctrine of Gita, i.e. 'selfless action'. He acted as his reason and conscience dictated, but was not overanxious about the results. Even when he was struggling against heavy odds, he would not throw up the sponge. "Satisfaction lies in the effort', he would say, "not in attainment. Full effort is full victory".

As the concluding part of this chapter we are producing certain pertinent thoughts of Gandhi collected from several sources.

By religion, I do not mean formal religion, or customary religion, but that religion which underlies all religions, which brings us face to face with our Maker.[10]

Let me explain what I mean by religion. It is not the Hindu religion which I certainly prize above all other religions, but the religion which transcends Hinduism, which changes one's very nature, which binds one indissolubly to the truth within and which ever purifies. It is the permanent element in human nature which counts no cost too great in order to find full expression and which leave the soul utterly restless until it has found itself, known its Maker and appreciated the true correspondence between the Maker and itself.[11]

I have not seen Him, neither have I known Him. I have made the world's faith in God my own, and as my faith is ineffaceable, I regard that faith as amounting to experience. However, as it may be said that to describe faith as experience is to tamper with truth, it may perhaps be more correct to say that I have no word for characterising my belief in God.[12]

There is an indefinable mysterious power that pervades everything. I feel it, though I do not see it. It is this unseen power which makes itself felt and yet defies all proof, because it is so unlike all that I perceive through my senses. It transcends the sense. But it is possible to reason but the existence of God to a limited extent.[13]

I do dimly perceive that whilst everything around me is ever changing, ever dying, there is underlying all that change a Living Power that is changeless, that holds all together, that creates, dissolves, and recreates. That informing Power or Spirit is God. And since nothing else I see merely through the sense can or will persists, He alone is.[14]

And is this Power benevolent or malevolent? I see it as purely benevolent. For I can see that in the midst of death life persists, in the midst of untruth truth persists, in the midst of darkness light persists. Hence I gather that God is Life, Truth, Light. He is love. He is the Supreme God.[15]

I know, too, that I shall never know God if I do not wrestle with and against evil even at the cost of life itself. I am fortified in the belief by my own humble and limited experience. The purer I try to become the nearer to God I feel myself to be. How much more should I be near to Him when my faith is not a mere apology, as it is today, but has become as immovable as the Himalayas and as white and bright as the snows on their peaks?[16]

This belief in God has to be based on faith which transcends reason. Indeed, even the so-called realisation has at bottom an element of faith without which it cannot be sustained. In the very nature of things it must be so. Who can transgress the limitations of his being? I hold that complete realisation is impossible in this embodied life. Nor is it necessary. A living immovable faith is all that is required for reaching the full spiritual height attainable by human beings. God is not outside this earthly case of ours. Therefore, exterior proof is not of much avail, if any at all. We must ever fail to perceive Him through the senses, because He is beyond them. We can feel him, if we will but withdraw ourselves from the senses.

The divine music is incessantly going on within ourselves, but the loud senses drown the delicate music, which unlike and infinitely superior to anything we can perceive or ear with our senses.[17]

But he is no God who merely satisfies the intellect, if He ever does. God to be God must rule the heart and transform it. He must express Himself in every the smallest act of His votary. This can only be done through a definite realisation more real than the five senses can ever produce. Sense perceptions can be, often are, false and deceptive, however real they may appear to us. Where there is realisation outside the senses it is infallible. It is proved not by extraneous evidence but in the transformed conduct and character of those who have felt the real presence of God within. Such testimony is to be found in the experiences of an unbroken line of prophets and sages in all countries and climes. To reject this evidence is to deny oneself.[18]

To me God is truth and love; God is ethics and morality; God is fearlessness. God is the source of light and life and yet he is above and beyond all these. God is conscience, He is even the atheism of the atheist.... He transcends speech and reason... He is a personal God to those who need His personal presence. He is embodied to those who need his touch. He is the purest essence. He simply is to those who have faith. He is all things to all men. He is in us and yet above and beyond us.... He is long-suffering. He is patient but he is also terrible.... With Him ignorance is no excuse. And withal he is ever forgiving for He always gives us the chance to repent. He is the greatest democrat the world knows, for he leaves us 'unfettered' to make our own choice between evil and good. He is the greatest tyrant ever known, for he often dashed the cup from our lips and under the cover of free will leaves us a margin so wholly inadequate as to provide only misth for himself.... Therefore Hinduism calls it all his sport.[19]

To see the universal and all-pervading spirit of truth face to face one must be able to love the meanest of creation as oneself. And a man who aspires after that cannot afford to keep out of any field of life. That is why my devotion to truth has drawn me into the field of politics; and I can say without the slighest hesitation, and yet in all humility, that those who say that religion has nothing to do with politics do not know what religion means.[20]

Identification with everything that lives is impossible without self-purification; without self-purification the observance of the law of *ahimsa* must remain an empty dream; God can never be realised by one who is not pure of heart. Self-purification therefore must mean purification in all walks of life. And purification being highly infectious, purification of oneself necessarily leads to the purification of one's surroundings.[21]

But the path of self-purification is hard and steep. To attain perfect purity one has to become absolutely passion-free in thought, speech and action; to rise above the opposing currents of love and hatred, attachment and repulsion. I know that I have not in me as yet that triple purity, in spite of constant, ceaseless striving for it. That is why the world's praise fails to move me, indeed it very often stings me. To conquer the subtle passions seems to me to be far harder than the physical conquest of the world by the force of arms.[22]

I am but a poor struggling soul yearning to be wholly good — wholly truthful and wholly non-violent in thought, word and deed; but ever failing to reach the ideal which I know to be true. It is a painful climb but the pain of it is a positive pleasure to me. Each step upward makes me feel stronger and fit for the next.[23]

I am endeavouring to see God through service of humanity for I know that God is neither in heaven, nor down below, but in every one.[24]

Indeed religion should pervade everyone of our action. Here religion does not mean sectarianism. It means a belief in ordered moral government of the universe. It is not less real because it is unseen. This religion transcends Hinduism, Islam, Christianity, etc. It does not supersede them. It harmonises them and gives them reality.[25]

Religions are different road converging to the same point. What does it matter that we take different roads, so long as we reach the same goal? In reality, there are as many religions as there are individuals.[26]

If a man reaches the heart of his own religion, he has reached the heart of the others too.[27]

REFERENCES

1. R.N. Tagore, quoted in *Mahatma Gandhi*, by Romain Rolland, pp. 122-23.
2. Romain Rolland; *Mahatma Gandhi*, p. 124.
3. B.R. Nanda, *Gandhi and His Critics*, p. 158.
4. Krishna Kriplani, *Gandhi: A Life*, p. 60.
5. B.R. Nanda, *Gandhi and His Critics*, p. 73.
6. Ravindra Kumar, "Secularism in a Multi-Religious Society, p. 32 in *Secularisation in Multi-Religious Societies*, Edited by S.C. Dube and V.N. Basilov.
7. Louis Fischer, *Life of Mahatma Gandhi*, p. 430.
8. V.P. Verma, *Modern Indian Polititat Thought*, p. 93.
9. *Gandhi and his Critics*, p. 145.
10. *The Mind of Mahatma Gandhi*, p. 85.
11. *Selection from Gandhi*, p. 223.
12. *Mahatma Gandhi*, p. 341.
13. *The Mind of Mahatma Gandhi*, p. 21.
14. *Ibid.*, p. 22.
15. *Ibid.*,
16. *Ibid.*,
17. *Ibid.*, pp. 22-23.
18. *Selection from Gandhi*, p. 9.
19. Mahatma Gandhi, *The Last Phase*, I, pp. 421-22.
20. *The Story of My Experiments with Truth*, p. 615.
21. *Ibid.*, pp. 615-16.
22. *Ibid.*, p. 616.
23. *Selection from Gandhi*, p.8.
24. *The Mind of Mahatma Gandhi*, p. 24.
25. *Selection from Gandhi*, p. 224.
26. *Ibid.*
27. *Ibid.*, p. 225.

APPENDICES

APPENDIX-I

WESTERN VIEW OF INDIAN LIFE

Max Muller (1823-1900), a celebrated German Indologist was the first scholar; who roused genuine interest for the Vedas among the people in the West and his expert knowledge of the facts of the Vedas invested his writings with asking of authority. His perception of the Vedic religion was essentially naturalistic, he believed that Vedic Poets always sought to perceive the 'divine', the 'supernatural', the 'infinite', behind the 'natural', and usually a name was given to god, which denoted the special characteristic of the nature (or form) of that god, such as Indra (from Indu-drop), the rainer, Rudra, the howler; Maruts, the thrusters and Varuna, the all-encompasser.[1] His special contribution to the study of Vedic religion is the 'theory of henotheism in Rigveda', which is neither polytheism nor monotheism. In fact monotheism precedes the polytheism of the Veda. He prefers to call henotheism or Kathenotheism, that is to say, 'a successive belief in single supreme god.'

Produced below are the excerpts from his famous book "*India—What it can teach us*", which is based on his lectures for candidates of the Indian Civil Service, on whom he wished to impress the importance of ancient Indian culture. He saw a break in the development of literature after the invasion of Sakas and the introduction of Buddhism and Jainism. A renaissance set with the Guptas who favoured Brahmanical religion and encouraged Sanskrit literature. His contribution towards Buddhist studies and classical

1 For details please see the author's book *Contribution of Western Indologists*, pp. 103-106.

literature is also quite stupendous. His monumental work in several volumes is "Sacred Books of the East", which is published in 50 Volumes. In this gigantic project his co-author was H. Oldenberg.

"What then, you may ask, we find in that ancient Sanskrit literature and cannot find anywhere else? My answer is, we find there Aryan man, whom we know in his various characters, as Greek, Roman, German. Celt and Slav, in an entirely new character. Whereas in his migrations northward his active and political energies are called out and brought to their highest perfection, we find the other side of the human character, the passive and meditative, carried to its fullest growth in India. In some of the hymns of the Rig Veda we can still watch an earlier phase. We see the Aryan tribes taking possession of the land and under the guidance of such warlike gods as Indra and the Maruts; defending their new homes against the assaults of the black-skinned aborigines as well as against the inroads of later Aryan colonists. But that period of war soon came to an end, and when the great mass of the people had once settled down in their homesteads, the military and political duties seem to have been monopolized by what we call a caste, that is by a small aristocracy, while the great majority of the people were satisfied with spending their days within the arrow spheres of their villages, little concerned about little outside world and content with the gifts that nature bestowed on them without much labour. Bhartrihari says :

"There is fruit on the trees in every forest, which everyone who likes may pluck without trouble. There is cool and sweet water in the pure rivers here and there. There is a soft bed made of the twigs of beautiful creepers. And yet wretched people suffer pain at the door of the rich !"

At first sight we may feel inclined to call this quiet enjoyment of life, this mere looking on, a degeneracy rather than a growth. It seems so different from what we think life ought to be. Yes, from a higher point of view, it may appear that those Southern Aryans have chosen the goad part; or at least the part good for them while we, Northern Aryans, have been careful and troubled about many things.

It is at all events a problem worth considering whether, as there is in nature a South and a North, there are not two hemispheres also in human nature, both worth developing the active, combative, and political on one side, the passive, meditative, and philosophical on the other; and for the solution of that problem no literature furnishes such ample materials as that of the Veda, beginning with the Hymns and ending with the Upanishads. We enter into a new world not always an attractive one, least of all to us; but it possesses one charm, it is real, it is of natural growth, and like everything of natural growth, I believe it had a hidden purpose, and was intended to teach us some kind of lesson that is worth learning, and that certainly we could learn nowhere else. We are not called upon either to admire or to despise that ancient Vedic literature; we have simply to study and to try to understand it.

There have been silly persons who have represented the development of the Indian mind as superior to any other, nay, who would make us go back to the Veda or to the sacred writings of the Buddhists in order to find there a truer religion, a purer morality, and a more sublime philosophy than our own. I shall not even mention the names of these writers or the titles of their works. But I feel equally impatient when I see other scholars criticizing the ancient literature of India as if it were the work of the nineteenth century; as if it represented an enemy that must be defeated, and that can claim no mercy at our hands. That the Veda is full of childish, silly, even to our minds monstrous conceptions, who would deny? But even these monstrosities are interesting and instructive; nay, many of them; if we can but make allowance for different ways of thought and language, contain germs of truth and rays of light, all the more striking, because of breaking upon us through the veil of the darkest night.

Here lies the general, the truly human interest which the ancient literature of India possesses, and which gives it a claim on the attention, not only of oriental scholars or of students of ancient history, but of every educated man and woman.

There are problems which we may put aside for a time, aye, which we must put aside while engaged each in our own hard struggle for life, but which will recur for all that, and which, whenever they do recur, will stir us more deeply than we like to confess to others, or even to ourselves. It is true that with us one day only out of seven is set apart for rest and meditation, and for the consideration of what the Greeks called to megista – "the greatest thing". It is true that seventh day also is passed by many of us either in mere church-going routine or in thoughtless rest. But whether on week-days, or on Sundays, whether in youth or in old age, there are moments rare though they be, yet for all that the most critical moments of our life, when the old simple questions of humanity return to us in all their intensity; and we ask ourselves: What are we? What is this life on earth meant for? Are we to have no rest here, but to be always toiling and building up our own happiness out of the ruins of the happiness of our neighbours? And when we have made our home on earth as comfortable as it can be made with steam and gas and electricity, are we really so much happier than the Hindu in his primitive homestead?

With us, as I said just now, in these Northern climates, where life is and always must be a struggle, and a hard struggle too, and where accumulation of wealth has become almost a necessity to guard against the uncertainties of old age or the accidents inevitable in our complicated social life, with us. I say, and in our society, hours of rest and meditation are but few and far between. It was the same as long as we know the history of the Teutonic races; it was the same even with Romans and Greeks. The European climate with its long cold winters, in many places also the difficulty of cultivating the soil, the conflict of interests between small communities, has developed the instinct of self preservation (not to say, self-indulgence) to such an extent that most of the virtues and most of the vices of European society can be traced back to that source. Our own character was formed under these influences; by inheritance, by education, by necessity. We all lead a fighting-life; our highest ideal of life is a fighting-life. We work till we can work no longer, and are proud, like old homes to die in harness. We point with inward satisfaction to what we and our ancestors have achieved by hard work, in founding a family or a business, a town or a state. We point to the marvels of what we call civilization — our splendid cities, our highroads and bridges, our ships, our railways, our telegraphs, our electric light, our pictures, our statues, our music, our theatres. We imagine we have made life on earth quite perfect:

in some cases so perfect that we are almost sorry to leave it again. But the lesson which both Brahmans and Buddhists are never tired of teaching is that this life is but a journey from one village to another and riot a resting-place. Thus we read:

"As a man journeying to another village may enjoy a night's rest in the open air, but, after leaving his resting-place, proceeds again on his journey the next day, thus father, mother, wife and wealth are all but like a night's rest to us wise people do not cling to them for ever."

Instead of simply despising this Indian view of life, might we not pause for a moment and consider whether their philosophy of life is entirely wrong, and ours entirely right; whether this earth was really meant for work only (for with us pleasure also has been changed into work), for constant hurry and flurry; or whether we, sturdy Northern Aryans, might not have been satisfied with a little less of work, and a little less of so-called pleasure but with a little more of thought, and a little more of rest. For, short as our life is, we are not mere Mayflies that are born in the morning to die at night. We have a past to look back to and a future to look forward to, and it may be that some of the riddles of the future find their solution in the wisdom of the past.

Then why should we always fix our eyes on the present only? Why should we always be racing, whether for wealth or for power or for fame? Why should we never rest and be thankful?

I do not deny that the manly vigour, the silent endurance, the public spirit, and the private virtues too of the citizens of European states represent one side, it may be a very important side, of the destiny which man has to fulfil on earth.

But there is surely another side of our nature, and possibly another destiny open to man in his journey across this life, which should not be entirely ignored. If we turn our eyes to East, and particularly to India, where life is, or at all events was, no very severe struggle, where the climate was mild, the soil fertile, where vegetable food in small quantities sufficed to keep the body in health and strength; where the simplest hut or cave or a forest was all the shelter required, and where social life never assumed the gigantic, aye monstrous proportions of a London or Paris, but fulfilled itself within the narrow boundaries of village communities — was it not, I say, natural there, or, if you like, was it not intended there, that another side of human nature should be developed—not the active, the combative and acquisitive, but the passive, the meditative and reflective? Can we wonder that the Aryans who stepped as strangers to some of the happy fields and valleys along the Indus or the Ganges should have looked upon life as a perpetual Sunday or Holiday; or a kind of Long Vacation; delightful so long as it lasts, but which must come to an end sooner or later? Why should they have accumulated wealth? Why should they have built palaces? Why should they have toiled day and night? After having provided from day to day for the small necessities of the body; they thought they had the right, it may be the duty, to look round upon this strange exile; to look inward upon themselves upward to something not themselves, and to see whether they could not understand a little of the true purport of that mystery which we call life on earth.

Of course, we should call such notions of life dreamy, unreal, unpractical, but may not they look upon our notions of life as shortsighted, fussy, and in the end, most unpractical, because involving a sacrifice of life for the sake of life?

No doubt, these are both extreme views, and they have hardly ever been held or realized in that extreme form by any nation, whether in the East or in the West. We are not always plodding — we sometimes allow ourselves an hour of rest and peace and thought — nor were the ancient people of India always dreaming and meditating on tamegista, on the great problems of life, but, when called upon, we know that they too could fight like heroes, and that, without machinery, they could by patient toil raise even the meanest handiwork into a work of art, a real joy to the maker and to the buyer.

All then that I wish to put clearly before you is this, that the Aryan man, who had to fulfil his mission in India, might naturally be deficient in many of the practical and fighting virtues, which were developed in the Northern Aryans by the very struggle without which they could not have survived, but that his life on earth had not therefore been entirely wasted. His very view of life, though we cannot adopt it in this Northern climate, may yet act as a lesson and a warning to us, not, for the sake of life, to sacrifice the highest objects of life.

The greatest conqueror of antiquity stood in silent wonderment before the Indian Gymnosophists, regretting that he could not communicate with them in their own language, and that their wisdom could not reach him except through the contaminating channels of sundry interpreters.

That need not be so at present. Sanskrit is no longer a difficult language, and I can assure every young Indian Civil Servant that if he will but go to the fountain-head of Indian wisdom, he will find there, among much that is strange and useless, some lessons of life which are worth learning, and which we in our haste are too apt to forget or to despise.

Let me read you a few sayings only, which you may still hear repeated in India, when, after the heat of the day, the old and the young assembly together under the shadow of their village tree-sayings which to them seem truth, to us, I fear, mere truism!

"As all have to sleep together, laid low in the earth, why do foolish people wish to injure one another?"

"A man seeking for eternal happiness (*moksha*) might obtain it by a hundredth part of the sufferings which a foolish man endures in the pursuit of riches."

"Poor men eat more excellent bread than the rich, for hunger giveth it sweetness."

"Our body is like the foam of the sea, our life like a bird, our company with those whom we love does not last for ever; why then sleepest thou, my son?"

"As two logs of wood meet upon the ocean and then separate again, thus do living creatures meet."

"Family, wife, children, our every body and our wealth, they all pass away. They do not belong to us. What then is ours? Our good and our evil deeds."

"When thou goest away from here, no one will follow thee Only thy good and thy evil deeds, they will follow thee wherever thou goest."

"According to the Veda the soul (life) is eternal, but the body of all creatures is perishable. When the body is destroyed, the soul departs elsewhere, fettered by the bounds of our works."

"As a man puts on new garments in this world, throwing aside those which he formerly wore, even so the self of man puts on new bodies which are in accordance with his acts."

"No weapons will hurt the Self of man, no fire will burn it, no water moisten it, no wind will dry it up."

"It is not to be hurt, not to be burnt, not to be moistened, not to be dried up. It is imperishable, unchanging, immovable, without beginning."

"It is said to be immaterial, passing all understanding, and unchangeable. If you know the Self of man to be all this, grieve not."

"There is nothing higher than the attainment of the knowledge of the Self."

"All living creatures are the dwelling of the Self who lies enveloped in matter, who is immortal, and spotless. Those who worship the Self, the immovable, living in a movable dwelling, becomes immortal."

"Despising everything else, a wise man should strive after the knowledge of the Self."

We shall have to return to this subject again, far this knowledge of the Self is really the Vedanta, that is, the end, the highest goal of the Veda. The highest wisdom of Greece was ""to know ourselves"; the highest wisdom of India is "to know our Self."

If I were asked to indicate by one word the distinguishing feature of the Indian character, as I have here tried to sketch it, I should say it was transcendent, using that word, not in its strict technical sense, as fixed by Kant, but in its more general acceptation, as denoting a mind bent on transcending the limits of empirical knowledge. There are minds perfectly satisfied with empirical knowledge, a knowledge of facts, well ascertained, well classified, and well labelled. Such knowledge may assume very vast proportions, and if knowledge is power, it may impart great power; real intellectual power to the man who can wield and utilize it. Our own age is proud of that kind of knowledge, and to be content with it, and never to attempt to look beyond it, is, I believe, one of the happiest states of mind to be in.

But for all that, there is a Beyond, and he who has once caught a glance of it is like a man who has gazed at the sun wherever he looks, everywhere he sees the image of the sun. Speak to him of finite things; and he will tell you that the Finite is impossible and meaningless without the Infinite. Speak to him of death, and he will call it birth; speak to him of time, and he will call it the mere shadow of eternity. To us the senses seem to be the organs, the tools the most powerful engines of knowledge; to him they are, if not actually deceivers, at all events heavy fetters checking the flight of the spirit. To us this earth, this life, all that we see, and hear, and touch in certain. Here, we feel, is our home, here lie our duties, here our pleasures. To him this earth is a thing that once was not, and that again will cease to be: this life is a short dream from which we shall soon awake. Of nothing he professes greater ignorance than of what to others seems to be most certain, namely what we see; and hear, and touch; and as to our home wherever that may be, he knows that certainly it is not here. .

Do not suppose that such men are made dreamers. Far from it! And if we can only bring ourselves to be quite honest to ourselves, we shall have to confess that at times we all have been visited by these transcendental aspirations, and have been able to understand what Wordsworth meant when he spoke of those

> "Obstinate questionings
> Of sense and outward things,
> Fallings from us, vanishings;
> Blank misgivings of a creature
> Moving about in worlds not realized."

The transcendent temperament acquired no doubt a more complete supremacy in the Indian character than anywhere else; but no nation, and no individual, is entirely without that "yearning beyond"; indeed we all know it under a more familiar name — namely Religion.

It is necessary, however, to distinguish between a religion and a religion, quite as much as in another branch of philosophy we have to distinguish between language and a language or many languages. A man may accept a religion, he may be converted to the Christian religion, and he may change his own particular religion from time to time, just as he may speak different languages. But in order to have a religion a man must have religion. He must once at least in his life have looked beyond the horizon of this world, and carried away in his mind an impression of the Infinite, which will never leave him again. A being satisfied with the world of-sense, unconscious of its finite nature, undisturbed by the limited or negative character of all perceptions of the sense, would be incapable of any religious concepts. Only when the finite character of all human knowledge has been perceived, is it capable for the human mind to conceive that which is beyond the Finite, call it what you like, the Beyond, the Unseen, the Infinite, the Supernatural or the Divine. That steps must have been taken before religion of any kind becomes possible. What kind of religion it will be, depends on the character of the race which elaborates it, its surroundings, nature, and its experience in history.

APPENDIX-II

PREACHINGS OF *HOLY QURAN*

Islam, as is well known, has two components—religious and social-cum-political-cum-economic. The Messenger of Allah started getting trance at Mecca and so he started preaching. Most of it was religious component. It is said that thirteen years period at Mecca was a period of trial and tribulation and almost humiliation. At Madinah on the other hand, the Prophet Muhammad became a ruler. Here also the trance and revelations continued to come but here guidance was more on social, political and economic affairs. It was the end of one period and starting of another glorious one which gave the Hijrah – June 20th , 622 D.A. to be more precise.

Experts opine that guidance given in matters of religion is more rigid and it should not be amended or modified but the guidance given on socio-politico-economic matters is not that rigid and it is quite flexible and dynamic.

Important preachings of the *Holy Quran* are as follows :

1. To Offer Namaz Five Times a Day

Salat means prayer which is enjoined upon the Muslims as a foremost religious duty. Prayers are of various kinds : Five obligatory prayers daily, Friday prayer, funeral prayer; Id prayer, etc.

Book on *Salat* (Prayer) has 1398 *Ahadis* which provide all the necessary guidance concerning prayers. Besides this book, reference on prayer is also found at other places. For example, Chapter on the Night Journey of the Messenger of Allah to Heaven, shows how due to intervention of the Prophet 50 Prayers a day were reduced to 5 a day without any loss but the prayers were made obligatory for every believer (*Hadis* 309 to 322). Exact words are:

"They are five and at the same time fifty." (*Hadis* 313).

There are *Ahadis* on Adhan (i.e., *Aazan*), on bodily movements, on Imam to lead and others to fallow, on not lifting eyes towards the sky in prayer, on formation of assembly and the importance of the first row, on prayer in a single garment, on forbidden to build mosques on the graves, on timings of five prayers, on observing punctuality in offering prayers, on when can one be away from the congregational prayers, on shortening of prayers, etc. Besides these, there are other do's and don'ts' like: In *Namaz* it is allowed, to spit on left side; wear shoes, not to wear a cloth which has designs, finish eating when about to start eating and then offer prayer, not to go to mosque after eating onions and garlic, etc.

Any number of verses are found in *Holy Quran* on Prayers. To mention a few : 13/14, 19/3, 62/9, 2/126, 9/84, 9/113, 12/101, 26/83, 27/19, 71/26 etc.

It is a matter of investigation, what percentage of Muslim population strictly observe these requirements. And if the finding is that the percentage is quite low, then it is for *Imams, Maulvis, Qazis* and *Ulmas* to think and decide what they propose to do. If Muslims do not abide by the *Holy Quran* and dictates of the Messenger of Allah in such an important matter as Prayers, then to take a stand by political leaders on lesser important things becomes meaningless.

2. To Give Zakat

"Of the fundamentals of Islam, *Zakat* occupies the second position, the first being prayer (*Salat*)." *Sadaqa*, i.e., *Zakat* means spending the wealth for the sake of Allah. It is believed in Islam that it purifies the heart of the man and affirms the truth that nothing is dearer to the man than the love of Allah. It is also a way to improve the economic condition of poor.

Zakat or *Sadaqa* in Islam is not a voluntary act of charity which a rich man gives to the poor out of his own sweet will, but it is an obligatory act. Thus, there is no obligation on one who receives *Zakat*, but, on the other hand, there is a sense of thankfulness and gratitude on the part of the giver because he could discharge his duty to Allah and the society.

This is what *Holy Quran* has to say :

> "Take alms of their wealth, wherewith thou mayst purify them and mayst make them grow. ..."
>
> — *Holy Quran* 9/103

> "Establish worship, pay the poor due, and bow your heads with those who bow (in worship)."
>
> — *Holy Quran* 2/43

Zakat is mentioned in *Holy Quran* at eighty-two places. This shows its importance.

Zakat should be paid after the end of the year at the uniform rate of 2.5 per cent of profit earned.

The minimum wealth on which *Zakat* is chargeable is known as *Nisab*. Normally it is 200 Dirhams, or 52.5 Tolas of Silver, or 7.5 Tolas of Gold. In modern times, with the prices of gold and silver touching sky, this limit will be much less.

Whom *Zakat* is to be paid by the state, after collection, is mentioned in *Holy Quran*. To quote —

> "The alms are only for the poor and the needy, and those who collect them, and those whose hearts are to be reconciled, and to free the captives and the debtors, and for the cause of Allah, and (for) the wayfarers; a duty imposed by Allah. Allah is knower, Wise."
>
> — *Holy Quran* 9/60

Kitab Al-Zakat (*Hadis* 2134 to 2360) gives all the necessary details, such as upto which amount *Zakat* is not payable, it is binding on every Muslim to pay at the end of the month of Ramadan, sin who does not pay, it is forbidden to beg, etc.

To the best of the knowledge of the present writer, Indian Muslims hardly pay *Zakat* or *Sadaqa*. Thus, they disobey not only the Messenger of Allah but Allah also. Should *Ulmas, Imams, Maulvis, Qazis*, etc. keep indifferent to it? Should they not, on one hand, persuade co-religionists to honestly pay *Zakat* @2.5 per cent to the Government of India and on the other hand, request the Government to make a law for Muslims to make payment obligatory. This *Zakat* should be paid to the Government of India alone and the government must be bound to pay it to poor, needy, under debt, bounded labour, etc.

3. To keep fasts during the month of Ramadan (Ramzan)

"After prayer and *Zakat* the third obligatory duty which every Muslim is required to perform is that of fasting during the month of Ramadan." The word *Sawm* has been used in *Holy Quran* for fasting.

Kitab Al-Sawm relates to fasting (*Hadis* 2361 to 2646). It guides when the fasting be commenced and when finished, the number of days of fasting, time of taking the meals, kissing in the day is allowed in the month of Ramadan but not sexual intercourse, who is exempted from observing fast, how to observe the *I'tikaf*, etc.

There are several verses on the subject in *Holy Quran*. For example :

> "The month of Ramadan in which was revealed the *Holy Quran*. ... And whosoever of you is present, let him fast the month, and whosoever of you is sick or on a journey, (let him fast the same) number of other days. Allah desireth for you ease; He desireth not hardship for you; and (He desireth) that Ye should complete the period, and that Ye should magnify Allah for having guided you, and that peradventure Ye may be thankful."
>
> — *Holy Quran* 2/185

Thus, there are exceptions when a fast may not be taken but it is to be compensated on other days. How many Indian Muslims do it?

Verse 2/187 permits people to have sexual intercourse in the night so that there may be no necessity to try to deceive oneself.

It appears that Allah knew better. Probably most of the Muslims are deceiving themselves even today by posing that they are on fast when the reality is different. Let the Muslim social leaders find out the truth and decide what should be done? If an average Muslim cannot be persuaded to observe this most important pillar of Islam then where is the logic on insisting on lesser important things.

4. To go to Hajj or Pilgrimage

The fourth most important fundamental of Islam is to go on pilgrimage. *Hajj* is not a new institution which the Messenger of Allah established. It already existed at Ka'ba (*Holy Quran* 2/127, 3/95, 14/37). He only "purged it of all evil practices and made it an obligatory act of piety by which one can develop God-consciousness".

It is said that the *Hajj* was started by the Prophet himself, in the present form, when he visited Mecca in A.D. 628 (or A.D. 630).

Kitab Al-Hajj gives all possible details on *Hajj* (*Hadis* 2647 to 3230): What to wear and what not to wear, what to apply and what not to apply, the place (or places) where the pilgrims enter upon the state of Ihram, prohibits hunting, which animals are permitted to be killed, when one is allowed to shave, or get the treatment for eyes, types of Ihram, kissing of black stone (*Al-hajaru'l aswad*) and taking seven circuits round the Ka'ba, casting the pebbles, making animal sacrifice, drink water of the well of Zamzam, clipping of haris, stoning at *Jamrat Al-Aqaba*, etc.

It is for the scholars to reply to the criticism that "pilgrimage to Mecca and the Ka'ba is close to being idolatrous." Kissing of black stone appears to be idol worshipping.

It is apparent that most of the Indian Muslims do not go to pilgrimage and thus do not observe an essential fundamental of Islam. *Imams, Ulmas, Maulvis* and *Qazis* should find out a solution. And if they fail they lose right to oppose several things taking the plea that it is un-Islamic.

5. Some other minor Do's

Holy Quran and *Hadis* mention some other Do's of lesser importance which a true Muslim is supposed to do. Some examples are given below:

(1) *To resort to Spell, Magic, Incantation, etc. when ill* — *Holy Quran* and *Hadis* after *Hadis* decree that when one is taken ill, one should seek help of megic (*Hadis* 5428 to 5429), Spell (*Hadis* 5424-5427), incantation (*Hadis* 5432 to 5438), Recitation of Mu'Awwidhatan (*Suras* CXII, CXIV, and *Hadis* 5439 to 5462), etc. One living in modern India, fails to understand how one can refuse to be treated by a qualified practioner and pin down faith on magic, spell, incantation, etc. Probably, Ulmas, Imams, Maulvis, Qazis will like to give their considered opinion. If they allow taking of modern medicines, will it not amount to disobedience to Allah and His Messenger. And once it starts, where will be the end.

(2) *To kill Dogs* — The Prophet announced that dogs are an evil. One must normally refrain from taming them except for specific purposes. The best course is to kill them. To quote —

> "...Allah's Messenger (may peace be upon him) ordered us to kill dogs..."
>
> — *Hadis* 3813 and 3809 to 3829

Even a penalty was imposed on keeping a dog (*Hadis* 3823). The selling of the dog was also prohibited. It was compared to the earnings of a prostitute (*Hadis* 3903 to 3808).

Is it possible or desirable to kill dogs? Can every Muslim be persuaded not to tame dogs?

(3) *To Cultivate Land and not to lease it out* — Muslim religion expects everybody to cultivate one's own land. In only exceptional circumstances, it should be given to another Muslim for cultivation but in that case no rent is chargeable. To quote —

"...He who has land should cultivate it, but if he does not find it possible to cultivate it, or finds himself helpless to do so, he should lend it to his Muslim brother, but he should not accept rent from him."

— *Hadis* 3719 and *Hadis* 3714 to 3757

Apparently Muslim religion differentiates between Muslims and non-Muslims. One should ponder whether in India, which is a multi-religion country, this stand is conducive to emotional integration and unity of the country. Further, it will be worthwhile to know how many Muslim cultivators have leased out their lands on rent and what Imams and Maulvis propose to do against them.

(4) *To fulfil Vows* — Imam Nawawi opines that it is quite essential to fulfil the vow in case it is taken for Islamic purposes, but if it is taken for un-Islamic ends, then its fulfilment is not binding. Vow taken by a dear and near one should be fulfilled even after the death (*Hadis* 4017 to 4037).

(5) *Poets and Poetry* — Allah did not like Poets and Poetry. To quote

"That it is indeed the speech of an illustrious Messenger." "It is not poets speech — little is it that Ye believe". "Nor diviners speech — little is it that ye remember."

— *Holy Quran* 69/40, 41,42

Hadis 5602 to 5611 also says so. To quote —

"...It is better for the belly of anyone of you to be stuffed with pus rather than to stuff (one's mind) with poetry."

— *Hadis* 5610

Consequently a number of poets were killed.

These *Do's*, need a close look by the Muslim Ulmas, Qazis, Imams and Maulvis so that they may be able to give proper guidance in the context of India which is a multi-religious country and where Muslims are in a minority.

Don'ts in Islam

Islam requires its followers not to do a number of things. These 'Don'ts' appear to be a negative doctrine but they show what a Muslim is ordered to leave or not to do. Some of the important 'Don'ts' are :

1. *Not to take intoxicants, or produce them, or sell them, or gift them*

Allah was not happily disposed of towards drinks and games of chance. So, he revealed :

> "They question thee about strong drink and games of chance. Say : In both is great sin, and (some) utility for men; but the sin of them is greater than their usefulness..."
>
> — *Holy Quran* 2/219

Again,

> "O Ye who believe ! Draw not near unto prayer when Ye are drunken..."
>
> — *Holy Quran* 4/43

And,

> "O Ye who believe strong drink and games of chance... are all infamy of Satan's handiwork. Leave it aside in order that Ye may succeed.
>
> — *Holy Quran* 5/90

When Allah was not in favour of drinks then His Messenger could not be indifferent to the issue of intoxicants. This is evident from Prophet's life. To quote —

> "...I was the cup bearer of some people in the house of Abu Talha on the day when liquor was forbidden. Their liquor had been prepared from dry dates or fresh dates when the announcer made the announcement. He (Abu Talha) said to me : Go out and find out (what the announcement is)... Behold, liquor has been declared unlawful. He said : The liquor (was split and) flowed in the lanes of Medina. Abu Talha said to me : Go out and spill it..."
>
> — *Hadis* 4882

Footnotes added to this *Hadis* say : "Whatever is the material from which liquor is prepared and whatever is the process of preperation, every intoxicant is liquor. ... In another *Hadith*, the Holy Prophet (may pace be upon him) is reported to have said : Every drink that induces intoxication is forbidden. ..."

Same footnote further says : "...the Holy Prophet (may peace be upon him) did not permit wine to be given to the non-Muslim as a gift..."

Again,

Aisha reported : "Allah's Messenger (may peace be upon him) was asked about Bit, whereupon he said : Every drink that causes intoxication is forbidden."

— *Hadis* 4956

Intoxicants cannot be taken even as medicine. To quote—

> "...asked Allah's Apostle (may peace be upon him) about liquor. He forbade (its case) and he expressed hatred that it should be prepared. He (Tariq) said : I prepare it as a medicine, whereupon he (the Holy Prophet) said : It is not a medicine, but an ailment."
>
> — *Hadis* 4892

It is forbidden to prepare vinegar from Khamr (wine). To quote—

"Anas reported that Allah's Messenger (may peace be upon him) was asked about the use of Khamr from which vinegar is prepared. He said : No (it is prohibited).

— *Hadis* 4891

Not only production and consumption of all intoxicants are prohibited but their sale is also not allowed. To quote—

"... A person presented to Allah's Messenger (may peace be upon him) a small water-skin of wine. Allah's Messenger (may peace be upon him) said to him : Do you know that Allah has forbidden it? He said : No. He then whispered to another man. Allah's Messenger (may peace be upon him) asked him what he had whispered. He said : I advised him to sell that, whereupon he (the Holy Prophet) said : Verily He who has forbidden its drinking has forbidden its sale also.... "

— *Hadis* 3836

To sum up, in Islam to produce any type of intoxicant, to sell it, to gift it, to consume it, to take it even as a medicine — all are strictly prohibited. So, a good Muslim should keep himself away from all varieties of intoxicants — their production, sale, gift and consumption. What the Ulmas, Imams, Maulvis and theologists are doing about it.

2. *Not to indulge in Games of Chance*

Similarly, a good Muslim should not participate in any type of games of chance. Gambling in any form is strictly prohibited. In modern times, it will include games of Cards, Lotteries, Forward Trading (Speculation), Chess, etc. To quote —

"He who buys foodgrains should not sell it until he has taken possession of it."

— *Hadis* 3640 and 3641 to 3653

Thus Forward Trading is prohibited in Islam.

Again,

> "...Allah's Apostle (may peace be upon him) said : He who played chess is like one who dyed his hand with the flesh and blood of swine."
>
> — *Hadis* 5612
>
> — Also *Holy Quran* 2/219, 5/90

Will Muslim theologists, Ulmas, Imams, Qazis, etc. give their considered opinion on it?

3. *Do not indulge in Debauchery, Adultery and Rape*

Allah strictly warns His followers not to indulge in adultery. To quote—

> "Lo! Allah forghiveth not that a partner should be ascribed unto Him. He forgiveth (all) save that to whom He will. Who so ascribeth partners to Allah, he hath indeed invented a tremendous sin."
>
> — *Holy Quran* 4/48 and also 4/116

Again,

> "As for those of your women who are guilty of lewdness, — then confine them to the houses until death take them..."
>
> — *Holy Quran* 4/15

> "And as for the two of you who are guilty thereof, punish them both...."
>
> — *Holy Quran* 4/16

The Messenger of Allah did not lag behind. *Hadis* 3553 to 3577 tell that the Prophet never liked charges of adultery. He imposed the severest penalty on the guilty. To quote—

> "... when an unmarried male commits adultery with an

unmarried female (they should receive) one hundred lashes and banishment for one year. And in case of married male committing adultery with a married female, they shall receive one hundred lashes and be stoned to death."

— *Hadis* 4191 and *Hadis* 4192 to 4210

One wonders whether it shall be possible for Muslim Ulmas, Imams, Qazis, etc. to condemn those Muslims who freely indulge in raping non-Muslim ladies. Will they be able to recommend the Government of India to make a special law for Muslims to punish them as per scriptures?

4. *Not to Commit Major Sins*

The Prophet and Allah Himself classified Sins into two — major sins and minor sins. Even the minor sins become major ones if "committed deliberately or is repeated without any qualm of consciousness and one feels no remorse over it" (Footnote of the title of Chapt. 39). The major sins "in Islam are very grave and these make a man either an unbeliever, or a Fasiq" on the other hand, minor sins "are washed off by daily prayers."

Major Sins

The Messenger of Allah mentions seven major sins. They are :

(i) *To associate anybody with Allah—Hadis* 158 mentions it and *Holy Quran* also reveals it. To quote—

"... that ye ascribe nothing as partner unto Him...."

— *Holy Quran* 6/152

This certainly is a religious duty and so there is no scope to debate on it.

(ii) *To disobey Parents — Hadis* 158 to 163, spell it. *Holy Quran* 6/152 also decrees so. It is social norm.

(iii) *To give false Testimony or make false utterance – Hadis* 158 and 189 *Hadis* explain it. It says : "... The tale-bearer shall not enter Paradise." Footnote says —"...means : slander, defamation, calumny, malicious and mischievous misrepresentation." This is also a social norm.

(iv) *To kill a person* — "Killing without sufficient cause and without having proved ones guilt and affording one an opportunity of defence" is prohibited in Islam — (Footnote of *Hadis* 160). *Holy Quran* also decrees : "... and that Ye slay not your children ... and that Ye slay not the life which Allah had made sacred. ..."

— *Holy Quran* 6/152

(v) *To consume the property of an orphan — Holy Quran* says :

> "... Those who devour the property of orphans wrongfully, they do but swallow fire into their bellies, they will be exposed to burning flame."
>
> — *Holy Quran* 4/10 and *Hadis* 161

(vi) *To consume usury — Hadis* 161, 3880, 3881 and also *Holy Quran* prohibits taking usury. To quote—

> "... whereas Allah permitteth and forbiddeth usury."
>
> — *Holy Quran* 2/275

One will have to pronounce a judgement on how far this is possible in the present time. Today, because of banks and also larger size of industry and business houses, taking loans and paying interest thereupon has become a necessity.

(vii) *To avoid Magic — Hadis* 161 says :

> "... the Messenger of Allah (may peace be upon him) observed : Avoid the seven noxious things. It was said (by the hearer) : What are they... He (the Holy Prophet) replied... magic..."

5. Not to Commit "Other" Sin : Minor Sins

The other minor sins are many but the important ones are :

(a) *Pride—Hadis* 164 says :

> "... the Apostle of Allah (may peace be upon him) observed : He who has in his heart the weight of a mustard seed of pride shall not enter Paradise. ... Pride is disdaining the truth (out of self-concept) and contempt for the people."

Again, this is what *Holy Quran* has to say:

> "And when we said unto the angels : Prostrate yourselves before Adam, they fell prostrate, all save Iblis. He demurred through pride, and so became disbeliever."
>
> — *Holy Quran* 2/34
>
> also *Holy Quran* 2/87, 7/40, 31/18

Hadis 192 explains that the Prophet did not like the "dragger of lower garments." He said that he will "neither speak (to them) on the Day of Resurrection, nor would took at them, nor would absolve them..." Footnote of *Hadis* 192 explains, "It is a sign of pride that people go about with their lower garment dragging on the earth..."

(b) *Theft* — "Aisha reported that Allah's Messenger (may peace be upon him) as saying : Cut off the hands of a thief for a quarter of a dinar and upward."

— *Hadis* 4175

And this is what *Holy Quran* has decreed :

> "As for the thief, both male and female, cut off their hands. It is the reward of their own deeds, and exemplary punishment from Allah. Allah is Mighty, Wise."
>
> — *Holy Quran* 5/38

Will Muslim Ulmas, Imams and Qazis will recommend such a legislation to the Government of India for Muslims alone?

(c) *To kill ones own child, i.e. To practice birth control* —

Hadis 156 says : "... I asked him (the Messenger of Allah) what the next (gravest sin) was. He (the Holy Prophtet) replied : That you kill your child out of fear that he shall join you in food..."

Commentator adds the Footnote :

> "...It is shirkfi'l-Rubu-biyah, i.e., man assumes the role of a nourisher and sustainer and thinks that he is responsible for the nourishment of his children.... The practice of killing children and other methods of birth control is in fact the denial of Rububiyah. ..."

Holy Quran also decrees :

> "Slay not your children, fearing a fall of poverty. We shall provide for them and for you. Lo! The slaying of them is great sin."
>
> — *Holy Quran* 17/31

It appears that in those times, abortion was the only technique of birth control. In the changed conditions —with other methods of birth control available, where neither abortion nor 'coitus interruptus' are needed, the theologists should put in their heads and decide the issue. Today, quite a good percentage of Muslim population is below poverty line. And the prophet ruled that only that man should marry who can afford a wife. So, a dynamic solution is needed.

(d) *To sell goods by false oaths—Hadis* 192 says :

> "... the Messenger of Allah observed : Three are the (persons) with whom Allah would neither speak on the Day of Resurrection, nor would look at them nor would absolve them and there is painful chastisement for them... They are.... the

seller of goods by false oath."

— *Holy Quran* also says so (3/76)

Will Muslim theologists recommend to the Government of India to make a separate law for Muslims of India in keeping with the scriptures.

(e) *To lay obligations on those on whom you have shown some favour*

Hadis 192 and *Holy Quran* 2/264 says so.

(f) *To Commit Suicide*

Any one who kills himself with a weapon, or by taking poison, or falling from the mountains, i.e. height, etc., will be burnt by the fire of Hell (*Hadis* 199).

These are some of the minor sins. A Muslim is prohibited to commit these sins.

A reading of these 'DON'Ts' give a feeling that since neither Allah nor the Messenger of Allah were rigid in their outlook and they changed their views on matters, socio-politico-economic, with changing times and situations, it is desirable for Ulmas, Imams, Maulvis, Qazis and Theologists to find out, in the light of scriptures, how many of them need modification. And thereafter, it becomes their duty to ensure that the followers of Islam honestly abide by the left over. 'Don'ts' not doing so will amount to a disloyalty to Allah and His Messenger. Will it not amount to become a disbeliever?

BIBLIOGRAPHY

Aurobindo, Shri, *Problem of Rebirth.*

——*The Life Divine*, American Edition (1951).

——, *Savitri* (Epic).

Aiyer, P.S. Sivaswamy, *Evolution of Hindu Moral Ideals*, Gian Publishing House, New Delhi.

Alvin Toffler, *Future Shock*, New York, Random House, 1970.

Ambedkar, B.R., *Annihilation of Caste*, 1936.

Brown, I.C., *Understanding other cultures.*

Barth, A., *The Religions of India*, London, 1882.

Bhandarkar, R.G., *Vaisnavism, Saivism, and Minor Religious Systems*, Grundriss der Indo-Arischen Philologie and Altertumskunde, Strassburg, 1913.

Bernard, H.M., Vlekke, *Nusantara : A History of Indonesia*, The Hague, 1959.

Carpenter, J.E., *Comparative Religion*, New York and London, 1912.

Clyde & Beers, *The Far East, A History of the Western Impact and the Eastern Response* (1830-1963), Prentice Hall, New Delhi, 1966.

Cora, Dubois, *Social Forces in Southeast Asia*, 2nd ed., Cambridge, Mass., 1959.

Cowell, E.B. and Gough, A.E., *The Sarva Darsana Samgraha or Review of the Different Systems of Hindu Philosophy*, by Madhva Acharya, Translated by E.B. Cowell and A.E. Gough, Second Edition, London, 1894.

Cumont, F., *The Oriental Religions in Roman Paganism*. Chicago, 1911.

Dasgupta, Surma, *Development of Moral Philosophy in India.*

Davids, T.W. Rhys, *Buddhism*, London, 1903.

Dayanand Sarswati, *Light of Truth*, Sarvadeshil Arya Pratinidhi Sabha, Ramlila Ground, New Delhi, Edition 1991.

Desai, A.R., *Social Background of Indian Nationalism*, Bombay, 1948.

Durant, Will, *The Story of Civilization,* Part I, Our Oriental Heritage, New York, Simon and Suchuster, 1954.

Dutt, V.P., *India and the World*, Sanchar Publishing Housing, New Delhi, 1990.

Edmunds, A.J., *Buddhist and Christian Gospels*, 4th ed. Philadelphia, 1908.

Fausboll, W., *The Dhammapada*, London, 1990.

Farquhar, J.N., *Outlines of the Religious Literature of India*, London, 1920.

Ferguson, J., *Moral Values in the Ancient World*, Methuen and Co., Ltd., 1938.

Prabhu, R.K., *Mind of Mahatma Gandhi*.

Gandhi, M.K., *Women and Social Injustice*, Ahmedabad, 1945.

Gupta, N.L., *Education and Values in the Mahabharat,* Concept Publication Co., New Delhi 1995.

——,*Humanistic Traditions of India*, Mohit Publications, 1999.

——, *Equality of Religions*, Mohit Publications, New Delhi, 1996.

——, *Contribution of Western Indologists*, Mohit Publications, New Delhi, 1996.

——, *Crosscultural Communication - Global Perspective*, Concept Publication Company, New Delhi, 1997.

——, *Women Education: Through the Ages*, Concept, 1999.

Gayor, E., *A Dictionary of Mysticism*, New York, 1933.

Gordon, G.A., *Ultimate Conceptions of the Faith*, Boston, 1903.

Gloria, Faizi, *The Bahai Faith*, Bahai Publishing Trust, New Delhi, 1992.

Gambhirananda (Trans.), *Eight Upanishads*, Vol. I-II, Advaita Asharam, Calcutta, ninth impression, 1992.

Hiriyana, *Outline of Indian Philosophy*.

Hume, E.R., *The Thirteen Upanishads*, Translated from the Sanskrit, with an Outline of Philosophy of the Upanishads and an Annotated Bibliography. Oxford, 1921.

Hutchinson, Gregory and Lydekker, *The Living Traces of Man-kind*, New York, 1902.

——, *The Religions of India*, Boston, 1895.

Herbert Passin, *China's Cultural Diplomacy*, New York, 1963.

Hindery, Roderick, *Comparative Ethics in Hindu and Buddhist Tradition*, Motilal Banarasidass, Delhi.

Hopkins, E.W., *The Great Epic of India, Its Character and Origin,* New York, 1902.

Huston Smith, *The Religion of Man, A Mentor Book*, New American Liberary, 1958.

Iyanger, S., *Hathayogapradipika*, Second Edition, Adyar, 1933.

Jayne, W.A., *The Healing Gods of Ancient Civilizations*, New Haven, 1925.

James, R. Ware, *Sayings of Confucious* (Translated), New American Liberary, New York.

James Oliver & Christina Scott (Ed.), *Religion and World History - A Selection from the works of Christopher Dawson*, Image Books, New York, 1975.

Jha Nirmala, *Law of Karma*, Capital Publishing House, Delhi.

John Chinnery and Wilkins (Trans.), *Hindu Mythology*, Calcutta, 1913.

Joseph, R. Levenson, *Confucian China and Its Modern Fate*, Vol. I, *The Problem of Monarchial Decay*, Brekeley, 1958-1964.

Keith, A.B., *The Religion and Philosophy of the Veda* —2 Vols., Cambridge, Mass., 1925.

Kane, P.V., *History of Dharmasastra*, Vol. I-III, Poona.

Macdonell, A.A., *Vedic Mythology* (Grundriss der Indo-Arischen Philologie and Altertum-skunde),Strassburg, 1897.

——, *A History of Sanskrit Literature*, New York, 1900.

Macdonell, A.A., and Keith, A.B., *Vedic Index of Names and Subjects*, 2 Vols., London, 1912.

Monier-Williams, M., *Brahmanism and Hinduism*, London, 1891.

Moulton, J.H., "*The Zorastrian Conception of a Future Life.*" Journal of Transactional of the Victoria Institut, XLVII, 233-52, London, 1915.

Miller, F. Max, *Sacred Books of the East*, Vols. I, XV, XXXII, XLII, XLVI.

Mukherjee, S.N., *India—History and Thought*, Subranrekha, Calcutta, 1982.

Naik, M.K., *et al.*, *The Image of India in Western Creative Writing*, Macmillan, Madras, 1971.

Nehru, J.L., *The Discovery of India*, 2nd ed., Calcuta, 1946.

Nicholson, R.A., *The Mystics of Islam*, London, 1914.

Pande, B.M., *India's Contribution to World Thought and Cultures*, Vivekananda Kendra, Madras, 1970.

Rao, U.R., *Collected Works of Mahatma Gandhi*, New Delhi, 1958.

Radhakrishnan, S., *Indian Philosophy*, 2 Vols., New York, 1922, 1927.

——, *Eastern Religions and Western Thought*, Unwin Books.

——, *An Idealistic View of Life*, Unwin Books, London, Paper-back ed., 1961.

——, *Hindu View of Life*.

Raymond, Dawson, *Confucious*, OUP Past Masters Series, 1981.

Richard, Butwell, *Southeast Asia Today and Tomorrow: A Political Analysis*, New York, 1961.

Robert, C. Bone, *Contemporary Southeast Asia*, New York, 1961.

Smith, Warren, *Confucianism in Modern Japan: A Study of Conservatism in Japanese Intellecutal History*, Tokyo, 1959.

——, *Shrimadbhagvad Gita*, Gita Press, Gorakhpur.

Sneath, E.H., *The Evolution of Ethics*, New York, Macmillian Co., 1927.

William, Monier, *Indian Wisdom*, Cosmo Publications, New Delhi, 1978.

Walli, Koshelya, *Theory of Karman in Indian Thought*, Bharata Manisha, Varanasi.

Whitehead, A.N., *Religion in the Making*, New York, 1926.

Yale, John, *What Religion Is—in the words of Swamy Vivekanand*, Phoenix House, London, 1962.

Yadava, B.R., *Vedic Cosmology*, Vijnan Prakashan, Aligarh, 1987.

INDEX